THE CHARITY BALL

The Charity Ball

HOW TO DANCE TO THE DONORS' TUNE

GARY JOHNS

Connor Court Publishing Pty Ltd

PO Box 224W
Ballarat VIC 3350
sales@connorcourt.com
www.connorcourt.com

ISBN: 9781925138221 (pbk.)

Cover design by Ian James

Printed in Australia

CONTENTS

Figures

Tables

Dedication and acknowledgements

I walked off the street when I was 18 and joined a political party. No one asked me to, I volunteered. I stayed for 30 years. I got lucky and it became a career. I also became an inaugural member of the board of Volunteering Australia and was, for many years, an office-holder of the Bennelong Society, a not-for-profit think tank on Aboriginal policy. Those who volunteer their time in pursuit of a cause, even a political one, have some claim to investigate the work of charities. For those who volunteer, including the professionals who stay, and for the many donors who supply the capital for charities, this book is for you. It is also for politicians who devise the rules within which donors and charities operate.

I would like to thank those many people who have contributed their time and thoughts to this project, in particular Cassandra Wilkinson, Les Hems, Ron Manners and numerous Mannkal volunteers who supported the research, and Don D'Cruz for his assistance in assembling data on significant 'policy research, advocacy, lobbying' charities. Special thanks are due to Dr Lauren Vogel for her work on the statistical analysis of the attitudes of charity activists and John Humphreys for his critique of the Social Return on Investment evaluation technique.

I have had the opportunity to present aspects of the book to various forums, including the John Curtin Public Policy Institute, Curtin University, Perth, the Centre for Independent Studies, Sydney, and the Biennial Conference of the District and County Court Judges of Australia and New Zealand, Brisbane. I have also attended a number of seminars held by the philanthropic sector – in particular, Philanthropy Australia and Givewell workshops on measuring charity impact. A version of the first chapter was published in the 2013-14 summer edition of *Policy* (Centre for Independent Studies).

I have also had the benefit of meetings with the Commissioner of the Australian Charities and Not-for-profit Commission, executives of the Fundraising Institute of Australia, Philanthropy Australia, a number of trust company representatives, lawyers and accountants operating in the field, and some charity CEOs, each of whom were able to enhance my understanding of the sector.

The academic and professional literature in the field is voluminous and very helpful. I have tried to make the most of it, hopefully without having it swamp the policy discussion. The Queensland University of Technology Business School made access to the literature possible during my year as visiting fellow. I would like to thank Professor Robina Xavier, Dean of the school for her support, as well as her predecessor, Professor Peter Little. I have also enjoyed discussions with Professor Myles McGregor-Lowndes of QUT and Professor Ken Wiltshire of the University of Queensland on the state of the charity market and charity regulation in Australia.

Thanks once again to my publisher, Dr Anthony Cappello, and his team at Connor Court. Special thanks for the fine editing of my colleague, Adjunct Professor John Nethercote. Any errors and all of the views expressed are mine alone.

Brisbane, April 2014

Sample and references

A sample of 200 charities has been used to illustrate key characteristics of Australian charities. Drawing the right sample should be straightforward. Unfortunately, because of the poor specifications of the central register, the task was difficult and time-consuming and could not, with statistical confidence, represent the population of Australian charities. Nevertheless, care has been taken in selecting the sample and therefore case studies used throughout the book to illustrate important characteristics of the sector should be reasonably representative.

In addition to the sample, many other charities have been selected to illustrate discussion about the sector. These have been discovered during the course of research for the book. For ease of identification, all charities and charitable trusts are in italics. In general, larger charities are required to produce audited accounts (although there is no requirement to make these public) so that the study concentrates almost exclusively on those charities whose accounts, and other material, have been presented on their website. Their transparency is to be applauded.

As it was essential to cover the important literature, annual and other reports, and data from a range of sources, the references are extensive. In order to keep the text flowing and provide guidance to sources, the following conventions have been observed. The literature has been referenced using the Harvard method (author, year, page) in the body of the text and names have been abbreviated. For example, (Australian Taxation Office, 2013) becomes (ATO, 2013). Where there is more than one author, and it is unambiguous in the bibliography, the first author only will be named. For example, (Chambers & Parvin, 2010, 96) becomes (Chambers, 2010, 96). The full reference is to be found in the bibliography. Charity annual and other reports are to be found in footnotes, without their web links, as these should be readily available to those who wish to follow up. Other web-based sources, which may not be permanent, are presented with links and the date at which they were accessed. References to newspaper articles are to be found in footnotes.

Abbreviations

ABS	Australian Bureau of Statistics
ACF	Australian Conservation Foundation
ACNC	Australian Charities and Not-for-profits Commission
ACOSS	Australian Council of Social Services
ACTU	Australian Council of Trade Unions
AIHW	Australian Institute of Health and Welfare
ANPHA	Australian National Preventive Health Agency
ATO	Australian Taxation Office
CBA	Cost-Benefit Analysis
CF	Charitable Fund
CI	Charitable Institution
DGR	Deductible Gift Recipient
FBT	Fringe Benefits Tax
HPC	Health Promotion Charity
HPCI	Harm Prevention Charitable Institutions
ICAC	Independent Commission Against Corruption (NSW)
NDIS	National Disability Insurance Scheme
NGO	Non-Government Organisation
PAF	Private Ancillary Fund
PBI	Public Benevolent Institution
PC	Productivity Commission (Commonwealth)
SROI	Social Return on Investment

1

Charity? What charity?

This book is a salute to charities who do good work and a straightener to those who do not. The trick is to know which is which. At the Charity Ball, charities dance to the tune of charity activists, government, and some big philanthropists and business. The vast majority of donors, and the vast majority of taxpayers, do not get to dance. The reasons are simple, their donations are so small and taxes so dispersed that they do not warrant paying attention to how charities perform.

Well-informed donors can drive charities to do their best work. As in any market, large numbers of buyers (donors) with some information can, collectively, drive sellers (charities) to better perform. Donors can become better-informed if the cost of becoming so is made cheaper. Governments can lower the price of information in a number of ways. One way is by not licensing charities that do little or no charity work, or spend too much time lobbying government for their pet projects, or who receive too much government money – in other words, who are not charities. Philanthropists and business can help drive a more powerful market by subsidising the cost to the donor of charity performance information. The data need not be overly sophisticated; sometimes it is enough to prime a donor with a probing question. 'Prove that you do what you promise' may be enough.

Government, philanthropists and business may find that their best effort in charity is to let charities alone to do their best, with a million watching eyes. In other words, to have charities dance to the donors' tune. In this way, they may lift the entire charitable sector to do its best work.

What charity?

According to a recent opinion poll, charities are the most publicly trusted of institutions, scoring 63 percent: business and government polled 58 percent and 48 percent respectively (Edelman, 2013). But are they all charities? Lindsay Fox, the trucking magnate, houses his vintage car collection in Melbourne's dockside. *The Trustee for the Fox Classic Car Collection* is a charitable institution (CI), open to the public, admission $10 per adult.[1] The *Chamber of Commerce & Industry of Western Australia Incorporated* is a CI. It proudly proclaims to have 'succeeded in influencing government policy and keeping public debate focused on key business issues, an area often overlooked or marginalised by politicians, the general public and special interest groups.'[2] Matchworks is an 'associate partner' (a sponsor) of Melbourne Heart, the professional soccer team.[3] Matchworks is a division of *Karingal*, a Public Benevolent Institution (PBI) with Deductible Gift Recipient status (DGR), in other words, a big charity.[4]

The *Victorian Women's Trust* placed a newspaper advertisement in praise of the first female to be Prime Minister of Australia, Julia Gillard, shortly after former Prime Minister, Kevin Rudd, had deposed her. The advertisement contained the sentence: 'the Victorian Women's Trust

---

1 Fox Classic Car Collection, http://www.foxcollection.org.au/opening-hours-and-tours.html accessed 27 January 2014.

2 Chamber of Commerce and Industry WA, http://www.cciwa.com/policy-advocacy/Board_Councils__Policy_Forums accessed 27 January 2014.

3 Melbourne Heart, http://www.footballaustralia.com.au/melbourneheart/ourpartners accessed 25 March 2014.

4 MatchWorks, http://www.matchworks.com.au/about-us/ accessed 25 March 2014.

wish to thank the generous and thoughtful women who provided us with the funds to place this statement on the public record – without the privilege of tax deductibility.'[5] The *Victorian Women's Trust* is a CI but does not have DGR status, however, the *Victorian Women's Action Trust* and the *Victorian Women's Benevolent Trust* do and they are administered by the one organisation.[6] *Christians for Biblical Equality*, whose mantra is God believes in feminism, is a CI.[7] *Animal Liberation* is a CI.[8] *The Conversation* is a daily commentary website sponsored by publicly-funded universities. It is a CI. The *Flying Fruit Fly Circus (Foundation)* is, well, a circus. It is also a CI. The trustee for the *Collingwood Football Club Community Foundation*, with its origins in the highly commercial and successful Collingwood Football Club in Melbourne, recently received an $11m grant from the Australian Government. It is a CI. The *Royal Institution of Australia* sponsored a World Vasectomy Day on 18 October 2013, with the catch cry, 'would you put your balls on the line?' It is predominantly government-funded, but is also a CI. *Sea Shepherd Australia* must consider itself unlucky. There it is, saving whales, but the Full Federal Court of Australia decided that that work did not constitute animal welfare and was not entitled to endorsement as a deductible gift recipient. But it is a CI.[9]

As a consequence of a decision of the High Court in 2010 in *Aid/Watch Incorporated v. Commissioner of Taxation*, charities are now free to lobby government and not do any charity work. When charities lobby government on controversial matters, using the privilege of charity status, does the taxpayer have a right of veto? Tim Costello, the CEO of *World Vision*, is fond of quoting from the UNICEF organisation's brief, that the 'number of deaths dropped from 40,000 to 19,000 per

---

5 'Credit Where Credit is Due', *The Australian* 5 July 2013.

6 Victorian Women's Trust, *Annual Report 2010-11*.

7 Christians for Biblical Equality, http://cbesydney.org.au accessed 5 September 2013.

8 Animal Liberation, http://animal-lib.org.au accessed 5 September 2013.

9 *Sea Shepherd Australia Limited v Commissioner of Taxation* [2013] FCAFC 68 (3 July 2013).

day [between 1990 and 2011].'[10] The issue, of course, is what has this promising change got to do with foreign aid? The global poverty rate may have been cut in half in 20 years,[11] but whether it was foreign aid that caused the decline is highly contested. It is more likely to have been as a consequence of economic growth, something over which foreign aid charities have no control, indeed, often oppose. At least *World Vision* gets its hands dirty. *Results International's* mission, for example, is simply to 'generate the public and political will to end poverty', and government pays them to do so.[12]

The *National Institute of Dramtic Art*, better known as NIDA, is an acting school. A charitiable institution heavily government-funded, it also accepts donations which are tax deductible. Student fees make up a little more than $1 million of its $23 million income and donations do not appear to make an appearance in the accounts.[13] The Peter Mac Clinic is a cancer research and treatment group with an income in excess of $300 million – $160 million comes from recurrent government spending, $30 million from government capital funding, $85 million from commercial activities and research, and $20 millon from donations and bequests.[14] A potential donor may be interested to know that the largest UK cancer charity raises £500 million per year and that there are 4,000 researchers and medical staff in the UK.[15] At least US$6 billion was devoted to cancer research in the US in 2012 alone (NCI, 2012, 56), and there are more than 8,000 PhDs in US universities every year in biological and biomedical sciences.[16] Should the extra Australian dollar be spent on care of the sick, or on research? These questions are at the heart of improving

10 Tim Costello, CEO of World Vision Australia, interview by Hamish McDonald, Channel 10 *Late News* 30 April 2013.

11 'Poverty: Not Always With Us', *The Economist*, 1 June 2013.

12 Results International, http://www.results.org.au/about-us/ accessed 15 March 2014.

13 National Institute of Dramtic Art, *Annual Report 2012*.

14 Peter Mac Foundation, *Annual Report 2012*, page 50.

15 Cancer Research UK, www.cancerresearchuk.org accessed 24 July 2013.

16 National Science Foundation, National Center for Science and Engineering Statistics, http://www.nsf.gov/statistics/sed/2011/data_table.cfm accessed 25 September 2013.

the impact of charity work. Sometimes charities ask these questions, but it is difficult to change direction when the purpose of the charity has a life of its own, and perhaps an historical mandate or purpose.

Australia's oldest charity, the *Benevolent Society*, which in 2013 celebrated its 200th anniversary, has an income of more than $80 million per annum. Almost 82 per cent of its income comes from government. Only 4 per cent comes from donations.[17] The *Society* may be described as a government sub-contractor. The *Society* is not alone: economically significant not-for-profits (largely charities) in Australia derive 33 per cent of their income from government (PC, 2010, 72). Charities have placed themselves in the hands of government, a predicament that some charity elders have described as a crisis of identity: 'They do not know who they are and they do not know why they are doing what they are doing' (Judd, 2012, 4). Others are businesses by another name. *Workways Australia* is a PBI that wins contracts from the Australian Government to find people jobs. Its contract revenue was $20 million in 2012, almost its entire income.[18] In what sense is it different to any other service provider? Does it provide a cheap service to government?

At a stretch, the non-profit sector makes up about four per cent of the Australian economy (ABS, 2009, 2). In Australia, the UK and Canada, the level of giving is about 0.7 per cent of GDP as measured against annual average income (PA, 2011, 17). If the amount of money donated to charities increased to that of the US, which remains just under two per cent (Lohmann, 2007, 440), it would not come near the monies that governments command of taxpayers' income to transfer to those who are in need. That being the case, can charity play much of a role in a country where the welfare state has a massive part to play in every Australian life, and many elsewhere, in receipt of Australian aid? Is it the role of charity to make up the short fall in the welfare state, or to be an innovator in programs, or to lobby government?

---

17 The Benevolent Society, *Annual Report 2012*, page 30.

18 Workways Australia, *Annual Report 2011-12*, page 40.

As the welfare state has grown, so have charities. Not-for-profits (largely charities) grew more than double the real growth rate of the economy in the seven years to 2006-07.[19] In 2007, there were 51,000 tax concession charities, 24,000 of which were eligible DGR charities. In 2005-06, individuals claimed $1.5 billion in deductible gifts (ATO, 2007, 96, 196). In 2011, there were 55,000 tax concession charities and 28,000 DGRs. In 2010-11, nearly five million Australians claimed $2.2 billion in deductible gifts (ATO, 2013, 101).

The total number of Private Ancillary Funds (PAF), a form of trust account, was 924 by the end of 2010-11, with 103 new funds registering for DGR status in that year.[20] PAFs have grown from donations of $53 million and distributions of $7 million in 2001-02 to donations of $304 million and distributions of $165 million in 2010-11. Donations reached a high of $780 million in 2007-08 before the GFC (figure 1.1). These amounts substantially understate the extent of giving. It is estimated that in 2004, Australians gave $5.7 billion in donations; about 50 per cent of the population gave another $2 billion through charitable gambling, charity auctions, dinners and other events where they received a benefit in return for their support. Around 92 per cent of this went to non-for-profit organisations (PMCBP, 2005, vii).

The ways in which charities raise funds is ever expanding. A Starwood preferred guest at a Meridien or Sheraton, or a host of other participating hotels, has the option to not donate to UNICEF through its checkout for children program. One dollar is automatically deducted from the guest's account for the donation, unless the guest, at checkout, declines to make the donation. A Coles or Woolworths customer may participate in a host of charities through donating to any number at the checkout.

A customer at *Typo* part of the *Cotton On* brand is encouraged to round up their purchase to the nearest whole cent or dollar with the difference

19 Growth in health, education and the environment sectors of the economy have been strongest, but the trend in charities is also unmistakable (PC, 2010, 63).

20 A discussion of PAFs is to be found at chapter 6.

Figure 1.1: Private ancillary fund donations and distributions ($m), 2002-11

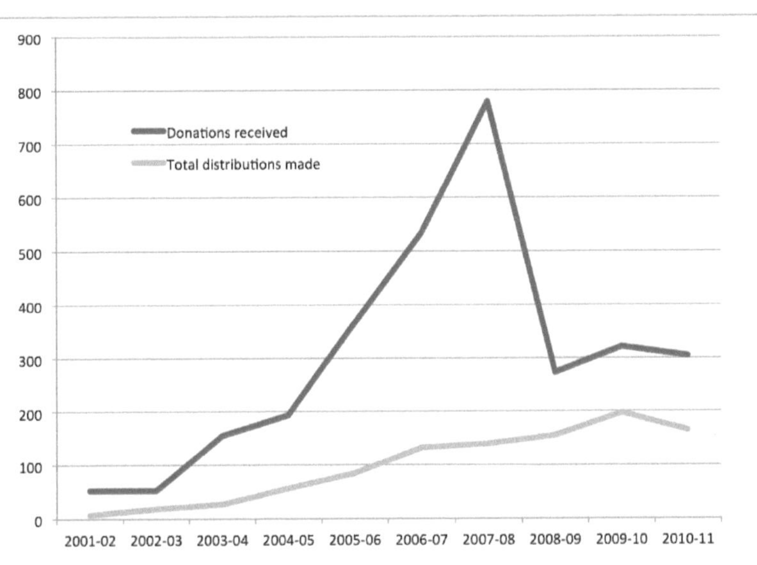

Source: (ATO, 2013, table 5).

being donated to the *Cotton On Foundation* (a PBI). The customer is nudged towards this outcome; it takes some act on the customer's part to say no. Moreover, the customer does not get bragging rights, but *Cotton On* does.[21] EFTPOS has organised an annual *Giveback* campaign at Christmas, during which time shoppers were asked to support charities 'by pressing CHQ or SAV at the checkout.'[22] *Diabetes Australia* and *Cancer Australia* were pledged $2 million in the 2013 campaign.

And there are the street corner charity 'spruikers', people paid to raise funds on the street, in place of volunteers. About 200,000 people sign on to become a regular donor through face-to-face marketing each year, committing $60 million to a plethora of causes, according to Cornucopia

21 Cotton On, http://shop.cottonon.com/cottonon-foundation/?ici=cof&icn=cof_131202_aunz_ipledge_HPgrid_02_13 accessed 4 December 2013.

22 EFTPOS Australia, http://www.eftposaustralia.com.au accessed 17 December 2013.

Consulting, a marketing firm that represents such charities as *Amnesty International*, the *Fred Hollows Foundation* and the *Red Cross*.[23] Donors secured through face-to-face marketing return, on average, 29 times their initial monthly donation over five years, according to the Fundraising Institute of Australia. The *Fred Hollows Foundation*, for example, has 118,000 donors.[24]

There has been a proliferation of marketing companies that hire salespeople to recruit donors and manage the sign-up process. Cornucopia Consulting, Ways Fundraising and 2evolve are among the most prominent. The marketing company generally receives a one-off fee per donor, forgoing the fee if the donor cancels in the first 100 days. The company also takes a proportion of the overall donation, with the amount varying according to the lifetime of the donor support. The sooner the donor cancels the gift, the higher the proportion that goes to the marketing company. Paul Tavatgis, a fundraising consultant at Cornucopia Consulting, says the average donor agreement lasts up to five years, and Cornucopia would usually take 20-25 per cent of the total given. Tavatgis says face-to-face fundraising has been part of a wider change in which charities have prioritised regular giving. 'The benefit of this method is that charities have a reliable and predictable source of income to fund their programs.'[25]

Regulate or better information for the market?

As the charity ball bounces along, government and philanthropists are beginning to ask questions about charity performance.[26] Donors believe that their contribution can make a difference (Bekkers, 2010, 942), and they are influenced by charities' performance, so it is in the interests of charities that their performance is scrutinised by donors (Kitching, 2009;

---

23 Julia May, 'The Hard Word on the Street', *The Sydney Morning Herald* 22 October 2013.

24 Fred Hollows Foundation, *Annual Report 2012*, page 2.

25 Julia May, 2013, as above.

26 Philanthropy Australia, for example, offers courses in assessing social impact.

Trussel, 2007). The problem is that relevant and reliable information is rarely available in Australia (Chen, 2009, 350). This absence needs not only to be addressed but also remedied.

A recent report on the sector by the Productivity Commission treated all dollars – donor dollars, tax-assisted donor dollars, and charity-government contract dollars – as charity 'inputs'. This view masks the essential tension in the relationship between government and charities, and between charities and private donors (PC, 2010, xxxv). After all, the 'source of funding will impact to whom charities are accountable' (Judd 2012, 304). Currently, private donors, often with tax-assisted donations, are generally not well informed about charity performance (PC, 2010, xxiii). Charity performance is now a product of the charity activist, often without the input of donors. Charity activists sometimes approach every problem with the same set of solutions; they are said to 'problem surf' (Boscarino, 2009). Some are also in the business of exaggerating problems for which they have 'the solution'. A headline, '1 in 4 Australians' (… fill in the problem) or some other bold claim, is a signal to be wary of the accuracy of the data. For example, although the number of homeless people in Australia is reported as 90,000, the actual number of people sleeping rough on the streets is 7,000. The definition of homelessness has been expanded to include, among others, those who live in supported accommodation, which is the solution for some causes of homelessness. Nevertheless, homelessness charities always report 90,000, never 7,000.

The *Australian Indigenous Education Foundation (AIEF)* claims it 'has found a way to make the best education available to the most marginalised children in [Australia] … by offering scholarships which cover their school or university fees.'[27] The founder has stated: 'Our program is not about cherry-picking the best and brightest kids, it's about giving opportunity to kids of all walks of life who want to make the most of

27 Australian Indigenous Education Foundation, www.aief.com.au accessed 25 September 2013.

those opportunities, irrespective of where they come from.'[28] Clearly, the charity is sensitive to the claim that such programs of assistance can appear to be successful by selecting people who would otherwise have succeeded, without such assistance. According to their own measure, however, their targets are 'the most marginalised', meaning disadvantaged. Selecting those who want to succeed is, of course, an important element in success. The *AIEF* state that they are looking for students who are 'tapped into the idea they could achieve more',[29] but they would presumably choose the most marginalised among those who show promise.

The two case studies that the *AIEF* allowed to be featured in recent extensive press coverage were students who did not appear to be at all marginalised.[30] The most marginalised students are those who live in remote Aboriginal communities – 20,000 children on Aboriginal lands attending Aboriginal schools. 'These students had by far the worst results, with failure rates often exceeding 90 per cent' (Craven, 2013, 14). The case studies promoted by the *AIEF* appear not to satisfy their goal. In addition, it is highly likely that scholarships could have been made available at less expensive schools, possibly in the region where students lived. Then again, the *AIEF* is entitled to argue that government should tackle the hard core students but, if that is so, *AIEF* loses credit for claiming to help those most in need.

Corporations, which presumably have built their wealth on merit and the marketplace, are at times peculiarly susceptible to naivety in their 'charity' work. A recent report for the *Smith Family*, sponsored by AMP, on the apparent failure on equality of opportunity in Australia failed to distinguish even in the most rudimentary of ways different

28 Andrew Penfold, 'From Locked Up, To Looking Up,' *The Weekend Australian* 9–10 February 2013.

29 Rick Morton, 'A $100 Million Plan to Deliver a Better Future,' *The Australian* 7 May 2013.

30 Patricia Karvelas and Justine Ferrari, 'Funds Secure Lifetime of Opportunity,' *The Weekend Australian* 11-12 May 2013.

conceptions of fairness: egalitarian, meritocratic and liberal. Instead, it assumed that different outcomes had to be amenable to fixing with more resources. The study published data suggesting well-known differences in outcomes for children based on class background which, despite the best efforts of massive government interventions across decades, have changed little except for the fact that bright children from poor classes and areas have a good chance of succeeding (Leigh, 2007). For a charity to suggest that it has solutions is somewhat naïve, or is simply a marketing tool (Cassells, 2011). The charity may well be able to help some children, selectively, to the limits of their donors' resources. All too frequently, when corporations attempt to intervene in Aboriginal policy they lose all sense of analytical probity. AMP, for instance, in a program designed to build 'cultural identity' argued that gender equality was a traditional Aboriginal strength (Doyle, 2012, 21). This would come as a surprise to many Aboriginal women.

A remedy

Competition among charities for informed donors should overcome the tendencies to 'problem surf', exaggerate claims and solutions, and lobby government. Suggestions of the type of information required range from the highly sophisticated, such as a predictive market in charity products, to the mundane, such as minimal registration information required by the Australian Charities and Not-for-profits Commission (ACNC) (Goldberg, 2009). The charity sector should not escape some form of accountability. Currently, governments impose a mild level of accountability because tax dollars are indirectly at risk. Donors, however, should impose a form of accountability as part-owners of charitable deeds.

Well-informed donors, especially philanthropists with an investment large enough to justify inquiring about charity performance, are the best chance of both forestalling further government regulation and fostering a better charity market. Donors can ask hard questions of charities. A child sponsor charity working in less-developed countries, for instance, should be asked whether they can name the village they have ceased working in because it is functioning well enough to look after its own as a result of charity.

Meanwhile, governments get on with regulation. The ACNC registers charities and requires an annual return to be lodged with the Commission, details of which will be shared with the public (ACNC (a), 2013). This year, 2014, larger charities will have to lodge a financial return, the details of which should enable public scrutiny of charity efficiency (ACNC (b), 2013). The Abbott Government has announced that it will abolish the Commission, but continue to 'support transparency and accountability of public funds'.[31] This stance may well be a reaction to the corporatist attitude of the sector and the previous Labor Government which had established a 'Compact' between the government and charities. The statement from the Compact – 'We believe a strong, independent not-for-profit sector is vital for a fair, inclusive society' (Australian Government, 2011, 7) may seem innocuous but is clearly a statement of egalitarian intent, a view not shared by all charities nor, indeed, is it consistent with the historical purpose of charities. The Productivity Commission report quoted the Compact on 14 occasions throughout its report, which indicates the influence it had on the Commission's report (PC, 2010). Typically, the Commission is the champion of markets, not of political compacts.

Whatever new body is established, it will be prompted by recommendations of the Productivity Commission to improve data collection about sector performance and its availability to the public. One suggestion is for the government to fund the establishment of a Centre for Community Service Effectiveness to promote evaluation (PC, 2010, 112), but this may be no more than a 'starter kit' on governance for new charities. Concentrating on the effectiveness of charity is a good

---

31 Kevin Andrews, 'Civil Society and the Role of Government,' *Centre for Independent Studies* 23 April 2013.

idea. Although donors are affected by efficiency in charity fundraising and disbursement (Bowman, 2006), these may not indicate an effective charity and are perhaps better suited to internal management purposes (Pallotta, 2008; Ryan & Irvine, 2012). After all, 'success in raising money' implies nothing about success in serving beneficiaries (Fiennes, 2012, 874). Nevertheless, work on a national standard chart of accounts for charities is well advanced so that comparisons in efficiency will, in time, be possible should that work proceed (ACNC (b), 2013).

One charity industry insider recently commented that charity tax deductions were 'chickenfeed' compared to government contracts.[32] The charity sector may well continue to be a supplicant and lobbyist to government, but it should seize the opportunity to allow donors to help drive performance. Government need not fund a centre for service effectiveness when the Australian National Audit Office is quite capable of scrutinising government service contracts. Charities and philanthropists should fund evaluations. In this way, the donor market may begin to deepen and mature, perchance once more to become a voice apart from government.

Lobbying

There is something unsatisfactory about taxpayers' money being used to fund charities that are campaigning for things that we may disagree with. (Seddon, 2007, 62)

As well as seizing the opportunity to promote a more effective market, charities should seriously review lobbying. The *Benevolent Society* lobbied government for better provision as early as 1862 when the NSW Government took responsibility for those once housed by the *Society* in the Benevolent Asylum. The *Society* proudly boasts that its president was a leading voice in the campaign for the old age pension introduced in

32 Private conversation with author.

1901.[33] The *Society* spends $2 million per year on charitable activities from its endowment fund, which comes from donations, $700,000 of which is spent on 'influencing social change by advocating for policy reform'.[34] The 'reform' aims to create a 'fairer' Australia and bewails 'growing disparity in income and job opportunities', an all-too-familiar cry among those disposed towards big government and redistribution. Such policies do not necessarily result in public benefit.

Olympic swimmer Ian Thorpe's *Fountain for Youth* is a CI. It receives a number of taxation advantages, as do donors, who are able to deduct the value of a gift from the income tax they would otherwise contribute to general revenue. *Fountain for Youth* raises funds through private donations, bequests, corporate partnerships and grant funding. As to the latter, *Fountain for Youth* has received three grants totalling $3.2 million (2005-2012) from the Australian Government for the [Indigenous] Literacy Empowerment Project.[35] Perhaps private donors are not concerned about how well their money is spent, but government, on behalf of the taxpayer, should be.

Unfortunately, there is no annual report available on the website and no report of the effectiveness of any programs. Upon request, a financial statement was made available.[36] As with many charities it is a financial audit, which is to say, the money flowed in and the money flowed out. But the question is: did it do any good?

Ian Thorpe's *Fountain for Youth* may do wonderful work, but someone other than the charity has to be the judge of its effectiveness. Only then can markets work. Maybe another charity could do a better job with the money? And, it does not only deliver literacy programs or, more

---

33 The Benevolent Society, 'Celebrating 200 years,' www.benevolent.org.au accessed 25 September 2013.

34 The Benevolent Society, *Annual Report 2012*, page 30.

35 Fountain for Youth, http://ianthorpes-fountainforyouth.com/about-us/funding accessed 12 November 2013.

36 Ian Thorpe's Fountain for Youth. (2013). *General Purpose Financial Report*, Sydney.

accurately, backpacks with books to children, it also dips its toe into political matters by linking to lobbyists against the NT Intervention in a campaign called Keeping Them Home.[37] Rightly or wrongly, both Labor and Coalition governments support the Intervention. These represent almost all voters. Does Thorpe's foundation have greater insights than those? Perhaps so, but why should the taxpayer, either directly or indirectly by subsidising donation tax deductions, fund such controversial activity? Perhaps it should be left to donors only. Let them pay for his foundation's megaphone.

Beacon Foundation is a charitiable institution whose mission is 'to influence the attitudes and culture of Australians so that each young person develops an independent will to achieve personal success through gainful activities'. It seems that *Beacon Foundation* was able to influence some Australians at least, because in 2011 it claimed to 'finally get traction with Federal Government after Tasmanian Independent Andrew Wilkie gave up his weekly agenda with the Prime Minister, in exchange for introducing *Beacon* and its work. This positive exchange has led to close to a million dollars in funding for *Beacon* to expand its work in a logical way.'[38] Now that is lobbying.

International studies suggest that 'political activity' or lobbying increases donations (Nicholson-Crotty, 2011, 591). The same may hold in Australia. Australia's foreign aid charities, for example, raise $1 billion per annum but it is unknown by how much lobbying has expanded its coffers. But the big prize is official foreign aid for which charities lobby. Official aid is $5 billion per annum and rising, and Australian charities receive $289 million of it.[39] It is clear where the best return on effort lies. A recent advertisement signed by 17 charities urged the Australian Government to spend more on foreign aid. The charities

37 As above.

38 Beacon Foundation, *Annual Report 2011*, page 5.

39 Australian Bureau of Statistics, *Yearbook Australia 2012*, pages 212–214. Some foreign aid organisations do not have charity status.

purported to represent 'more than two million Australian households who generously support international aid organisations each year'.[40] The two million presumably agreed to donate their private funds to charities. Perhaps they were aware that taxpayers supported their donations, but it is arguable they gave the charities permission to press government to spend more on foreign aid.

Advocacy courses for those working in charities are offered at universities. RMIT University offers Advocacy and Social Action in a Global Context, which teaches advocacy and social action to promote 'social justice for disadvantaged groups'. The course outline makes the wholly incorrect assertion that, 'Over the past two decades global capitalism has rapidly expanded and the Australian welfare state – like other welfare states – has contracted.'[41] The course chides government that 'welfare recipients (and many others) are under more obligations to demonstrate their deservedness to receive assistance'. Perhaps taxpayers are very keen that they do so. Some charitable foundations support this work as, for example, the *Bertha Activist Fellows Program*, which 'will nurture and support a network of activists who are challenging the status quo, in order to elevate, deepen and expand the impact of their work.'[42] Less ideological perhaps is The Graduate Certificate in Social Impact, offered by the Centre for Social Impact in partnership with three business schools: Melbourne Business School, the Australian School of Business at The University of New South Wales and Swinburne University of Technology's Faculty of Business and Enterprise.

Charities in Australia have always been free to lobby so long as they maintained charity work as their dominant purpose. The High Court decided that a charity engaged in 'lawful means of public debate

40 'Foreign Aid Must Reach the World's Poor,' *The Australian* 21 December 2012.

41 RMIT University, http://www.rmit.edu.au/courses/012110 accessed 18 July 2012.

42 The Bertha Foundation, http://www.berthafoundation.org/activism.html accessed 18 July 2013.

concerning the efficiency of foreign aid directed to the relief of poverty is a purpose beneficial to the community'.[43] Justice Heydon, in the minority judgment, found that 'Aid/Watch did not have the goal of relieving poverty. It provided no funds, goods or services to the poor.'[44] Justice Kiefel, in the minority, decided that Aid/Watch's 'pursuit of a freedom to communicate its views does not qualify as being for the public benefit'.[45] If the Australian Taxation Office (ATO) had challenged a charity set up to cut foreign aid, arguably a public benefit, the High Court would have run a mile. The Australian Government has written the substance of the High Court decision into law to legitimise 'promoting or opposing a change to any matter established by law, policy or practice in the Commonwealth, a state, a territory or another country'.[46] Advocacy and lobbying will become charitable purposes. Charities will be less constrained to lobby and less constrained to do less charity.

Given that common law has been changed to accommodate lobbying, a statute prohibiting lobbying may be the only way to constrain this use of funds, as is the case in other common law jurisdictions. The Abbott Government has agreed to repeal the legislation, although not necessarily to undo the High Court decision, if indeed that is possible. There are organisations such as the Centre for Independent Studies and the Institute of Public Affairs (where the author was a senior fellow) that have charity and DGR status. They are deemed research institutions and their purpose is to further public discourse, which includes promoting or opposing changes to law. Research institutions that rail against government provision and its debilitating effect on liberty – IPA and CIS – should be especially wary of promoting a culture of paid lobbying among charities. They may well argue, of course, that they would be at

43 *Aid/Watch Incorporated v Commissioner of Taxation* [2010] HCA 42 (1 December 2010), [47].

44 As above, [60].

45 As above, [86].

46 The Parliament of the Commonwealth of Australia, *Charities Act 2013*, Part 3 Division 1(12).

a competitive disadvantage to not accept DGR status. It is clear that no other charities lobby for less government.

Political parties have been publicly-funded since 1984, and the idea that government should pay organisations to play politics has entered the Australian culture. It is important, though, that subsidised lobbying should never be able to displace charity. There is, indeed, something unsatisfactory about using the power of government to do the bidding of charities. The law privileges one group of voters who, having covered the costs of organising their 'voice' on the basis of charity reputation and government privilege, proceed to lobby government, placing them and their views ahead of other citizens' voices. Recent UK polling suggests that donor attitudes to lobbying are closely aligned to political allegiances. While the UK public is largely positive about charities lobbying government, 78 per cent of Conservative MPs and 23 per cent of Labour MPs opposed charities 'being political' (nfpSynergy, 2013, 4).

A modest foil to governments funding the loudest lobby, those who can cry poor or create the greatest scare, is to specify that charities declare any and all monies they receive from government, and spend on lobbying. Thousands of donors making better informed choices should achieve a better reflection of a wider set of values, and provide some surety for taxpayers that not only charity activists' values are supported.

Taxation

Some have argued that, the key element of charitable activity is the simple mechanism of a person being motivated by the need of another or a cause, and responding to it. (Judd, 2012, 82)

So why do charities need taxpayers' help? After all, charities would survive on after-tax dollars and would not be beholden to government, or subject to scrutiny, if they got off the drip. The cost of foregoing tax advantages, however, is that the cost of philanthropy may rise and less of it would flow to charities. By lowering the price of giving, tax incentives potentially increase the amount donated and the number of individuals donating. The same, of course, could be said of any industry. There is, after all, an opportunity cost of philanthropy and charity. There are alternative beneficial uses for these resources.

In addition to those other beneficial uses, the critical taxation question is whether additional giving induced by taxation deductions is greater or less than the value of the tax deductions provided. Best estimates suggest that 'a one per cent decrease in the cost of giving [as a result of the taxation deduction] results in a 0.51 to 1.26 permanent rise in the amount of giving' (PC, 2010, 174). At the low end, this means individual giving rises by less than the value of the tax subsidy so that there is some 'crowding out' and only a minor increase overall. At the high end, giving rises by more than the value of the tax subsidy, resulting in a higher level of giving by the individual and a major increase overall. There is evidence to suggest that high-income individuals are more likely to give more than the value of a tax deduction.

Regardless, in political terms, no government is about to remove tax assistance for all or most charities. They may, however, look at changing the 'incentive' target and the nature of the assistance. A recent report on the matter to the Australian Government recommended, among other things, that DGR status should be extended to all charities, but use of tax deductible donations 'should be restricted to purposes and activities that are not solely for the advancement of religion, or the advancement of education through child care and primary and secondary education, except where the activity is sufficiently related to advancing another charitable purpose' (TCWG, 2013, 6). Putting to one side debate about the efficacy of grants or rebates as opposed to deductions (PC, 2010, appendix G.32; Scharf, 2010), two questions need to be addressed – whether some charities deserve assistance and whether the balance between the donor and the charity (or charity employees) is right.

Some charity activities such as lobbying are of doubtful public benefit but profitable for the charity. Some charitable purposes are doubtful on other grounds. There are almost 5,000 school or college building funds that are DGR status charities. A case could be made that these are self-regarding, rather than for the public benefit. Since when is giving to one's child's school a charity? The same could be said for public hospitals and Technical and Further Education institutions and universities. These are, to all intents and purposes, commercial activities with paying clients and considerable direct government assistance. The benefits accrue to individuals and only indirectly to the public. Why throw in an extra subsidy? Again, politics, not logic, decides these matters. No government will disturb these constituencies, but in failing to do so they weaken the case for 'other-regarding' and public benefit charity.

Charities and donors receive taxation benefits. The balance of these is worth investigating. A range of taxation advantages such as payroll tax and stamp duty concessions from State government assists charities (PC, 2010, appendix E). The Australian Government provides fringe benefits tax (FBT) exemptions for employees of eligible institutions and deductible gift exemptions for donors to charities with DGR status. Some in the charity sector would like to have fewer funds used in FBT and more access to DGR (CCA, 2012, 6). They do so to rebalance support for large rather than small charities. They also argue that most FBT benefits accrue to well-paid employees. These arguments are unproven. There is little reason to suspect that small charities are better than large charities or that higher paid workers are not worth their benefits. In broad terms, however, taxation should assist the donor, not the charity worker.

Accountability and its limits

A key part of the charity ball is that government has rarely been prepared to ask what charities do with donated money (and charity is keen to remain free of regulation). But every dollar that has little or no public benefit is a dollar misspent. Well-informed donors could drive a better charity market. The Productivity Commission has charted a path to a better charity market, though with a significant weakness: a less than complete appreciation of the donor.

The Commission's formulation suggests that apart from access to capital, there are several main constraints to improving productivity in the charity market: a danger of excessive regulation (Kurti, 2013); lack of information and evidence on outcomes; and weak mechanisms to reallocate resources to more productive charities. There is one other. Although the Commission argued that competition plays 'at best a weak role as an incentive for productivity improvement in charities', charities nevertheless compete (PC, 2010, 228). Among other things, charities compete for government contracts – their major source of income – and for donors.

In common with most associations (including political parties), activists, not donors, are the driving force. Political parties that seek to maximise votes, however, must balance the desires of active members with the desires of voters. Businesses that seek to maximise profits must balance the desires of owners with the desires of consumers. It is not clear-cut what charities seek to maximise (Andreoni, 2011), but, ideally, charity should maximise 'impact'. Impact is such a contestable idea, however, that it is likely only to emerge out of the struggle for control between the organisation which runs the charity and those who support its causes through donations (of time and money). Account should be taken of recipient wishes where these can be identified, but that applies equally to the charity and the donor. The political essence of the well-informed donor theory is that the donor can act to offset the enthusiasms of charity activists, and the fear that governments hold of program evaluations in its own programs (Cobb-Clark, 2013, 90).

The economic essence of the theory is that donors can drive an effective market by choosing which charity to support. It can strengthen the reallocation of resources to more efficient charities, and improve allocations across charitable causes by supporting the most effective charities. Evidence suggests that charity ratings do affect donor behaviour (Chen, 2009; Sloan, 2009). At present, information about charitable works is held by charities and it is not easy to convey to others. To achieve greater 'symmetry' of information in the charity market, ways must be found to allow reporting good information. The burden of information should not, however, be so great as to divert large resources from charitable works or prove a disincentive to donate (Null, 2011).

Most donors are insufficiently organised or have insufficient investment to demand scrutiny of charity performance. Fortunately, big philanthropy is turning its attention to market function. There are few measures of charity market function, where ideally a major portion of monies flows to the most needy via competition between charities for donations. There is little concept, for example, of the optimum number of charities or whether more charities result in greater public benefit (Barla, 2005). There are few measures of charity performance, although the costs of fundraising and disbursement as well as impact are beginning to be counted. Nevertheless, it is worthwhile observing that well-informed consumers and investors drive markets. While consumers of charity services are not likely to be in a position to choose their 'product', donors should be in a position to choose which charity to support or, at the very least, to ask pertinent questions.

Which donors are likely to drive a better charity market? In Australia, 40,000 individuals gift $5,000 a year, and nearly 15,000 individuals gift $15,000 or more a year, to charities. In addition, there are the PAFs, mentioned above, that distribute about $200 million per year (ATO, 2012, 109). In time, these donors would probably constitute the informed market. Large trust companies are beginning to 'engage' with philanthropists to maximise the social impact of their clients' investment in charity (TTC (b), 2012). These changes could drive not only existing charities to respond, but also stimulate greater competition among charities or the growth of new charities.

Then there are the big hitters. Twiggy Forrest, Bill Gates, Warren Buffett, and others, for example, have promised to donate half their wealth to charity through the *Giving Pledge*.[47] The public benefit of these generous actions is welcome but not obvious. There are opportunity costs, because it means their money will no longer be available for wealth creation. When a donor of the resources of those mentioned above steps into the charity arena they could overwhelm the charity. In essence, they become the charity. They could, however, drive sophisticated cost-benefit analysis to guide charitable priorities and 'highest impact' philanthropy (Buteau, 2011; Tuan, 2008).

A donor guide – DonorInform Limited

The common way to measure the impact of charity is to tell stories about the people helped by a charity. *WaterAid Australia*, for example, displays on its website, in the main, many smiling faces of African people assisted by their newfound access to clean water, an undoubted benefit.[48] How great the benefit is compared to another water intervention, or another form of intervention in those same lives, or, indeed, the intervention's endurance (Munk, 2013), are the real evaluations missing in the charity field.

It is not sufficient, for example, to have charities report in a narrow band of financial ratios. There is no reason to assume that charities with higher fundraising costs, for example, are 'worse buys' (Steinberg, 1986, 348). Alternatively, just because a charity may be an efficient fundraiser does not mean it is effective in directing resources to the causes it serves (Berber, 2011, 2). But while donors need not consider fundraising costs as the determining factor in their decision to invest, there is no need to have an 'empty policy locker' either. The donor needs to know about fundraising costs in conjunction with program delivery. Together, these provide powerful information for improving performance.

47 Giving Pledge, http://givingpledge.org accessed 25 September 2013.

48 WaterAid Australia, http://www.wateraid.org/au/what-we-do/our-impact/stories-from-our-work accessed 27 November 2013.

A recent inquiry by a committee of the Australian Senate recommended that the [then foreshadowed] ACNC investigate the costs and benefits of a GuideStar-type system in Australia to encompass all not-for-profit organisations (SCE, 2008, 3). *GuideStar UK*, an information repository, provides information about all registered charities in England and Wales.[49] The quality of the information is not adequate to inform donors in a way that would have them decide how their monies will be best used. A survey in 2006 of 73 of the United Kingdom's largest charities reporting on *GuideStar* concluded, 'Charities more readily provide descriptive information … about organizational motives … stakeholders have little indication of the effectiveness and efficiency with which charities are operating' (Dhanani, 2009, 186).

The sector, as a whole, has resisted performance monitoring. There are, however, signs that performance monitoring by other agencies is possible. For example, the private company *Givewell Australia* believes that a 'more informed and generous giving will lead to a more accountable, efficient and effective charitable sector'.[50] *Givewell* was formed in 1997 to 'foster a better culture of giving in Australia'. It researches charities and generates ideas on better ways to give. Regrettably, *Givewell* has ceased to operate as an information site.

A great deal of experience in performance measurement of charity is available, mostly in the United States. *GiveWell USA (GW USA)*, for example, claims: 'Unlike other charity evaluators, which focus solely on … assessing administrative or fundraising costs, it focuses on how well programs actually work.'[51] *GW USA* only recommends charities that can make a strong case that they are significantly improving lives in a cost-effective way and can use additional donations to expand their proven programs.

Another independent operator, *Charity Navigator* (CN), serves more

49 GuideStar UK, www.guidestar.org.uk accessed 25 September 2013.

50 GiveWell Australia, the website is now defunct.

51 GiveWell US, http://givewell.org accessed 25 September 2013.

than three million unique visitors and informs approximately $10 billion of charitable donations each year. *CN* rates charities by financial health and accountability and transparency.[52] Evaluations on financial health are based on information each charity provides in its tax returns. From the data, *CN* generates measures of financial efficiency; it also intends to rate results and drive change by rewarding charities that publish rigorously collected feedback from their beneficiaries.

Providing metrics for results is the most difficult part of the performance exercise. There are signs of development. There are professional bodies and an international association supporting social impact analysts.[53] These indications of movement towards rigorous external scrutiny to increase competition between charities in the name of better use of donor monies are to be applauded.

The idea that Australia should have a national register of charities to inform donors better is well-established and the ACNC has embarked on that journey. What information such a register should contain is, however, to be settled. The contention is that donors should shape the charity market with their choices. Rating charities by means of objective performance is a worthy goal, but it can be resource intensive and may not answer donors' questions. Rather than establish a charity rating agency and website, it may be more feasible, and preferable, at least as a start, to establish a donor guide on a website. To this end, the concept of DonorInform Limited [54] will be explained in chapter 7.

Donors want a warm inner glow from giving and they have biases as to the cause they may give. A donor's preferences may, to some extent, be influenced by the frequency of events or 'distorted by the prevalence and emotional intensity of the messages to which they are exposed' (Kahneman, 2012, 2467).

---

52 Charity Navigator, www.charitynavigator.org accessed 25 September 2013.

53 Social Impact Analysts Association, http://siaassociation.org accessed 25 September 2013.

54 DonorInform Limited is a not-for-profit company limited by guarantee. Gary Johns, Cassandra Wilkinson and John Humphreys are directors.

Charities want to find and solve problems; they identify needs, sometimes with 'attitude'. They have their agendas and they sell their cause. Satisfying donors, and, perhaps, correcting their biases may be achieved by creating tools to allow donors to work out to whom they want to give, and why. A charity rating will not answer the most fundamental questions about which cause is most important to the donor, unless they are first exposed to a wider set of data about the relative merits of causes. The latter would be one purpose of the donor guide.

According to the most recent large survey of donor attitudes in Australia, undertaken in 2004, 87 per cent of Australians gave to charity; most of the money went to charitable organisations (PMCBP, 2005, 36). Almost half the donors gave because they identified with the cause and the people whose assistance is the object of the cause. Close to a third said they gave because of a sense of reciprocation for services already provided, or anticipation that help might be needed in future. For just under one-eighth, the main reason was a desire to strengthen the community or, more generally, to make the world a better place. Identifying with a cause may be a perfectly understandable, if shallow basis, on which to decide to spend money. Charities work on simple messages of hope, but their messages assume a great deal of knowledge. For example, whether sponsoring a child in Africa is the best way to assist a child, and why in Africa?

Overall, 34 per cent of givers claimed some sort of direct affiliation with the organisation to which they were donating. For 25 per cent, this affiliation was that they (or members of their family) used the service it provided (some of these were also members of the organisation or volunteered for it). Affiliation could be held to be self-serving, a form of insurance for the future.

People give to what they know. If they know more, or differently, they may give differently. Those in the survey who answered that they did not give were doubtful about the money's use or that too much would be soaked up in administration, or that too little would reach those in need.

These doubts displayed a lack of trust in charities, although they may have been convenient reasons not to give. Nevertheless, they were factors that may have been overcome with better information. Matching the desires of donors and charities is something to which markets are well-suited. Markets are at their best when donors and charities freely interact, and where donors are well-informed of the most important aspects of the operation of charities and the policy context in which they work.

There is a way to deflate the charity ball and relieve, to some extent, the burden of government regulation on charities. If donors wish to continue to donate knowing the charity already receives large grants from government, and/or spends a great deal of time lobbying government – a recent UK survey found that 32 per cent of respondents thought that charities should lobby government to change law or policy (Wixley, 2014, 8) – then the donor can judge whether the charity is worthy of their support. Governments are reluctant to set rules for such matters, so better to let the donor decide. Some proportion of the charity dollar is likely misallocated or misspent. Throwing open the market to better-informed donors can help to solve these weaknesses in the present market. The beneficiaries of charity have the most to gain.

Government can help by making a simple annual return of purpose, activities and income a compulsory part of charity registration. Government should also make available a list of all grants to charities and insist that charities make this a part of their annual financial statement. A donor advisory service and website, funded by the philanthropic sector itself, can do the rest.

Some would be uncomfortable with the idea that charity operates in a marketplace. But it surely does: charities compete for donors on behalf of those whom the charity deems need help. They compete by tugging at heartstrings, by telling stories of woe – 'cerebral palsy is more common than cancer, stroke, appendicitis and road traffic accidents' [55]

55 Cerebral Palsy League, *Annual Report 2011-12*, page 5.

– and sometimes by describing how they will solve the problem. Proof that they do solve the problem better than any other charity is sometimes hard to find. The charity market is messy. The object of this study is not to make it any less messy, only to make it work better. To make it work better requires a few rules and many prying eyes and inquiring minds. The objective is to lower the cost of finding what charities do with the money given to them by donors and taxpayers. Donors, in conjunction with charities, can drive better charity.

2

Charity market – donations for information

A not so different market

Apart from do-it-yourself charity, of which there is plenty, charity usually flows through charities. Charities sell a means to fulfil a donor's desire to assist the needy and donors buy satisfaction and assurance that their desire will be fulfilled. Charities need donors' money and donors need charities' organisation. The exchange of money and services to satisfy those needs constitute a market.

While charities may not behave in the way that business does, they nevertheless display 'economic behaviour'(ABS, 2009, 32). For example, they seek to attract customers (the needy or a 'cause') and, indeed, to represent them, and investors (donors). Their behaviour is influenced variously by financial support from philanthropic trusts and donors, small and large, and government.

Charities are the agent of the donor, but donors are rarely in the driver's seat. They rely on the charity to report the use of the donation. They are often constrained by lack of information about the best use of their donation. There are costs that the donor has to incur to constrain the activities of the charity, and there are costs that the charity has to incur to convince the donor that their wishes are being met.

The big question is what will the donor pay to find out whether the charity fulfils their wish? The answer is unnerving: not a lot. Where the cost of information outweighs the benefit derived from knowing about the impact of the donation, it is rational for a donor to remain ignorant. Citizens may also be rationally ignorant about the size and activities of government, but some research suggests much less fiscal illusion and rational ignorance about education funding than other social spending functions, perhaps because education directly affects more people than any other social program (Garrett, 2010, 118). Nevertheless, donor ignorance may keep the level of donations anchored below what the donor judges to be 'go away' money when charities ask for donations. The same should not be true of philanthropists and governments, who have a greater investment in knowing outcomes, but sometimes they forget to ask, or fail to share the information.

Charities, on the other hand, also have their own values and traditions and, often, definite ideas about what to do to 'solve problems'. Charities also have to overcome donor reticence. Donors are likely to want to do other things with their money which, after all, is not 'taken from under a mattress and introduced into the economy as new money'.[1] There would be some associated welfare benefits in leaving it in the bank. As difficult as it may be to measure, in order to make a positive contribution to welfare, charities need to do something better than the alternative uses to which donations could be put. Those who do not 'understand the long-term effects or efficiency of donating to a charitable cause should think twice before depriving the world of investment by giving to charity'.[2]

A well-functioning charity market would ensure the highest level of satisfaction among donors for the least amount of effort. There should be, for example, an efficient number, or size and number, of charities. The highest level of satisfaction among donors should be consistent with allocation of funds to those in greatest need as decided by donors,

1 Fransen, 'The "Opportunity Cost" of Philanthropy.' http://www.philanthropydaily.com 9 April 2012 accessed 18 February 2014.

2 The Freakwenter, 'The Opportunity Cost of Philanthropy.' http://zacharychild.blogspot.com.au/2008/09/opportunity-cost-of-philanthropy.html accessed 9 April 2012.

or to programs of the highest value to recipients (Schizer, 2009, 242). Achieving a well-functioning market without prices and profits is difficult. Nevertheless, where people choose to support one cause over others, and where charities compete for donations using various strategies, mainly information about the cause, or perhaps information about their performance in pursuing the cause, there is an exchange – donations for information. While the interests of donors and charities may not be the same, they can be aligned by monitoring charity performance (Van Puyvelde, 2011, 435). The trick is to minimise the cost of monitoring and reporting performance as a way of fostering a well-functioning market.

Government is a third and major player in the charity market. Governments set conditions for who shall and shall not be allowed to enter the market. They assist charities by forgiving them taxation they would otherwise pay, and assist donors by forgiving them taxation when they donate to eligible charities. Government also displaces charity through welfare and other programs and arguably has 'crowded out' the role of charity. The nature, amount and balance of assistance may affect the overall functioning of the market. In these many respects, the charity market is a market not so different to any other.

Size and nature of the market

One thing is certain, without government intervention there would be precious little data by which to understand the charity market. Most of the characteristics of the market are gleaned from taxation statistics. There are, for example, more than 10,000 charities of significant capacity (those receiving fringe benefit tax exemption) in Australia and annual donations from individuals to charities have grown from $800 million in 2001 to more than $2.2 billion in 2011 (ATO, 2013, 98). Broader statistics about government grants to charities and contracts with charities are not well known but funding received from government has risen from 30 per cent of sector income in 2000 to 33 per cent in 2007 (PC, 2010, 54).

Which are the biggest charities and how long they endure are difficult to assess. Unattributed data suggests that the 'top 25 Australian charities by revenue have been around for an average of over 85 years' (Judd, 2012, 289), and that between 1998 and 2008 gross revenue averaged an annual growth rate of 9.4 per cent (Givewell (Australia), 2009). The causes or fields in which charities compete change over time. In a wealthy country such as Australia and where incomes are growing, perhaps contrary to expectations, the call for funding has also grown. Economic progress creates higher demands for causes such as environmental pollution, health issues such as psychiatric illness, and diseases that become more prevalent with longevity (Daza, 2010, 93). It seems that charity will never go out of business.

Measured by the number of tax concession charities (table 2.1), the greatest rates of growth between 2007 and 2012 occurred in charities in the fields of health (41 per cent), the natural environment (37 per cent) and culture (24 per cent). The lowest rates of growth occurred in traditional fields of social and community welfare (four per cent). These numbers may indicate that the market in the latter is satiated and that opportunities are opening in new fields such as the environment, as well as new parts of continuing fields, such as health.

Table 2.1: Number of tax concession charities 2007 and 2012

Main charitable purpose	Per cent increase	2007	2012
Social and community welfare	4	23,154	24,006
Religion	8	11,615	12,664
Education	9	8,609	9,412
Health	41	1,608	2,742
Culture	24	1,310	1,716
Natural environment	37	420	670
Other	23	3,913	5,069
Total	10	50,629	56,279

Source: (ATO, 2007, 97; ATO, 2013, 99).

Whether the right number of charities is in the market is difficult to judge. Businesses come and go on a frequent basis in the profit sector. They do so in response to the needs of buyers, barriers to entry and benefits to be gained through growing bigger. Ideally, the right number of businesses exists to serve the needs of the market; too few and needs go unmet; too many and the cost of satisfying the market is too high.

A thought experiment on assessing the efficient number of charities would run thus. Assuming that the objective is to maximise contributions to some common causes, and that contributions are made through charities, the number of charities is affected as follows. If there were no costs in establishing a charity, and if the government were in favour of the charitable cause in question, there would be a charity for each individual that shared the same values. With set-up costs, the number of charities has to be reduced. Theoretically, one charity suffices (Pestieau, 2006, 2). In essence, the conditions of entry and the amount of subsidy determine the number of charities. Governments control, in a fashion, the number of charities by granting the privilege of charitable status and tax breaks.

Rob Edwards, chief executive of the Fundraising Institute of Australia, has observed that while giving has levelled off, the number of charities has rocketed. 'You only have to look at charities in the cancer space – even more specific cancers for example, like breast cancer' – where the *Breast Cancer Network*, the *National Breast Cancer Foundation*, the *Jane McGrath Foundation* and the *Cancer Council*'s high-profile Pink Ribbon Day all compete.[3] Data appears to support this observation. Australian charities increased by 1.9 per cent per year between 2007 and 2012 (annualised, based on table 2.1) compared to businesses, which increased by 0.4 per cent from 2011 to 2012.

A possible explanation comes from a recent US study which suggests that, while entry rates are lower than those of for-profits in services, there are low exit rates, which result in net entry rates nearly three times

3 Julia May, 'The Hard Word on the Street', *The Sydney Morning Herald* 22 October 2013.

larger than that in for-profits. In addition, those leaving the field are not only few but decline with age and size, which is consistent with the endurance of the relatively few large charities in Australia (Harrison, 2008, 7). In Australia, the entry rate for business was 13.5 per cent for the 2011-12 financial year, higher than the exit rate (13.1 per cent), resulting in an increase in the number of businesses. Of the new business entries during 2008-09, 51 per cent were still operating in June 2012 (ABS, 2013, 6). Unfortunately, entry, exit and longevity figures for charities are not available from the Australian Bureau of Statistics (ABS) although the South Australian Government provides a list of expired and revoked charities, but not in a form that would allow annual comparison.[4]

Both theory and research appreciate that there is an optimal number of charities and that government can affect that number. Governments could, for example, raise the costs of establishing new charities thereby driving donations into existing charities. They could also increase the costs of compliance for existing charities, for example, by insisting on better reporting, which would drive out small and/or possibly inefficient charities. Nevertheless, in the absence of knowing with any precision, the optimum numbers of charities governments are unlikely to alter existing rules substantially in order to achieve that remote goal. Rather, as with other markets, a minimal degree of regulation, coupled with an informed market, should come nearest to solving the problem of too many or too few charities.

Mission, money, and magnitude drive charities

There is some evidence that charity accountability practices are motivated by a desire to legitimise their activities and present their organisation's activities in a positive light. These results are said to 'contradict the raison d'etre of charities and the values that they espouse' (Dhanani, 2012,

4 South Australia Attorney General's Department, Consumer and Business Services, http://www.charities.sa.gov.au/default.asp?action=nonCurrent_charities_list accessed 19 April 2014.

1140) or that 'short-term growth may be achieved at the expense of long-term survival as an independent organization with distinctive ways of working and contributing to the common good' (Harris, 2001, 105).

Some observers characterise charities as brokers, which seek funding from whatever source in order to advance the organisation's philanthropic mission (Baber, 2001, 330). Statutory funders and institutional donors demand more accountability and transparency from charities in their resource allocation and performance outcomes than private donors. They scrutinise charitable causes like potential business investments and expect 'value for money' in the work that charities undertake. This raises the questions: who and what drives charities?

It is predictable, for example, for CEOs to suggest that their aim is to 'do good'. But it is also difficult to separate that goal with growth in the organisation. David Barbagallo, CEO of the *Endeavour Foundation* in Queensland, for example, argues that 'being a not-for-profit does not mean that you cannot earn money, it just means that it is not distributed, it gets ploughed back into the goal.'[5] There may be no conflict between growth in the charity and the 'goal' but, then again, as Barbagello would readily agree, the two are not synonymous. Charities tend to reward their CEOs to maximise the charitable objective (Baber, 2002, 691), but these objectives can be difficult to quantify. There is a temptation to seek more objective or, at least, measurable criteria such as revenue. On this, there is some US evidence to suggest that charities leave considerable slack in their fundraising potential and stop once revenue goals are met (Andreoni, 2011, 339). By contrast, in some fields, for example, development giving, greater spending on fundraising by charities appears to be driving growth in 'excess incomes' (Atkinson, 2012, 185).

Professions

If the size of the charity and the charitable purpose are difficult to distinguish, so, too, is the goal itself. Doing good is complex. For example,

---

5 The author attended and spoke to David Barbagallo at Givewell, 'Social Impacts and Outcomes Forum', 31 May 2013, Brisbane.

Jack suffers from multiple sclerosis. He is active in a charity because he wants to raise funds for medical research to find a cure. His mother, on the other hand, wants the charity to fund care for Jack. How does a charity respond to these two conflicting demands? Charity boards represent the 'owners' of the charity and may well decide, but their employees will no doubt have a great deal to say about how money is spent. Clearly, the donor and, where feasible, the recipient of charity, has a say as well. Charities may be the agent of donors, but their active players – trustees, volunteers and, increasingly, professional employees, have the best information to drive charities. Medical scientists will more than likely drive medical research charities (Leggat, 2011). The old saw applies, 'to a hammer every problem looks like a nail.'

Perhaps the question of what drives charities is more a question of who owns the charity. Charities may be driven by an historical mission of enduring purpose, such as caring for the poor, or their desire to find problems to solve, perhaps in a particular way, labeled 'problem surfing' (Boscarino, 2009). They may be driven by the intention of the founders, a large benefactor, or they may be subject to professional capture, or an influx of new members. Through time, the way the mission is achieved, as well as the mission itself, may vary considerably. One reason is that experience may teach new ways and means of helping. Another is that others, for example, government, have solved some of the problems once addressed by charity.

Another aspect is that the source of funds may change. As senior charity officials in Australia have written, 'The source of funding will [determine] to whom charities are accountable' (Judd 2012, 304). When governments become a large source of funds, whether through grants, which often have some strings attached, or contracts, which usually have many strings attached, the result may be a 'crisis of identity'. Some Australian charities are said to 'not know who they are [or] why they are doing what they are doing' (Judd, 2012, 4). But these officials and observers offer no satisfactory solution, neither to give up the (government) money, nor change the purpose. They appear to ignore the fact that government money is not donor money. By contrast, a recent UK study found little evidence of mission drift or loss of independence in charities (Bruce, 2011).

Like Australia, government heavily funds the UK charitable sector. Contracts, as opposed to grants, make up nearly 70 per cent of statutory funding, with more than two-thirds of these provided for public service delivery work (NCVO, 2009). There is also a trend to growth in earned income and commercial activities. Half of the total income of UK charities in 2007 derived from earned income (for example, fees for services, income from sales of goods and merchandise), an increase of nearly 70 per cent since the beginning of 2000. There is, furthermore, an increased orientation towards trading activities that are unrelated to charitable missions, where profit-making from 'customers' is acceptable.

Positioning

A recent study of UK charities suggested that charities tended to avoid direct competition with other charities, instead selling their mission to donors and supporters. Charities will have, whether explicitly or implicitly, a 'positioning strategy' to gain advantage in the marketplace. The aim is to find the charity's place among its competitors, its funders and its recipients (Chew, 2007, 31). Some research has concluded that the charity's mission may be preeminent in determining the positioning strategy, but that a charity will also have a product derived from its mission. The mission may be a view about how to solve a societal problem, their 'theory of change', and the product is the charity's 'solution' to the problem, perhaps to sponsor a child. The mission may reflect the skills of those in the organisations, so that, for example, ophthalmologists will concentrate on providing services to those with eye disease.

Rise and fall – development charity market

However charities compete, whether for donors or among themselves, it helps to be in a growing market. The amount of donations to development, or foreign aid, charities in Australia, for example, more than doubled in real terms between 2000 and 2010. Moreover, the distribution of funds among development charities is highly concentrated, so that the top 15 development charities receive about 80 per cent of all donations to development charities. *World Vision Australia* dominates the sector. Although its share has started to decline (33 per cent down from over 40 per cent in 2000), *World Vision Australia* has consistently received 30-40 per cent of all donated funds, more than four times larger than the charity with the next largest share during the decade 2000-10.

Figure 2.1 shows how individual shares of the other 14 charities have changed over the decade. The figure in brackets following each charity represents growth in real terms 2000-2010. The rise of a new group of charities can be detected. A high growth group started the decade much smaller than the low growth group, but ended it bigger. Of the five biggest charities at the turn of the century (*World Vision*, *Oxfam*, *ChildFund*, *Caritas*, *Compassion*), only *Oxfam* and *Compassion* have increased their share of donations. It has been suggested that some new charities – *MSF* and *Fred Hollows Foundation*, for example – have grown quickly because they have a simple 'we save lives' message. The sector is evenly split between child sponsorship agencies and others. *ChildFund*, *Compassion*, *PLAN* (Australia) and *World Vision* are the main agencies that practice child sponsorship. They make up 46 per cent of the sector, but only *Compassion* is in the high growth group.[6]

6 Sophie Roden, Michael Wulfsohn and Stephen Howes, 'The Other Scale-up: Australian Public Donations for Development Over the Last Decade.' http://devpolicy.org accessed 10 September 2013.

Figure 2.1: Share of donations top 15 charities (excludes World Vision Australia)

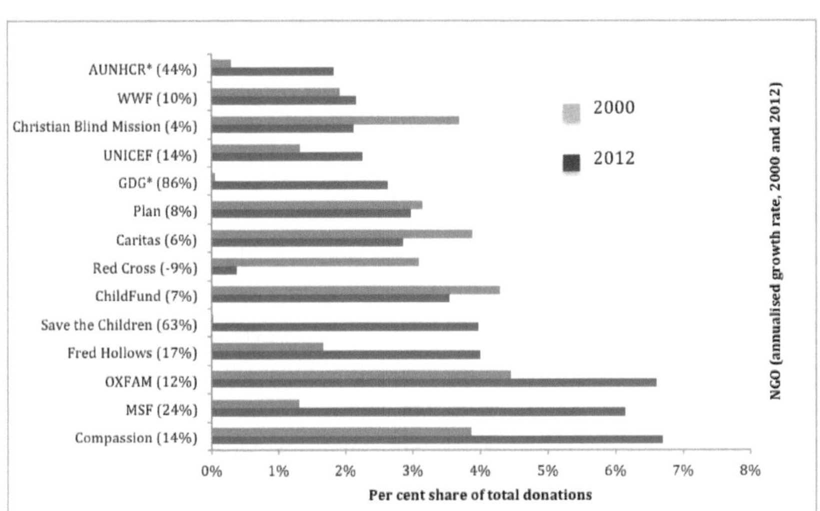

Source: http://devpolicy.org reproduced with permission.

* GDG Global Development Group: AUNHCR, Australian office, United Nations High Commissioner for Refugees.

Voluntary failure

Charity fortunes vary as they compete for donors with product and mission, and as the cause which they advocate or service changes in the public consciousness. Some find the competition too much. In a rare case of voluntary failure, the once pre-eminent New Zealand charity, the *Council of Organisations for Relief Service Overseas* (CORSO), collapsed after years of decline.

Initially, *CORSO* appeared to have sufficient resources to meet its mission. Yet it shunned these reliable resources and support to make an initially controversial mission change in the direction of development (rather than aid) in 1972. Delivering aid for government was a factor in its success in its early years, as was its broad membership base. Voluntary failure occurred when *CORSO* lost government support. It also lost donor support when international charities established a competitive donor 'market'. Its supporters' unwillingness to 'buy-in' to its change of mission to focus on local poverty was another factor in its collapse. Over the years *CORSO* has come to be viewed as a fringe group promoting a radical agenda (Sutton, 2010, 223).

Altruism is but one value that drives donors

It can be argued that the key to charitable activity is 'the simple mechanism of a person being motivated by the need of another' (Judd, 2012, 82). Being motivated by the need of another is, however, neither simple nor the sole means of motivation for making a donation. And while charity is defined as donations given to the needy (Daza, 2010, 92), who are the 'needy' is hard to define. As with charities, what drives donors is complex.

At least eight reasons have been identified as to why people donate money to charities (Bekkers, 2010). The first two are a particular concern of charities – people have to become aware of a need for support, and most donations occur in response to solicitation. Charities serve to increase awareness of need and to solicit support. Information about need is a very large part of the charities armoury, which will be analysed in chapter 5. The need for charities to spend money in order to make money is also a very large part of their operations, which is considered in chapter 6.

Self-interest

On the donors' side, there are five distinct motivations for giving. The first, perhaps uncomfortably, is self-interest. For example, a person may donate to medical research in order to maintain or enhance services for their own needs, at some later time. Indeed, in determining whether a gift is charitable in Australia, the law is that the motive of the donor in making the gift is immaterial. As long as a gift results in public benefit it does not fail to be charitable because there is some incidental benefit to the donor, although a donor 'cannot render a predominantly selfish purpose charitable where an element of charity is incidental only' (Halsbury, 2013, 75(45)). Nevertheless, it may come as some surprise that donations may be for self-regarding reasons, for example, the donor's children's school building fund. The need of 'another' may be thought to motivate charity, but the 'other' may in fact be the donor at a later date, or the donor's family.

Indeed, it appears that 'donors value someone like themselves far in the future as much as they value someone like themselves in the present [but] discount someone unlike themselves in the present' (Core, 2010, 277). In other words, the act of giving may be charitable but it does not rise very far in the humanity stakes. Even though ethical considerations suggest that recipients' level of need should be the dominant factor in allocating gifts, donors also express preferences for benefits arriving sooner rather than later, and for recipients who are 'closer' rather than farther away. Only if charities and donors act with 'low time preference' and 'low distance preference' may they appropriately use ethical language such as 'intergenerational equity' and 'equality of persons'(Core, 2010, 282).

Caring

The second and an obvious reason why individuals may contribute money to charities is because they care about the organisation's output, or the consequences of donations for beneficiaries, that is, they are altruistic. It appears, however, that the characteristics of those who are altruistic are quite distinctive. A very large US study concluded that a majority of citizens are charitable, but a sizable minority is conspicuously uncharitable. The first group is religious; does not support government income redistribution; works; and has strong intact families. The minority is secular; supports government income redistribution; does not work; accepts income from government, and does not have strong intact families (Brooks, 2007b, 182).

Elsewhere, for example, those of higher education and a higher level of religiosity seem to influence international giving more than they do domestic giving (Rajan, 2008, 437). Those who gave to religion were found to give more to education and charity than those not giving to religion, and higher education households were more likely to give to religion than households with less education. These findings point to an enduring, internal motivation for giving rather than an external, 'What do I get for what I give' motive (Showers, 2011, 181).

Values

These motivations are closely aligned to a third distinct motivation, donors' values. These can be placed along a socio/political continuum of at one end 'changing the world' to, at the other end, 'providing comfort'. Values express a means to reach a desired state of affairs that is closer to a view of the 'ideal' world, for example, equality, to reduce poverty, empower women, safeguard human rights, protect animals, wildlife, and so on. Donors may also have objectives that are partisan or even harmful. Altruism and values may play a very large part in a donor's acceptance or non-acceptance of charity lobbying government for more resources or programs which suit their preferred state of affairs, observations which are reviewed in chapter 4.

Conspicuous compassion and warm glow

The fourth motivation is known as 'conspicuous compassion', where donors receive recognition and approval. This may explain the recent advent of ribbons and wristbands in a number of charity campaigns such as 'Make Poverty History'. The fifth motivation is known as 'warm glow', which expresses the observation that helping others produces positive psychological consequences for the helper. There is substantial evidence that money giving 'unleashes substantial benefits' to the givers themselves (Brooks, 2007a, 410). Indeed, the entire foundation of the market in charitable deeds is predicated on the donor receiving some benefit from their actions.

As noted earlier, 87 per cent of Australians gave to charity and most of the money they gave went to charitable organisations (PMCBP, 2005, viii and 36). Half the donors gave because they identified with the cause and the people whose assistance is the object of the cause. Another one-third say they gave because of a sense of reciprocation for services already provided, or anticipation that help might be needed in future. For one-eighth, the main reason was a desire to strengthen the community or, more generally, to make the world a better place.

Thirty-four per cent of givers claimed some sort of direct affiliation with the organisation to which they were donating. For 25 per cent, this affiliation was that they (or members of their family) used the service it provided (some of these were also members of the organisation or volunteered for it). Affiliation could be held to be self-serving, a form of insurance for the future.

Efficacy

Matching the desires of donors and charities is something that markets are well suited to resolve. Markets are at their best when donors and charities freely interact and where donors are informed of the most important aspects of the operation of charities and the policy context in which they work. These various motivations are not necessarily mutually exclusive, and most, if not all, who are variously motivated to donate to a charity will also be concerned with the eighth and final motivation: efficacy. Efficacy expresses the desire that the contribution makes a difference to the cause.

Providing donors with information (especially financial) about the effectiveness of contributions has been found to have a positive effect on philanthropy. There is research, for example, to suggest that 'among gifts costing the same, the donor will choose that which will produce the most utility to the recipient' (Mourâo, 2008, 25). The question of what to report is taken up in chapter 6.

Favour the donor or the charity?

Behind the apparently simple money-for-information charity market, and complexity of the character of charities and donors, there is government. Governments play an important part in the charity-donor relationship. This occurs in three ways: the degree to which taxation affects giving by lowering the cost of giving; the extent to which tax advantages favour donor or charity; and the degree to which government effort 'crowds out' private efforts.

Charities and donors receive taxation benefits. The Australian Government provides FBT exemptions for employees of eligible institutions and deductible gift exemptions for donors to charities with DGR status. The value of reportable fringe benefits in 2009-10 was $5.6 billion and the value of individual gifts (including distributions from PAFs) in 2009-10 was $2.2 billion (ATO, 2012, 106-09). A range of taxation advantages such as payroll tax, land tax and various stamp duty and fee concessions from State government also assists charities. Taxation expenditure for four states in 2008-09 amounted to nearly $1.7 billion (PC, 2010, appendix E).

Taxation advantages are not uniform across all charities. There is a hierarchy of charities, which is reflected in the value of their taxation assistance. Further, charities receive Australian and State government taxation assistance in many forms, whereas donors receive taxation assistance in one form only, tax deduction on their income for donations to eligible charities. Table 2.2 sets out the taxation assistance to which different types of charity are eligible. The major form of assistance is the FBT exemptions, for which Public Benevolent Institutions (PBI) and Health Promotion Charities (HPC) are eligible. Almost all PBIs and HPCs are also endorsed for DGR status, so that donor-assisted donations favour these charities. Some others are also eligible for DGR status. Taxation also varies among charities with the same purpose, as shown in table 2.3 because the form, rather than the purpose, of the charity generally determines the advantage.

Table 2.2: Tax concessions and types of non-profit organisations

Tax concessions	Types of non-profit organisations				
	Charities			Income tax exempt funds	Other non-profit organisations
	PBI&HPC	Charitable institutions	Charitable funds		
Income tax exempt	✓	✓	✓	✓	✓ Certain types
exemption	✓				✓[1] Certain types
FBT rebate		✓			✓ Certain types
GST concessions for charities and gift deductible entities	✓	✓	✓	✓	✓ Certain types
GST concessions for non-profits	✓	✓	✓		✓
Deductible gift recipients	✓[2]	✓	✓	✓	✓ Certain types
Refunds of franking credits	✓	✓	✓	✓	✓ Certain types

Notes:[1] Public and non-profit hospitals eligible.[2] Must be endorsed.
Source: Adapted from (ATO, 2011, 4).

Table 2.3: Main charitable purpose of tax concession charities, 2010-11

Charitable purpose	Number of tax concession charities	Income tax exempt	FBT exempt	FBT rebatable	GST concession
Social and community welfare	24,006	23,911	8,482	11,639	23,585
Religion	12,664	12,643	6	12,440	12,312
Education	9,412	9,404	7	8,204	9,119
Health	2,742	2,725	1,438	494	2,592
Culture	1,716	1,711	0	1,385	1,599
Natural environment	670	668	0	533	612
Other	5,069	5,042	12	3,329	4,742
Total	56,279	56,104	9,945	38,024	54,561

Source: (ATO, 2013, 99).

The relationship between charity type and eligibility for DGR status is not close. Indeed, it seems more broadly that 'there is still no generally accepted rationale for charitable purpose tax exemptions' (Harding et al, 2011, 22). The reason may be that while there are economic justifications for taxation exemptions for charities the eligibility criteria and the taxation exemptions to which charities are eligible are essentially political decisions. It is likely that while 'tax concessions [are] driven by economics and the overall principles of fair taxation, [they are] rarely situated within an articulated political philosophy concerning the role of the [charity] sector' (Harding et al., 2011, 65). In other words, they are a mystery.

While generally the greater weight of taxation monies is granted to charities, rather than donors, the balance differs depending on the nature

Table 2.4: Deductible gift recipients, by type, 2010-11

DGR type	Number
Public benevolent institution	11,688
School or college building fund	4,775
Ancillary fund	1,777
Public library	1,700
Public fund on the register of cultural organisations	1,395
Health promotion charity	1,281
Private ancillary fund	1,030
Public library, public museum and public art gallery	923
Public fund for persons in necessitous circumstances	605
Public fund on the register of environmental organisations	573
Scholarship fund	460
Public hospital	371
Public fund for religious instruction in government schools	323
Government special school	223
Overseas aid fund	218
Specifically listed in the *Income Tax Assessment Act 1936*	207
Animal welfare charity	179
Approved research institute	155
Public institution for research	105
Other	1,058
Total	29,046

Source: (ATO, 2013, 100). Note: Definitions vary between ATO tables 10.1 and 10.4 of the same report.

of the charity. Charities with DGR status are allowed to receive tax-free donations; these are charities with the highest 'status'. Table 2.4 provides a guide to the type of charity supported by tax-assisted donations. The number of such charities does not indicate fields of charity, nor amounts donated, which are not available, but nevertheless provides a sense of the menu of causes. Whether the spread of causes and the level of their support would be different without tax-assisted donations is worth considering. Figure 2.2 (page 51) illustrates the non-exclusive nature of charitable categories and the range of taxation benefits.

The type of charity determines the extent of the taxation benefit and is broadly defined, with examples of each, as follows:

Charity

Charity has a special meaning under law. To be a charity, an organisation must:

- be not-for-profit
- have a charitable purpose
- be for the public benefit (other than where the charitable purpose is the relief of poverty)

A charity may be a fund or an institution.

Charitable Institution

There are 40,072 Charitable Institutions (CI). These are established and run to advance or promote a charitable purpose. Examples include:

- religious groups
- not-for-profit aged care homes
- homeless shelters
- disability service organisations
- universities and colleges
- animal welfare societies
- artistic or cultural groups.

Beacon Foundation, for example, is a CI with DGR status. *Beacon* is a company that is primarily involved in working with schools nationally to develop and implement programs to help inspire and motivate students either to stay in school or transition to employment, further education or training. Its income in 2012 was $3 million, derived from sponsorships, grants and donations, but the sources are not distinguished.[7]

Charitable Fund

There are 6,042 Charitable Funds (CF). These are established under an instrument of trust or a will for a charitable purpose. Charitable funds mainly manage trust property, and/or hold trust property to make distributions to other entities or persons. Examples include religious institutions, aged persons homes, homeless hostels, schools run by churches, organisations relieving the special needs of people with disabilities and societies to promote the fine arts.

The *Art Gallery of NSW Foundation*, for example, is a charity (with DGR status) and holds funds for the gallery. It had accumulated funds of $28 million and granted $2 million in 2012.[8] The *Art Gallery of NSW* income in 2011-12 was $67 million, derived from government grants $30 million, sale of services $13 million, and donations $20 million.[9]

Public Benevolent Institution

There are 8,909 PBIs. Their main purpose is to work directly to relieve poverty, sickness, suffering or disability. It must provide its services directly to people in need of relief. The meaning of direct has been interpreted in recent cases such that peak bodies, fundraising groups and those not closely involved in direct work have attained PBI status.[10]

PBIs are organisations that:

7 Beacon, *Annual Financial Report 2013.*

8 Art Gallery of NSW Foundation, *Financial Report 2011-2012.*

9 Art Gallery of NSW, *Annual Report 2012.*

10 See *Hunger Project Australia V Cmr Of Taxation* – BC201310980 at [126]. 'I do not accept that it is a requirement that a public benevolent institution engage directly in the activities making up the object of its benevolence. On the other hand, … the benevolent objects of an organisation [need] to be more than merely abstract.'

- provide hostel accommodation for the homeless
- treat sufferers of disease
- provide home help for the aged and the infirm
- transport the sick or disabled
- rescue people who are lost or stranded.

BoysTown, for example, is a PBI that runs a range of programs aimed at young people (and their families), including phone counselling, education, employment readiness, refuge services and parenting skills. Its annual income in 2012 was $85 million, derived from an art union $48 million, $15 million government grants, $15 million services (not clear if grants and services are, in effect, government contracts) and $2 million from donations, bequests and appeals. The important point about PBIs is that they are rewarded with the greatest level of taxation assistance on the proviso that they deliver services 'directly'.

As noted earlier, some in the charity sector would like to have fewer funds used in FBT and more access to DGR (CCA, 2012, 6). They make the case in support of small charities. They also argue that most FBT benefits accrue to well-paid employees. The holes in the arguments are that there is no reason to suspect that small charities are better than large charities or that higher paid workers are not worth their benefits. Nevertheless, it is reasonable to argue that taxation should assist the donor, not the charity.

Health Promotion Charity

There are 1,256 HPCs . These are non-profit CIs whose principal activity is promoting the prevention or control of diseases in human beings. Examples of activities that can promote the prevention or control of disease include:

- providing relevant information to sufferers of a disease, health professionals, carers and to the public
- researching how to detect, prevent or treat diseases

- developing or providing relevant aids and equipment to sufferers of a disease.

Unlike PBIs, HPCs receive the greatest level of taxation assistance, but are not required to deliver services directly.

Figure 2.2: Relationship between potential DGRs and charities

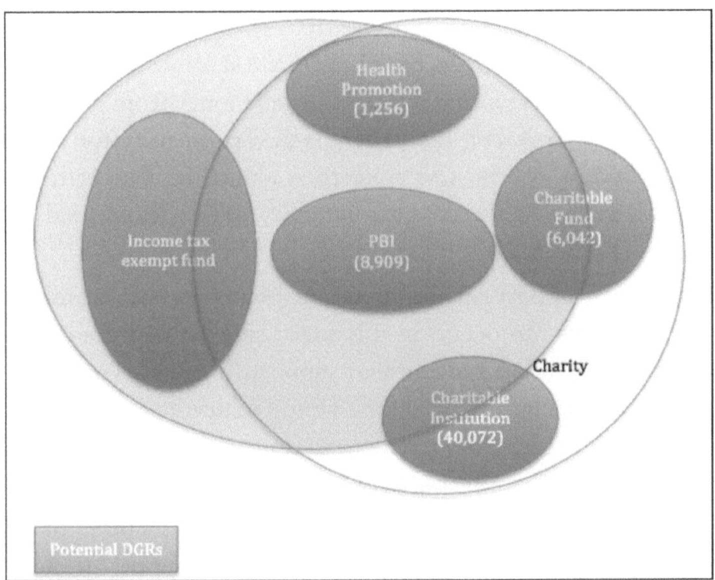

Source: Based on (Auditor General, 2010, 16) with 2010-11 figures from (ATO, 2013, 98).

Note: Health promotion organisations, PBIs and CIs may also separately operate charitable and income tax exempt funds.

Public hospitals, for example, are not charities although they benefit from FBT exemption. Many hospitals will have foundations associated with them. These are charities, possibly HPCs or PBIs, depending on their charter. An example is the Ipswich Hospital Foundation, which is a HPC. It has an income of more than $1million; most of its income

– $800,000 – is derived from operation of a car park; the remainder – $200,000 – from donations.[11]

Government is the biggest donor: does it crowd out charity?

As noted earlier, economically significant not-for-profits (largely charities) derive 33 per cent of their income from government and only nine per cent from philanthropic sources (PC, 2010, 72). Government is a big part of the donor base of charities, but charities are sensitive that donors will reduce donations where a charity has accepted money from government. This is known as crowding out. There is also propensity for crowding in. That is, donors will be less concerned about the true activities of a charity knowing that the charity's activities will be monitored by the government (Khanna, 2000, 1555).

Nevertheless, almost all the literature points to the sensitivity of crowding out. This can occur on the donor side, so that donors spend less on a charity that has government support. It can also occur on the charity side, by reducing the need for charities to devote so much of their attention to fundraising from private sources.

Guide Dogs NSW/ACT, for example, raised almost $22 million in 2012, almost all in bequests and donations. They make a point of telling prospective donors that they derive all 'financial support through the generosity of the people of NSW and the ACT. We receive no funding from the State or Federal Governments.' They have expressed the fear of crowding out when the National Disability Insurance Scheme (NDIS) is fully implemented. They anticipate that the NDIS 'may provide support for less than 20% of our existing clients. As a result we will continue to need support from the community to provide services to more than 80% of our clients who we expect will not be covered by the NDIS.'[12]

11 Ipswich Hospital Foundation, *Annual Report 2011-2012*.

12 Guide Dogs NSW/ACT, *Annual Report 2012*, pages 4 and 64.

In figure 2.3 the charity is hard pressed to convince the donor that it receives no government money when it is a deductible gift charity and, in that regard, the taxpayer subsidises the donor's choice. *St Vincent de Paul Society Canberra* reports that, 'While the Society receives considerable financial support from governments, fundraising remains vital in order for us to carry out our mission.'[13]

Figure 2.3: 'Informing' donors that charity receives no government money

Source: Letter of appeal to the author, 27 February 2013.

On its website, the children's charity *Variety Queensland* states that it 'receives no direct government funding.' The financial report appears to bear this out, although there is a large amount of income sourced from grants, but it is presumed these are private.[14] The point is that some charities readily point out that they receive no [direct] government support, presumably, because they want to appeal to donors. Most others

13 St Vincent de Paul Society Canberra, *Annual Report 2011-12*, page 10.

14 Variety, *Annual Review 2012*.

in the sample of 200 charities for the study, however, made no statements, perhaps because so many were in receipt of income from government that that fact is taken for granted.

Murdoch Children's Research Institute pleads that, 'As government and other grant-making bodies tend to support established research, philanthropic and corporate funds are vital to providing the start up funding we need to bring bold and innovative research ideas to life.'[15] Nevertheless, 48 per cent of its $96 million income in 2012 came either from government or from other peer-reviewed grants. Donations were net $6 million.[16]

On the donor side, the critical taxation question is whether additional giving induced by taxation deductions is greater or less than the value of the tax deductions provided. Best estimates suggest that, permanent rises in the level of giving are attributable to tax assistance to the donor (PC, 2010, 174).

There are a number of explanations why there is not a perfect substitution of public for private donations. The most common reason is that public charity is not a perfect substitute for private charity in consumption. A more specific version, and one most commonly associated with charitable donations, argues that charity provides private benefits to the donor as well as public benefits to the community. This has come to be known as the case of 'impure altruism' (Ferris, 2003, 399). Another is that the cost of providing assistance differs between private and government suppliers. The standard finding of less than complete crowding may reflect only the relative cost of delivering the two methods of providing assistance. Individuals may view charity as a 'super normal good', increasing their private charitable contributions more than proportionately following a rise in real income. There is

15 Murdoch Childrens Research Institute, http://www.mcri.edu.au accessed 1 December 2013.

16 Murdoch Childrens Research Institute, *Annual Report 2012*, page 44.

evidence that individuals care about leakages involved in transferring funds to the deserving through government, but also that individuals have responded to compensate for the changes in those costs (Ferris, 2003, 412).

Another explanation is that a person's income and likelihood of future need of charity may also determine the extent of the crowding out. For example, low income individuals with less education and skills may be more inclined to contribute voluntarily to income support and social programs because their probability of needing such support is higher. High income, two-wage earning families are less likely ever to need welfare, and, consequently, are less inclined to contribute voluntarily to such programs (Benzing, 2004, 212).

On the fundraiser side, if charity managers find fundraising a 'necessary evil', or fear it may hurt their evaluation from charity watchdog groups, then a government grant would allow them to redirect efforts from fundraising to providing charitable services. This means that after receiving a grant, charities may simply cut back fundraising. There is research evidence to suggest that if donors are largely unaware of fluctuations in the grants received by charities, then reductions in fundraising become a sensible explanation for crowding out. A requirement that charities match a fraction of government grants with increases in private donations could be a feasible response to crowding out. Whether such a requirement is welfare enhancing is an open question and depends on what is assumed about the marginal cost of raising public funds (Andreoni, 2011, 342).

An alternative explanation is that government grants impose additional costs on fundraising, since government grants reduce the efficiency of fundraising. All else being equal, given government grants, public charities spend more to generate the same amount of revenue from fundraising because of the reduced efficiency. Charities are not passive repositories, but active players, and additional government funding, in reaction, may reduce the charity's incentive to be efficient in fundraising (Yi, 2010, 474).

Displacement

A variant on the crowding out discussion is that of displacement. All donations may displace government funding. In doing so, government may spend on less important services. For example, fungibility is a risk to development effectiveness if aid displaces government expenditure, which is then used for less productive ends. This can especially be a problem in aid–dependent economies. Fungibility can undermine support for the aid program, especially if the recipient government is seen to be misusing its own resources. Fungibility is difficult to measure and control, but donors should be aware of it (Hollway, 2011, 285).

Cost of regulation

Australian charities receive one of the most significant preferential tax treatments in the world. (Judd, 2012, 282)

According to the Productivity Commission, direct funding of the charity sector is substantial and growing, but that sometimes entails 'excessive conditions and compliance requirements impose unnecessary burdens' (PC, 2010, 275). That is the complaint of many in the sector. Broad statements about regulation need to be made specific to the source and form of income. The complaints usually stem from the fact that charities receive income from many sources and in many forms and regulation varies according to sources and forms. In addition, the legal entity also determines different regulation, by different governments. The most common legal entities are incorporated association, which is State-based, or a company limited by guarantee, which is Commonwealth-based.

Charities receive income from government in three forms – grants, contracts and taxation forgiven on earnings and donations. Each requires a different form of obligation and acquittal. Grants may require little acquittal; contracts, by contrast, nearly always require a great deal. Taxation status requires almost none after an initial acceptance of status by the ATO. Fundraising rules for private donations are State-based. Monies received from trusts are federally based. Complexity probably stems from the divided responsibilities and multiple sources of income. For example, in all jurisdictions except the Northern Territory, there is legislation which makes it unlawful to make an appeal to the public for donations or subscriptions unless the charitable organisation is registered and the fundraising activity has been approved (Halsbury, 2013, 75(1240)).

Apart from proof of an annual audit, there is no requirement for most DGRs to report regularly to the ATO. Taxpayers do not have to identify recipients of their donations in tax returns. As a result the ATO has very limited internal information on which to assess the risk that income tax deductibility is only promoted in respect of fundraising activities associated with DGRs or, more broadly, that taxpayers are claiming for donations that are not made to DGRs. The potential for such risks materialising is illustrated by the Australian National Audit Office's identification of some 350 organisations that may be undertaking fundraising activities under State/Territory legislation but are not DGRs (Auditor-General, 2010, 27).

Nevertheless, there is State legislation that governs aspects of, in particular, fundraising so that, for example, the Best Practice Guidelines of the Office of Charities in NSW indicate that charity accounts must contain the following comparisons:

1. Compare total costs of fundraising to gross income from fundraising
2. Compare net surplus from fundraising to gross income from fundraising

3. Compare total costs of services to total expenditure
4. Compare total costs of services to total income received (Office of Charities, 2002, 70).

Moreover, 'Persons or organisations conducting appeals for donations only must take all reasonable steps to ensure that total expenses payable do not amount to more than 50 per cent of the gross proceeds' (Office of Liquor Gaming and Racing, 2010, 3). The information is not readily available publicly, although financial statements may, at the request of any person, be supplied (for a fee) to the person by or on behalf of the Minister.[17] In the sample for this study, only one report referred to the legislation and reported explicitly in the prescribed manner, and it failed by a large margin to ensure that its expenses did not exceed 50 per cent of gross proceeds. Figure 6.1 (page 162) is a comparatively rare exemplar of reporting ratios.

Governments expect that charity boards and donors will hold the charity to account. And, by and large, they do. Charities, however, do not always account in a meaningful way to their non-government donors who willingly give funds to support the charity's purpose. As senior charity officials report, 'charities may well have complied with all the regulations but that doesn't mean the donor public knows how the money is spent' (Judd, 2012, 263). And again, 'who makes sure the organisation you have donated to uses the money properly, for the right things? … no one really if the trustees or board of directors are not doing their job' (Judd, 2012, 260).

Contract will drive scrutiny

There is one area that will drive scrutiny, however. This is where charities win contracts to deliver government services. The NSW Independent Commission Against Corruption (ICAC) was very critical of the non-

17 *Charitable Fundraising Act 1991* (NSW), Section 47.

government organisation (NGO) sector, of which charities are a major component. It reported that, every year, in NSW, billions of dollars are provided to 2,000 NGOs, which amount to more than 7,000 different agreements to deliver human services on behalf of the government: 'Such large sums of money spent across so many agreements by so many agencies presents a formidable test of any control system' (ICAC, 2012, 4).

ICAC reported that while the vast majority of NGOs and staff are dedicated to helping others, there are those that see money from government as an opportunity for self-interested behaviour. The Commission was aware of a number of allegations and problems in NSW and other jurisdictions, including staff using government monies and resources for their own benefit. Sometimes this evolved over time with ever-increasing salaries, cars and benefits being appropriated by NGO staff. On other occasions, there was a deliberate intention to misappropriate funds and using funds to deliver a different service from that agreed with the government agency. This practice amounts to obtaining money under false pretences or fraud.

ICAC also reported that some NGOs obtained funding for the same service from multiple programs, agencies and jurisdictions. This was particularly an issue where NGO activities span borders, making it possible for an NGO to obtain funding from two States and/or the Australian Government, in the knowledge that there is little coordination between NSW and other States. There were also instances in specific funding agreements for capital works where construction was delayed in order to bank the funds and earn interest. The interest on several million dollars can then be used as income by the NGO. There were examples of government-funded assets belonging to an NGO being stolen or, in one case, used by NGO staff to run a business providing services to favoured clients from the same family or community as the NGO managers.

There was also collusion between government frontline staff and

NGO staff either to obtain funding or to agree to weak or minimally-specified delivery outcomes in return for funding. In either case, the NGO income is enhanced, falsely reporting to the government that services have been delivered when they have not, or delivering at a lower quality than required. There appear to be occasions where NGOs cover up critical client incidents to ensure continuation of funding (ICAC, 2012, 5).

Further, audit reports were not always an unbiased evaluation of NGO activities. In economically-depressed areas, for example, the bulk of the work of auditors was often with NGOs. While professionally independent, the auditors relied on continued business from NGOs, creating a significant conflict of interest. In some cases, the independence of audit was lost completely as the auditor also took on the role of book-keeper for the NGO (ICAC, 2012, 11). In remote areas of NSW, it has taken particular efforts of agency frontline staff to assist others in setting up an NGO to deliver a service. In many cases, the NGOs are fully funded by the government, potentially leading to devious behaviour around renewal of funding. Even where an agency is able to go to tender, some NGOs bid below the real cost of delivering a service because they are able to obtain additional funding from other agencies (ICAC, 2012, 14).

In communities with severe social problems, it is more likely NGOs will be funded to play some part in solving problems. ICAC is aware of one NSW town of about 500 residents where there is a ratio of one NGO funding agreement for every 10 residents. In such an environment, it is difficult to specify precisely what each NGO is to deliver as their part of the solution or to hold any one NGO accountable for community outcomes (ICAC, 2012, 17).

There is a lack of accountability on the part of charities for public donor costs and private donor privileges. Even in contract compliance, requirements to measure outcomes are generally poor. With respect to scrutiny, charities have little to complain about that is different from competitors in the for-profit sector. Notwithstanding, in political terms, no government is about to remove tax assistance for charities and they are also unlikely to impose greater compliance costs associated with greater scrutiny. The challenge is to increase scrutiny without too great a burden of compliance.

3

What about the taxpayer?

The history of taxation of charities demonstrates that the issue has always been politically contentious, the development haphazard, and that once introduced tax concessions are very difficult to remove. (Chia & O'Connell, 2010, 2)

Charities and government

Hospital of St Cross and Almshouse of Noble Poverty in Winchester, UK, is one of the oldest charities in the world. Bishop Henri de Blois, William the Conqueror's grandson, started the hospital in 1136.[1] It still stands but government and patients now pay for its services. The charitable function is but a remnant. Dutch philanthropy in the seventeenth and eighteenth centuries was legendary. Nowhere in the Europe of that time, and possibly in the world, was the level of charitable expenditure as great as it was in the Netherlands. Charitable responsibilities shared by church, state and citizens survived until introduction of the *Social Security Act 1965* (Van Voss 2012, 177). Australia's oldest charity, the *Benevolent Society*, which in 2013 celebrated its 200th anniversary, has drawn from the European attachment to charity and has adapted to the welfare state.

In 2012, the *Benevolent Society* had an income of more than $80 million, almost 82 per cent of which came from government and only four per cent came from donations. The *Society* lobbied government for better

1 The Hospital of St Cross and Almshouse of Noble Poverty, http://stcrosshospital.co.uk/history/ accessed 29 September 2013.

provision as early as 1862 when the NSW Government took responsibility for those once housed by the *Society* in the Benevolent Asylum. In 2012, it spent $2 million on charitable activities from its endowment fund, which came from donations, $700,000 of which were spent on 'influencing social change by advocating for policy reform'.[2] The 'reform' aims to create a 'fairer' Australia and bewails 'growing disparity in income and job opportunities'. The *Society* may be described as a charity-contractor-lobbyist. It has this status in common with many charities in Australia and elsewhere where the reach of government has extended into every part of society.

Charities have been described as hybrid organisations where boundaries between public, private and voluntary organisations are blurred, blurring which risks 'social mission drift, confused accountability and erosion of charitable values' (Bruce, 2011, 156). As discussed earlier, charities[3] receive 33 per cent of their income from government, slightly more than 10 per cent in self-generated income, and nine per cent from philanthropy (PC, 2010, 72). Even if they once did, charities no longer constitute a realm separate from government. On the contrary, they are now so tightly bound into the machinery of government that it is sometimes difficult to distinguish them from government, and yet they retain the privileges of charities.

Some governments have facilities for voluntary taxation which, if widespread, would presumably displace (tax-assisted) charities entirely. For example, 41 US states have 'check-off' programs through which taxpayers can make voluntary contributions to public programs by indicating their preferences on their state income tax forms. The popularity and success of these programs indicates a willingness on the part of taxpayers to pay additional voluntary taxes when they have control over how the money is used. A recent 'real donation' experiment, however, suggested that while individuals are not averse to 'donating' to

2 The Benevolent Society, *Annual Report 2012*, page 30.

3 The Productivity Commission referred to 'economically significant not-for-profits'.

government for nominated causes, charities could be trusted as much or more than government, and that the compulsory nature of taxation was the inhibitor to giving (Li, 2011). An Australian example of a 'check-off' program is the monies raised for restoration of the Brisbane City Hall, completed in 2013, through the donation facility on the rates account received by Brisbane ratepayers. One-fifth of Brisbane ratepayers, 60,000 people, donated $2 million worth of tax-deductible donations, mostly through $15 payments on rates bills, to the restoration of City Hall.[4] Governments are powerful, yet charity persists. Long may they both live, but is the relationship as beneficial as it could be?

Dilemmas in government-charities relations

When citizens pay taxes they are compelled to provide funds for public benefit, but governments cannot compel 'voluntarily' charitable purposes. 'It is the motive for the gift or the participation, not the manner in which the public is benefited, that distinguishes charitable from government purposes' (McG-Lowndes, 2012, 829). The charitable motivation is in danger of being lost, or smothered, where government contributes most of the money. Governments must satisfy the taxpayer, whose money it is, that the money is well spent. As important, where a charity can leverage government money, either by lobbying or by using tax-assisted donations, it is using involuntary monies for its voluntary purposes. Using someone else's money where it is not explicitly for purpose is not charity. Moreover, such monies are as liable to public scrutiny as any government grant or contract.

Contested purpose

Where government should spend money may be very different to where charity should spend. Official foreign aid should follow Australia's national interest and operate in its 'sphere of influence'. Private aid may

---

4 Rose Brennan, 'Public A Key Building Block To Brisbane's City Hall', *The Courier-Mail* 7 March, 2012.

have historic reasons to seek wider fields. By lobbying, however, the charity may induce government to spend money on matters other than the national interest and farther afield than would otherwise be the case. The propensity for such lobbying could increase where departments 'twin' with charities. The Department of Foreign Affairs and Trade, for example, maintains the list of approved overseas aid funds, although AusAID is the mother ship in terms of funds. Indeed, AusAID funds charities to advocate for all manner of causes, which saves the charity from spending its resources. Other lists include environmental organisations, cultural organisations and various health organisations, some of which have allied agencies such as the Australian National Preventive Health Agency. There are 69 Harm Prevention Charitable Institutions (HPCI) and more than 1,000 HPCs. The Abbott Government has recently abolished AusAID and moved its operations inside the department, perhaps as a way to minimise this charity influence.

Scrutiny is not simply a matter of accounting for expenditure. The use to which those monies are put, that is, the nature of public benefit, should be proved. This can be doubtful for some causes. For example, the case for exempting donations to churches, museums, opera houses, community centres, public parks, universities, elite private schools from taxation may be questionable because they have little 'income-augmenting' effect. The lost revenue from such exemptions reduces the resources available for 'direct redistribution', while also possibly 'exacerbating welfare inequality' (Dasgupta, 2009, 19). Poor government gatekeeping has consequences.

Given that tax-assisted donations tend to contradict the voluntary nature of charity, it can be argued that it is especially important that charities not pursue heavily contested purposes. Governments should be reticent about tax assistance to organisations that seek to promote viewpoints on issues upon which there is reasonable disagreement in the electorate. In other words, 'governments should not support one reasonable conception of "the good" over any other' (McCormack, 2010,

1025). It is difficult to distinguish what is a reasonable disagreement on how much redistribution of societies resources is justified (Chambers, 2010, 96). In some ways, these matters are judged over long periods through democratic means but, nevertheless, it is arguable that the more controversial the cause, the less generous should be the privilege afforded to the charity. Donors may well query a charity's motivation, for example, in selling its wares for 'the relief of poverty' when it is in fact lobbying to undermine the market system which arguably is the most powerful tool to relieve poverty. Few overseas development charities lobby governments in favour of the World Trade Organisation, for example, which, all things being equal, abhors trade subsidies. Instead, charities leave trade subsidies alone and seek aid subsidies to 'match' the trade subsidies.

Private benefit

In addition to the voluntary-compulsory dilemma faced by charities, and the risk of losing democratic support in controversial causes, a further risk arises where a charity delivers private and personal benefit. In law, it is fundamental that charitable trusts 'be for purposes and only indirectly for persons'. Individuals who come within the scope of the charitable purpose may be the recipients of the benefit but cannot be the direct objects. Making some contribution to the cost of nursing home services, for example, does not destroy the charitable intent of a not-for-profit institution (Halsbury, 2013, 75(10)). As is clear from analysis of the motivations of donors, in the previous chapter, however, donors may make a donation in anticipation of need later on or, indeed, of one's family. These donations are self-interested, but not direct. Similarly, schools and hospitals are deemed charitable but donors may well ask whether a donation is for the education of others or for their own child, or for their health.

In 2012, Goodman Fielder, one of Australia's largest food manufacturers, promised that, for every loaf of bread the company sold, it would in the future donate one to charity. The company reported that 'the consumer response was … terrific.'[5] The key to this story is that the company chose to make a donation on behalf of its owners. As Goodman Fielder is a public company, the owners are shareholders. Presumably they were informed of the donation. They had a choice to agree to the donation or, if they disagreed, to sell their shares or complain to the management. Consumers also had a choice to buy or not. Such choices are not available to the taxpayer when a fellow taxpayer privately donates to a DGR charity. The taxpayer is in effect underwriting someone else's charity dream. From a liberal perspective, it seems extraordinary that governments provide incentives for people 'to exercise their liberty to give their money away' (Reich, 2013, 2).

But provide incentives they do, so much so that Treasuries treat these as 'public expenditure' (C & AG, 2013, 5) because government 'effectively co-contributes to the donation in terms of tax revenue foregone' (PC, 2010, G.21). There are those who dispute that charity costs government revenue (Reich, 2013, 3). It is true that the impact of deductibility can be variable, and weak for some causes but, as discussed previously, best estimates suggest an overall rise in the level of giving as a consequence of taxation assistance to donors.

Tax relief costs

The cost of extending DGR status to all charities in Australia, which has been canvassed widely by the sector (CCA, 2012, 6), may increase tax expenditures by almost $1 billion (PC, 2010. H.6). Giving also seems to have been responsive to tax relief in the UK. With changes to repayment of tax to charities, and tax reliefs provided to individuals, the total 'cost' of tax relief doubled in real terms between 1990 and 2012 (C & AG, 2013, 18). To a Doubting Thomas, there is always a direct response. The owners of the more than 30,000 DGR charities (table 2.4, page 47) have been lining up to gain this prized status for decades, and more knock on the door of the ATO or ACNC every year.

5 Mitchell Nadin, 'Companies Use Their Loaf to Help Feed the Hungry', *The Australian* 31 October 2013.

In addition to the implied transfers from one taxpayer to another, often without the explicit scrutiny that comes with government programs, there is the issue that the preferences of the donor may not match that of the taxpayer. Consider the argument that the duty to help the poor is a moral duty to perform acts of charity, not a political obligation to comply with state redistribution (Chambers, 2010, 94). If democracy is a wish to reflect the motivations of the electorate accurately, why are some motivations privileged? There is evidence to suggest, for example, that high-income individuals are more likely to give more than the value of a tax deduction (PC, 2010, G.4). Tax-assisted donations reflect preferences of the donor and, while wealthy donors are more likely to monitor the work of charities to which they donate, these preferences – opera, museums, and other cultural institutions – are unlikely to reflect broad popular preferences (Schizer, 2009, 224).

While middle-aged individuals and women tend to donate more often, older individuals and men tend to donate more. Income is also a critical factor in the giving of money, with the share of the adult population donating and the average donation size increasing with income (PC, 2010, G.3). Larger donors – charitable foundations or philanthropists – often have a greater interest in their investment. If not, they certainly have a stake in ensuring the money is well spent. Bill Gates and others have pledged – *Giving Pledge* – to give half of their wealth to charity. An email exchange between Bill Gates and a prospective Pledge candidate, Robert Wilson, had Wilson observe that family-controlled foundations 'become, more often than not, bureaucracy-ridden sluggards.'[6] The super-philanthropist involvement in charity is so great that it is often the case that the donor becomes the charity.

A recent survey in Australia (PA, 2011, 26) suggested that 'high net worth' individuals wish to control how and where money is spent, but hesitate to be tied to 'restrictive' funding conditions (often associated with

6 *The Times*, 'Gates Campaign Deemed Futile', reprinted in *The Weekend Australian* 4-5 January 2014.

government involvement). At the same time, however, they wanted the tax break. Indeed, some seek 'co-investment' (Kramer, 2009; Whitman, 2009) from government. Donors receive a cross-subsidy from the taxpayer; very wealthy donors, much like car manufacturers, may demand co-investment. There is no direct Australian evidence that larger donors, for example, those who operate a private ancillary fund, have different preferences to other donors. Figure 3.1 displays the spread of donations – welfare receiving the highest distribution from PAFs and Sports & Recreation recording zero distribution – but there is no comparable spread for other donors, or taxpayer preferences. Nevertheless, a public subsidy to private donors is not to be treated as if it was the same as expressing the 'public's' values in charitable giving.

Figure 3.1: Private ancillary fund distributions by category ($m), 2010-11

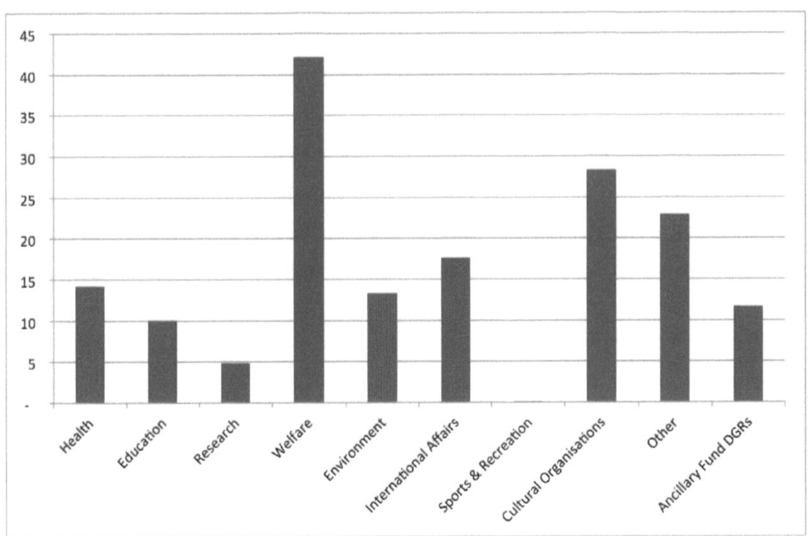

Source: (ATO, 2013, table 5: Charities and Deductible Gifts).

Because incentives to encourage people to give away their money are common, and as tax deductibility 'is potentially the only direct way that individual taxpayers … can allocate government revenue to causes that they … would like to see funded' (PC, 2010, 157), it is important that there be some means to account for expenditure. Perhaps most important is that success depends very much on whether 'the goods produced by charitable recipients are of broad social value' (Reich, 2013, 7). If charity incentives cost the taxpayer money via foregone revenue, 'the point of charity law had better be a good one' (Harding, 2011a, 2).

The intrusion of government into the charitable realm and, indeed, the intrusion of charities into the government realm through lobbying, along with the controversial nature of some causes and the self-regarding nature of others, bears close scrutiny. In policy terms, however, there is no benefit in rewinding the historical clock to rediscover the true purpose of charity as practised by charities. There is, however, benefit in unravelling parts of the charity-government relationship, if only to see whether the privileges are warranted. Government involvement seems to have spawned new roles for charities and a number of unintended consequences for government support for donors.

It is questionable, for example, that delivering government services is a public benefit deserving of privilege. If there is a strong argument for public benefit then, presumably, government should be supplying them (including by contract). If not, then, presumably, there should be proof that delivery by charities is superior to public service or for-profit delivery. Among charities there is much disquiet about regulation that stems from the contractual relationship for the delivery of government services. In terms of service delivery, however, charities are not-for-profit businesses. Reasons for being treated differently to for-profits, or not-for-profit non-charities, are thin. As for lobbying, a charity that derives a substantial income from government contracts may be lobbying on its own behalf, which, despite recent legislative change removing the last vestiges of constraint on lobbying, is hardly charitable.

Government charities

It may be arguable that charities undertake 'crucial work across the country that would otherwise fall on government'[7] but, if such work were the responsibility of government, a doubtful assumption, and government funded it, it would be subject to the full scrutiny to which government programs are subject. There are very few charities that do not receive government funds. Moreover, an organisation can be denied charitable status where, 'because of government control over its functions or due to an otherwise very close association with government', it can be seen as being little more than an arm of government. Nevertheless, the fact that charities deliver governmental services does not, as a matter of principle, undermine its charitable status (Halsbury, 2013, 75(xx)).

Charities are unlikely to be responsive to donors, however, when donations account only for a very small proportion of income. Many nursing homes, for example, are almost wholly-owned by government. These are historic institutions no longer running independently of government. Hospitals are not charities, but they receive monies from hospital trusts that receive donations, mostly for research. But in all other regards hospitals are not charities, yet they receive the greatest subventions, FBT exemptions, of all of the charities. Health Promotion Charities and Harm Prevention Charitable Institutions are very strange inclusions. Every citizen has free access to hospital care and highly subsidised access to General Practice care at which they can be advised about their health, including all of the issues that HPCs and HPCIs 'promote'. Why subsidise further, less professional, advice?

There are numerous examples of charities that are, in effect, government agencies, where private citizens have been given the privilege to use government funds as well as tax-assisted funds. In some cases the scrutiny is not the same as for government departments; in other cases,

---

7 Words attributed to Senator Rachel Siewert, http://www.probonoaustralia.com.au/news/2013/12/andrews-announces-move-end-acnc# accessed 6 December 2013.

the scrutiny is, but there seems to be no point to the charitable status other than granting some voters a political favour.

Alzheimer's Australia

Alzheimer's Australia, as a PBI, is supposed to deliver direct services. Instead, its income, which it reports as 'revenue', was $18 million in 2013. Details of the sources of revenue are not provided, although most are from government. Its principal activities were to represent the State and Territory associations in 'co-ordination of national projects, lobbying, promotion and advice to government.'[8]

Its principal argument is that 'people living with dementia, their families and carers have the right to services' and, 'whenever possible, services will be provided free and no person with dementia or their family or carer will be denied access due to their inability to pay'.[9] Lobbying began in earnest in July 2011 when *Alzheimer's* decided to take action to reverse the termination of the Dementia Initiative in the 2011 Federal Budget. The response was to advocate for action in a Fight Dementia Campaign with the aim of getting $200 million over five years allocated in the 2012-13 Federal Budget to tackle dementia and to achieve an emphasis on dementia in the reform of aged care.[10] With funding from the Department of Health and Ageing, *Alzheimer's* 'consult[ed] with people with dementia and their family carers across Australia about their experiences in accessing services.'[11]

With the guidance of Interbrand, a leading international branding consultancy, *Alzheimer's* developed a 'revolutionary' new look brand and image. They instructed Interbrand 'to let off "a great explosion" to combat the lack of understanding and support for dementia in the community.' To ensure this 'great explosion' had the desired effect they engaged Porter Novelli, a leading public relations agency. On 20

8 Alzheimer's Australia, *Annual Report 2012-13*, page 37.

9 As above, page 4.

10 As above, page 8.

11 As above, page 9.

April 2012, in response to the Fight Dementia Campaign, the Prime Minister and the Minister for Mental Health and Ageing announced an 'investment' of $268.4 million over five years to tackle dementia. The Government did not make any commitment to increase funding for dementia research, so the Fight Dementia Campaign continued to seek $200 million over five years for dementia research.[12]

As part of the campaign, *Alzheimer's* held a 'Fringe Event' at the Australian Labor Party's 46th Annual Conference on 2 December 2011. The theme, Dementia: The Chronic Disease of the 21st century, was chosen to encourage politicians to support the Fight Dementia Campaign.[13] In addition, one of the big economic consultancies was engaged to provide figures on how much dementia is costing Australia. This is, however, of little use, unless it is compared with all other problems and if the costs of solutions are known. In this particular instance, the report concentrated on 'prevalence' of the disease and reported by every federal electorate – not very subtle (DA Economics, 2011). There are 21 other registered charities listed under 'Alzheimer' on the ACNC register.

The *Alzheimer's* case study does not suggest that the disease is not important, but there are many others whose advocates, and sufferers, would also like the support of a large subvention of taxpayers' dollars. This really is a case of a government lobbying itself with taxpayers' money. In the health field, there seem to be as many charities as there are body organs, but not all charities receive similar privileges. The *Australian Kidney Foundation* proudly declares that it is independent of government. It raises $12 million per year, almost wholly private, for advocacy, education, research and support for people with kidney disease. It has generated a significant number of advocacy pieces and submissions to State and Australian governments.[14] The *Australian Lung Foundation*, on the other hand, receives most of its money from government. Department of Health and Ageing funds its awareness campaigns for the National

12 As above, page 11.

13 As above, page 30.

14 Kidney Health Australia, *Annual Report 2012*, page 6.

Lung Health Community Awareness and Promotion Campaign and the Chronic Lung Disease Self Management Project.[15]

Welfare business models

The *Sacred Heart Mission St. Kilda* boasts that 'more than 45 per cent of our overall income comes from op shop customers, donors, trusts and foundations, bequestors and people who use our fee-based services.' The majority of the income, however, comes from government grants.[16] Could higher fees, more government funding, or more fundraising satisfy their clients? What is this mix of private donations, government funding, and fee for service based on?

The *Sexual Assault Support Services of Tasmania* trumpets the fact that its 'services are government-funded and provided free of charge!'[17] In what sense is it a public benevolent institution? If the government provides the services free of charge, then why are the services not explicitly government services? *Beyondblue*, the national depression and anxiety initiative, touts as an 'independent, not-for-profit organisation working to increase awareness and understanding of depression and anxiety in Australia and to reduce the associated stigma.' It is proud of the fact that it is a bipartisan initiative of all governments 'supported by the generosity of individuals, corporate Australia and Movember.'[18] It seems to be a campaigning organisation using government money to leverage more government money and corporate and private donations.

Anglicare Victoria is a PBI helping the poor and disadvantaged throughout Victoria. The income in 2012 was $64 million, of which $8 million came from its own fundraising. The Most Reverend Dr Philip Freier, Archbishop of Melbourne, writes in the Annual Report 'about the mission of [*Anglicare*] to create a more just society by expressing

15 The Australian Lung Foundation, *Annual Report 2012*, page 3.

16 The Sacred Heart Mission St.Kilda, *The Sacred Heart Mission Annual Report 2013*, page 56.

17 Sexual Assault Support Services, *Annual Report 2011-12*, page 25.

18 Beyondblue, *Annual Report 2011-12*, page 1.

God's love through service, education and advocacy.' Which is all well and good, but it is government-funded, save for the fees it charges for its services. With these monies, *Anglicare Victoria* 'undertakes research to better understand social problems and to inform our advocacy and engagement strategies.' The expenditure on research and advocacy was $537,000 in 2012-13. $1.7 million was spent on building relationships with community, schools, parishes and media.[19] There are a number of research projects reported on the website.[20] A saving grace perhaps is that they claimed to measure the benefit of their programs and services.[21] Unfortunately, the results were not available.

Carbon Neutral is a CI that advises organisations on how to minimise or offset their carbon dioxide emissions. They report that, as a consequence of a change to a government program, 'we have lost a number of larger long-standing clients. However, it is pleasing to report that we have attracted 42 new commercial clients in this reporting period.'[22] Are they a business consultancy and, if so, why not a for-profit organisation?

NQ Dry Tropics is a CI, which claims to be a 'community-based, not-for-profit organisation'. It helps farmers, urban, rural and coastal residents, organisations, Traditional Owners, and community groups 'to improve their land and water management practices and help ensure a sustainable future'. Most of the funding received by *NQ Dry Tropics* originated from government contracts. The government contribution to the company's revenue was $12.8 million for the year, or 97 per cent of total revenue.[23]

Government by another name

From time to time Parliament will place an organisation on to the list

19 Anglicare Victoria, *Annual Report 2012-13*, page 41.

20 Anglicare Victoria, http://www.anglicarevic.org.au/index.php?pageID=7894 accessed 28 November 2013.

21 Anglicare Victoria, *Annual Report 2012-13*, page 25.

22 Carbon Neutral, *Annual Financial Statements 2012*, page 2.

23 NQ Dry Tropics, *Annual Community Report 2011-12*, pages 2 and 14.

of charities by naming it in the Act. Those charities named in the Act are a special category indeed. These may not have been able to satisfy the already broad provisions of the Act for charities. *Cancer Australia* is a statutory authority that is also named in the Taxation Act as a charity and is registered under the Charitable Fundraising Act 1991 (NSW) to conduct fundraising activities. The net surplus from donations and fundraising was $70,000 out of total cash received of $14 million in 2013.[24] The reporting requirements are stringent. The report was prepared in accordance with the *Financial Management and Accountability Act 1997* (Cth), which requires it be tabled in Parliament. It reflects the requirements for annual reports approved by the Joint Committee of Public Accounts and Audit under the *Public Service Act 1999* (Cth). There is nothing to complain of in an accounting sense, but is it a charity?

By contrast, *Worldskills Australia*, a public company whose purpose is to 'promote and build a skills culture by inspiring young people, [by] providing them with an opportunity to showcase their trade and skill talent,' organises competitions at a regional, national and international level. Beyond that, it is difficult to know because it is not clear where the money comes from or who the clients are. An annual report is not available on the website and there is no acknowledgment of government funding, if indeed it has any.[25]

Madec is a PBI that operates as a labour training and labour hire cum TAFE College servicing labour needs in the South Australian, Victorian and NSW inland. It appears to be entirely funded by its revenue.[26] It is unclear why it is a PBI.

Foundation Housing in West Australia is a PBI. It runs former public housing properties, collects rent and maintains them. 'With the completion of a number of major development projects and the

24 Cancer Australia, *Annual Report 2012-13*, pages 9 and 98.

25 Worldskills Australia appears on the charity sample list under 'Named in the Act', industry category.

26 Madec Australia Limited, *General Purpose Financial Statements 2013*.

successful transfer of over 300 properties from the Department of Housing, this year has seen *Foundation Housing* increase our housing portfolio to over 1300 properties, providing upwards of 1700 tenancies.' The main source of income is rental and it is seeking to 'establish new commercial opportunities to help fund on-going long term maintenance commitments whilst ensuring that Foundation Housing's PBI status is fully protected.'[27] Is it a business?

Outcare is a PBI almost wholly owned by government. 'Outcare's charter [is] to make Western Australia a safer place to live by providing rehabilitative and supportive services for offenders, ex-offenders and their families.' Contract and grant income was $7.5 million, which came from 14 different agencies. Its membership, donations and fundraising were $25,878.[28]

The *Silver Chain Group*, one of the largest not-for-profit health and community care organisations, provides a range of services to assist people in their homes throughout Western Australia, South Australia, Queensland and New South Wales. The main skills are nursing. Government funding is 85 per cent. Fourteen per cent is raised in fees, and one per cent of income from donations. They tender for government services; they are able to garner some volunteer help to assist. Would a for-profit company with subsidy provide better value?

SEQ Catchments Ltd is an Australian company and a CI, including DGR status. It received more than $11 million in 2012 and no donations. SEQ Catchments claims to be 'a community-based, not-for-profit organisation helping to build a sustainable community that cares for and values the natural resources and biodiversity of South East Queensland, and that recognises the impact of personal and collective actions on the environment.'[29] Its partners are Energex, Powerlink, SEQ Water, which are government-owned corporations, as well as local, State and Federal

27 Foundation Housing, *Annual Report 2010-11*, page 9.

28 Outcare, *Annual Report 2012*, page 10.

29 SEQ Catchments Ltd, *Audited Financial Statements 2012*, page 13.

governments, all of whom grant monies for environmental works. Does the charitable status help?

The *Regional Australia Institute* claims to be an independent, not-for-profit organisation developing 'real solutions to key policy issues through research and an ongoing conversation with Australian communities.'[30] The *RAI* is a CI and has DGR status. It does not advertise its charitable status, or seek donations, or mention government funding on its website, and only sparingly in its annual report. It derives all its money from a government grant. In what sense is the Institute independent?

Self-regarding charity

Full marks for bravado. A Victorian business lobby, the Victorian Employers' Chamber of Commerce and Industry recently petitioned the Supreme Court of Victoria to declare it a charitable and not-for-profit institution for taxation purposes, which would make it exempt from paying State taxes. It wants the 'promotion of commerce' defined as a charitable endeavour.[31] It has every chance of succeeding because, as noted previously, the *Chamber of Commerce & Industry of Western Australia Incorporated* has had charitable status for some years. There are many other entities whose charitable status, although well-accepted, seems less than obvious.

There are more than 5,000 school funds, hundreds of public hospitals and an unknown number of nursing homes (table 2.4, page 47), and much else besides, which are predominantly government funded and/or heavily subsidised. *Cressbrook Committee for the Royal Children's Hospital Brisbane*, for example, is a PBI, which has raised funds over the years for the support of patients, especially accommodation for country

30 Regional Australia Institute, *Annual Report 2012-13*, page 1.

31 Chris Vedelago, 'Victorian Employers' Chamber of Commerce and Industry Seeks Charity Status', *The Age* 12 January 2014.

children attending the hospital.[32] Most Queensland families are eligible for assistance through the Patient Travel Scheme. Why they should be regarded as charities, or be subject of charity arrangements, is an historic legacy of questionable value. There is another very powerful reason for not regarding many of these organisations as charities. Many are self-regarding.

Why is aged care a charitable object?

Charity law deems that a charitable trust for the relief of the aged is for the needs arising from old age. There is no need for some other element such as poverty or impotence, although a gift limited to the wealthy aged will destroy the charitable nature of the gift. Bequests for the aged will be valid if the requisite public benefit is present. The mere fact that a charge is made for services rendered to the aged does not overturn the charitable nature of those services, unless there is an element of private profit (Halsbury, 2013, 75(90)).

The laws governing charity for the aged are mostly irrelevant in an era of pensions and extensive government subsidies for nursing homes and other aged care programs such as the Commonwealth's Home and Community Care scheme. As always there is controversy about the extent to which benefits should be means tested and the degree to which the aged should pay for their own care, including bonds from their estate. As the following case studies suggest, most aged care charities no longer run on charity. Besides, the needs of the aged are almost always related to health, not age per se. Indeed, age, as a category of relief, may well be discriminatory or, at the very least, insulting.

Benetas aged care services is a PBI. It places great emphasis on the history that properties were donated, or built using funds received from bequests and donations. They are 'mindful of [their] obligation to fulfil the vision of the Christian (Anglican) benefactors. It now operates as

32 *Cressbrook Committee for the Royal Children's Hospital*, http://www.cressbrookcommittee.com.au/leonardlodge.com.au/Home.html accessed 6 March 2014.

a not-for-profit organisation employing 1,400 staff and 350 volunteers. *Benetas* supports 4,000 older people in aged care homes and community services throughout Victoria. It has an annual income of $78 million, and receives 71 per cent of this from government, eight per cent from investment revenue, 17 per cent from client service fees and just one per cent from donations and bequests. It concentrates overwhelmingly on the provision of services but, nevertheless, has 'an extensive Research and Advocacy Agenda.' 'Benetas has also been advocating strongly, including at two parliamentary committees, for the creation of one peak body for aged care, to produce one single voice for the industry.'[33]

Similarly, *Villa Maria* is a PBI that looks after the disabled and aged. Its income in 2013 was more than $68 million, 84 per cent of which is from government, 11 per cent in fees, and two per cent of its income is from donations and bequests.[34] Wesley Mission is a Presbyterian (now Uniting Church) organisation of long-standing and provides a range of services to those in need, including the aged. It receives 60 per cent of its income from grants and subsidies; donations and offerings are four per cent.[35] Each of these services is highly regulated by State and Commonwealth governments, such that there is no independent direction, and there are no donors to speak of. More important, each of the residents is in receipt of some government funds and some pay fees. Where is the charity?

Why are hospitals treated as charities?

In similar vein, gifts to hospitals are charitable regardless of patient income. They are deemed to be 'as for relief of impotent persons, in the sense of being in relief of needs arising from distress or other disability.' Trusts for provision of hospital staff and other medical purposes are also charitable. Charging patients for admission does not deprive it of a charitable character unless it operates primarily for private gain. This is

---

33 Benetas, *Annual Report 2011-12*, various.

34 Villa Maria Society, *Annual Report 2013*, page 43.

35 Wesley Mission, *Helping Create Sustainable Communities: 2012 Review*, page 35.

so even where the charges mean that the facilities 'may only be used by people of some means', or that the benefits accrue to those who run the institution, provided that the profits are not available to the members (Halsbury, 2013, 75(100)).

Why is education a charitable object, without proof of public benefit?

The law for education charities is that advancement and propagation of education and learning are valid charitable purposes irrespective of the financial position of the beneficiaries, provided that the requisite element of public benefit is present. If a gift is clearly educational in its object, however, there is no need for evidence that the public will benefit by it, or as to the efficiency of the form of education (Halsbury, 2013, 75 (105). In other words, the gift could be entirely useless for purposes of education and have used taxpayer resources to so do. Nor is it necessary that those who obtain the benefit of an educational charity to pay less for that gift than the value of the services they receive.

There are almost 5,000 school or college building funds that are DGR status charities. A case could be made that these are self-regarding rather than for the public benefit. Is giving to one's child's school a charity? The same could be said of public hospitals, Technical and Further Education institutions, and universities. These are, to all intents and purposes, commercial activities with paying clients and considerable direct government assistance. In some instances, the benefits accrue to the donor. Why throw in an extra subsidy? Politics decides these matters, not logic. As argued in the introduction, government will not disturb these constituencies but, in failing to do so, they weaken the case for 'other-regarding' and public benefit charity.

Controversial values

Controversial charitable objects usually centre on whether charity has distributive aims or simply relief aims or, in the words of a former UK charity commissioner, 'preservation, alleviation or transformation'

(Hind, 2011, 202). Distributive aims are not widely supported outside the charitable sector; for example, many charities expound the virtues of social justice, which is an ideology suggesting that there is a knowable fair distribution of resources.

The *Reichstein Foundation*, for example, has undergone a transformation under a new generation of the family of the original benefactor. It has shifted from a traditional supporter of established charities, to one of 'social change' philanthropy. The mission is to achieve 'a more equitable distribution of wealth and power and a healthy and sustainable environment'. The *Foundation* has launched a 2013-14 public grants program focused on promoting 'economic rights and reducing inequality'. It is the first time the *Foundation* has offered grants towards advocacy and policy reform projects around economic rights. The *Foundation* rationale is that the 'top 20 per cent of Australians possesses 62 per cent of the nation's wealth.' The 2013 grants program are touted to invest in 'smart advocacy, reforms and innovations that address tough social and economic disadvantage.' The *Foundation* says it is looking for causes that are focused on legislative, policy, regulatory or funding reform and innovative projects that address the causes of disadvantage and economic inequity.[36]

Whether agreement could ever be achieved on the notion of fairness is moot. For example, it is unlikely that a fair or 'just' distribution will be achieved by free choices of individuals who are more likely to consider merit and market as better arbiters of a fair distribution (Johns, 2012, 8). It may be that from an 'egalitarian liberal perspective, the point of charity law is not distributive' (Harding, 2011, 26), but that does not stop many charities operating as if redistribution is the only purpose of charity.

C20

The charity sector is quick to defend its political work, famously citing the churches' support for abolition of slavery. It is slow to defend its

---

36 Reichstein Foundation, http://www.reichstein.org.au/about-us accessed 12 September 2013.

support for prohibition, public policy that resulted in criminalising the manufacture and sale of alcohol and, in the process, created crime and destroyed lives. Doing good is often contestable. Doing good with other people's money, that is, with taxpayer subsidies, is dubious. Some charity leaders proceed on the basis that such controversies are settled. The former Prime Minister, Julia Gillard, for example, in appointing a C20 committee to organise the civil society part of the G20 conference in Brisbane in 2014, said self-described justice campaigner Tim Costello; CEO of *World Vision*, 'will help the G20 gather the views of civil society and convene a C20 summit to develop recommendations for G20 leaders' consideration.' Costello welcomed his 'fellow committee members who have been drawn from across the breadth of Australian civil society'.[37]

The committee members are, in effect, professional lobbyists for multiculturalism, Aboriginal separatism, church progressivism, neo-feminism, anti-smoking, eating, drinking campaigners, greens, and anti-development anti-free trade foreign aid lobbyists. Nowhere on this committee is to be found a traditional charity such as Meals-on-Wheels, the Salvation Army, Lifeline, or Rotary. The latter are civil society; the former are people who rely on the inclusive institutions of the Western liberal democracies, institutions that encourage creation and redistribution of wealth, to argue for its antithesis. They would stand little chance of being elected to parliament. A rare example is Dignity for Disability's Kelly Vincent, elected in 2010 to the Legislative Council in South Australia.[38] The C20 leader will instead argue that 'inequality remains one of the defining features of our world today. It not only holds back poor and vulnerable people, trapping them in poverty, it also holds back economic growth on a global scale.'[39] Costello argues, in effect, that wealth is to blame for poverty, a somewhat controversial position.

37 Quoted in Gary Johns, 'PM's C20 Committee is Unelectable', *The Australian* 18 June 2013.

38 Parliament of South Australia, http://www2.parliament.sa.gov.au/internet/desktopmodules/memberdrill.aspx?pid=4364 accessed 26 March 2014.

39 Johns, as above.

Equality of opportunity

The idea of equality of opportunity is very controversial in education circles because student success comes from two different sources: matters for which students should not be held responsible (circumstances) and matters that fall within individual responsibility (effort). Two distinct ethical principles support these positions. Compensation, which states that differences in outcomes due to circumstances are ethically unacceptable and should be compensated; and reward, which states that differences due to effort are to be considered ethically acceptable and do not justify any redistribution (Aaberge, 2011, 194).

In education, the two principles are fought over at every election, with the default position that both are 'rewarded' by government, but by different means. Charity should steer clear of such controversy; instead, governments encourage such charity by allowing universities and schools endless subventions, and charitable status for research and buildings.

Sexual politics

There are long-standing controversies where charities are eager participants. *Family Planning NSW* is a publicly well-funded HPC. *Family Planning NSW* believes that 'abortion should be removed from the Criminal Code of NSW and should be managed as any other medical procedure.'[40] Its income in 2011-12 was $11.5 million.[41] *Working it Out* is a PBI, and advocate for same sex couples. Its sole purpose appears to be 'education' in order to create a more positive image in the public's perspective for Lesbian, Bi- and Trans-sexual Tasmanians.[42] It has participated in marriage equality rallies within Tasmania. The Queensland Minister for Health, Lawrence Springborg, accused the Queensland HIV/AIDS organisation, *Queensland Association for Healthy Communities*, a PBI, of using taxpayer funds on political campaigns and gay activism.

40 Family Panning NSW, http://www.fpnsw.org.au/sofp_abortion.pdf accessed 2 December 2013.

41 Family Panning NSW, *Annual Report 2011-12*, page 63.

42 Working It Out, *Annual Report 2012*, page 12.

'Unfortunately, over time, it morphed into an organisation based on sectional political advocacy for gay issues.' The minister claimed the group had dipped into its $2 million of taxpayer funding to pursue a high profile gay rights agenda, 'contaminating the focus on HIV/AIDS awareness'. The minister recently announced a new agency, the *HIV Foundation Queensland*, to replace the Association, which lost its funding in August 2012.[43]

Reconciliation

Reconciliation Australia is a government charity dedicated to a particular view of Aboriginal policy. Its income in 2011-12 was $6 million, of which government provides about 60 to 70 per cent, but opaque reporting on project funding makes it difficult to be accurate. It declares that it is 'an independent, non-government organisation and the proportion of our income from non-government sources is on the increase.' However, the bulk of its funding has come from the Department of Families, Housing, Community Services and Indigenous Affairs (FaHCSIA) and the Department of Education, Employment and Workplace Relations.[44] It receives some funding from BHP Billiton.[45]

More controversially, the group, *Recognise*, is the officially sanctioned propaganda arm of the Australian government. *Recognise* self-promotes as 'the people's movement to recognise Aboriginal and Torres Strait Islander peoples in our Constitution.' It is hardly a people's movement because *Recognise* is part of *Reconciliation Australia* which, despite being a CI is, as noted, heavily funded by the Australian Government. In February 2013, *Reconciliation Australia* was promised $14.4 million for four years to assist in its task of, among other things, changing the Constitution.[46]

43 'AIDS Group Lost Prevention Focus', *The Australian* 11 November 2013.

44 In the Abbott Government these are now, the Department of Social Security, and the Department of Employment, and Education.

45 Reconciliation Australia, *Annual Review 2011-12*, page 18.

46 Australian Government, 'Continued Funding for Reconciliation Australia', http://www.indigenous.gov.au/continued-funding-for-reconciliation-australia/ accessed 20 September 2013.

Governments are bound to fund both sides of a referendum question, but there is no charity funding for the no case.

Family

Relationships Australia is a federation of community based, not-for-profit organisations providing relationship, community and family support services in each Australian State and Territory. It is 'committed to social justice and inclusion, and respect the rights of all people, in all their diversity, to live life fully within their families and communities with dignity and safety, and to enjoy healthy relationships.' *Relationships Australia* had a total income in 2011-12 of around $120 million, aggregated across all member organisations.

The majority of its income came from the Commonwealth departments of FaHCSIA and Attorney-General, as well as from State and Territory governments. *Relationships Australia* is a CI, which is eligible for GST concession, FBT rebate and income tax exemption but is not eligible to receive tax-deductible gifts.[47] The ordinary work that is undertaken by *Relationships Australia* may be perfectly good, but if it were to be made available to the non-poor, its charitable status would be highly questionable.

Research centres named in the Act

There is a number of research centres named in legislation that may not otherwise qualify for charitable status. The *Green Institute* and the political parties research arms, the *Centre for Independent Studies* and the *Institute of Public Affairs*, or, more accurately, *The Trustee for Institute of Public Affairs Research Trust*, are self-funded, but each has DGR status. By contrast, the *Grattan Institute* commenced with a $15 million endowment from each of the Australian and Victorian Governments. BHP Billiton provided $4 million. The *Grattan Institute's* board controls the endowment in order 'to safeguard [its] independence'. The funds are invested and *Grattan* uses the income to pursue its activities.

47 Relationships Australia, *Annual Report 2011-12.*

In addition, the University of Melbourne contributes support in kind, most importantly by housing the *Institute* in a building just off Grattan Street in Carlton, opposite the University. The *Institute* also benefits from significant support from companies and philanthropic organisations such as the *Myer Foundation.* The *Institute* has DGR status.[48] The Australian Government provided $25 million to support the founding of the *United States Studies Centre,* University of Sydney. The New South Wales Government provided $2 million of financial and in-kind support to the *Centre.*[49]

Environmental charities

The *Climate Institute* is a $3.4 million Australian public company established for the express purpose of reaching a 'zero-carbon global economy'. It is also a CI which receives GST concession, income tax exemption, FBT rebate and the *Climate Institute Gift Fund* may receive income tax deductible donations. Its major sponsor is Westpac. It receives 13 per cent of its income from government, and most of its money comes from philanthropic grants and donations, principally the Kantor family trusts. It works with *Greenpeace,* the ACTU, GetUp! and others to lobby government to change legislation, specifically to abate carbon dioxide emissions in Australia.[50]

The *Climate Institute's* work is not charitable; it is wholly political. Nor is it unambiguously a public benefit. Cassandra Goldie (ACOSS), Don Henry (*ACF*) and John Connor of the *Climate Institute* wrote an 'opinion piece' during a federal election campaign supporting renewables: 'We must not flinch in our determination to move to a low carbon economy …' and, by implication against the Coalition.[51] No more ideological or

48 Grattan Institute, http://grattan.edu.au/about-us accessed 29 November 2013.

49 US Studies Centre, http://ussc.edu.au/about/partners-supporters-collaborators accessed 6 March 2014.

50 The Climate Institute, *Annual Review 2011-12.*

51 Ged Kearney, Cassandra Goldie, Don Henry and John Connor, 'Efficient Power for Poor', *The Australian* 21 August 2013.

controversial statement could be made, and this prior to the changes to the Act allowing lobbying as a charitable purpose.

The *Graeme Wood Foundation* holds about $20 million in assets and gives away about $1 million a year to a range of arts, youth and environmental causes, $8 million to the University of Queensland, where he studied, and $15 million to establish its *Global Change Institute.*[52] *Global Change* covers 'global sustainability' challenges including climate change (carbon mitigation and adaptation); human population growth and shift; resource security and consumption; stewardship of biodiversity and natural ecosystems; and, responses on ecosystem health, social resilience and economic prosperity. The director is Professor Ove Hoegh-Guldberg.[53] Wood funds the *Global Mail* online; the estimated cost of the start-up is reported to be $2-3 million a year. 'The Global Mail is a philanthropically funded, not-for-profit news and features website.'[54]

The *Poola Foundation* (Tom Kantor Fund) has granted approximately $10 million to the *Australian Conservation Foundation.*[55] About $14 million has been granted to the *Climate Institute* to lobby for action on climate change.

Proof of the dangers of allowing charities to pursue controversial public policy issues, as charities, is the Greens protest against a charity on the other side of the environment movement's views of the efficacy of renewable energy. The *Waubra Foundation* is a small HPC and it highlights the health problems allegedly caused by wind turbines. The Greens have made a complaint to the ATO and the ACNC alleging the *Foundation* should

---

52 Paddy Manning, 'Net Millionaire Bankrolled Green Revolution, *The Sydney Morning Herald* 8 January, 2011.

53 Global Change Institute, http://www.gci.uq.edu.au/about accessed 12 September 2013.

54 The Global Mail, http://www.theglobalmail.org accessed 12 September 2013. Now rumoured to be closing Sally Jackson, 'Wotif Founder Graeme Wood to Close Global Mail News Site,' *The Australian* 30 January, 2014.

55 Crikey, 'The Power Index', http://www.thepowerindex.com.au/rich-crusaders/eve-kantor/201202261084 accessed 6 March 2014.

not be declared a charity.[56] This is a case of the pot calling the kettle black, as it was the Greens and fellow travellers that successfully rallied in support of *Aid/Watch's* freedom of speech in the High Court.

The expanding nature of public benefit

Charities have grown in their remit, their scope of activity and their willingness to take government money, and ask for more, often for controversial objectives. These changes are reflected in charity law. Charity law in Australia has recently been consolidated under the *Charities Act 2013* (Cth). The Abbott Government has vowed to repeal the statute, but how, when and why is unknown.[57] The Act nevertheless closely follows the common law and remains the best guide to its interpretation (Halsbury, 2013).

The common law meaning of charity has developed over 400 years, largely based on the Preamble to the Statute of Charitable Uses (known as the Statute of Elizabeth), enacted by the English Parliament in 1601 and consolidated in the terminology of the *Commissioners for Special Purposes of Income Tax v Pemsel* [1891-1894] in the UK. The *Pemsel* decision specified five heads of charity and that these purposes were for the public benefit:

(a) preventing and relieving sickness, disease or human suffering
(b) advancing education
(c) relieving the poverty, distress or disadvantage of individuals or families
(d) caring for and supporting the aged or individuals with disabilities
(e) advancing religion.[58]

56 Jake Sturme, 'Greens Challenge Charitable Status of Anti-Wind Farm Pressure Group.' http://www.abc.net.au/news/2013-11-08/hold-for-am-wind-turbine-story-jake-sturmer/5077592 accessed 11 November 2013.

57 Kevin Andrews MP, http://kevinandrews.com.au/parliament/house-speech/charities-bill-2013 accessed 15 July 2013.

58 *Charities Act 2013,* section 7.

The new Act has expanded the charitable purposes following the common law 'creep' over many years, by widening the purview of the five heads of charity where the nature of the public benefit (but not charitable purpose) is assumed, and adding others where it is not assumed:

(a) advancing health

(b) advancing education

(c) advancing social or public welfare

(d) advancing religion

(e) advancing culture

(f) promoting reconciliation, mutual respect and tolerance between groups of individuals that are in Australia

(g) promoting or protecting human rights

(h) advancing the security or safety of Australia or the Australian public

(i) preventing or relieving the suffering of animals

(j) advancing the natural environment,

(k) any other purpose beneficial to the general public that may reasonably be regarded as analogous to, or within the spirit of, any of the purposes mentioned in paragraphs (a) to (j).[59]

Charities, with a purpose that falls under the deemed list (a) to (e), have less to prove in order to receive their status and taxation advantages than those under (f) to (k). Where there is doubt about public benefit it is a matter of evidence. A court must decide, first, whether the objects of a trust will benefit the public in general and, second, whether the trust is beneficial to the community in a way which the law regards as being charitable. To substantiate an entity's charitable purposes, the activities of a charity may be considered. It is the role of its activities and the extent to which they further the entity's purpose that is relevant, not

59 *Charities Act 2013*, section 12.

the nature of the activities. In considering activities to substantiate the charitable purpose, it may be necessary to go beyond governing rules to operating rules and activities to substantiate its stated objects.[60]

Most important, the assessment as to purpose (whether the entity is a charity) is a continuing one and consideration has to be given to the purpose for which it continues to be conducted, not just the purpose for which it was established.[61] Once a gift is held to be beneficial to the public, it is not relevant to enquire whether the conditions of the gift represent the most effective means of achieving its purpose. This position is at the heart of the critique, that some of that which is held to be charitable may be of little public benefit. The presumption of public benefit in the heads of charity was removed in the UK *Charities Act 2006*, although the government has now supported its readmission.

Figure 3.2: Taxpayer preferred charity surface

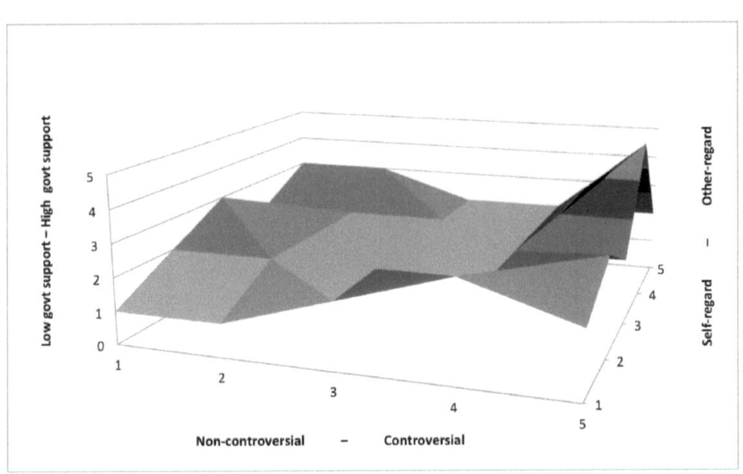

Source: Author.

60 *Charities (Consequential Amendments and Transitional Provisions) Bill 2013*, Explanatory Memorandum 1.27.

61 *Charities (Consequential Amendments and Transitional Provisions) Bill 2013*, Explanatory Memorandum 1.34.

Figure 3.2 plots the characteristics of a preferred charity in three dimensions: the level of government income; the degree of controversy; and the degree of self and other regard. Where the level of support strays from the ideal, which is where government support is low, where charities have a high propensity for other-regarding deeds, and are non-controversial, there could be a legitimate complaint from taxpayers. Further elements such as the direct nature of charity work could also be considered as, for example, PBIs, which are highly favoured in terms of taxation treatment because these must engage in direct work, but often do not.

Figure 3.3 suggests a surface that is a reflection of the actual activities and circumstances of Australian charities. While a number of charities that are non-controversial and other-regarding receive high government support, too many are dependent on government and promote causes that are not widely supported, and are self-regarding. The various elements of charity performance and behaviour are perhaps best summed up by the term 'public benefit'. Charities, by and large, should be for the public benefit, as well act in a charitable manner. Unfortunately, the test of public benefit has become bloated and fails to serve its purpose, part of which is to protect the public purse.

Figure 3.3: Actual charity surface

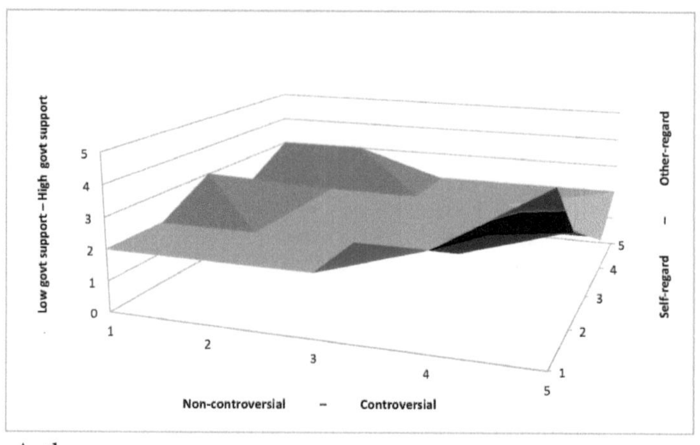

Source: Author.

Public benefit must be proved

The idea of public benefit needs to be tested and trimmed. To assume that certain causes are of public benefit if undertaken in a charitable manner is folly. There are organisations that are little more than government outposts, charities in name only, where money from government swamps any donor input, and charities that canvass matters that are not well supported in the electorate and should, therefore, not be supported by the taxpayer.

The ideas expressed in the law of public benefit, that it be beneficial for a sufficient number, are too ambiguous. For example, an effort to save one refugee is humane, whereas an effort to save one million refugees, presumably through a change of policy, may not be. Large numbers of refugees may change the nature of the host country, to its detriment. There should be, for all charities, clear verification of public benefit in the sense of an overall gain to the sum of well-being.

Refugee advocates rarely answer the question of how many is too many. Philanthropists Renata and Andrew Kaldor established the Centre for International Refugee Law at the University of New South Wales in 2013.[62] The Centre's founding director, Professor McAdam, has said the Centre aims to bring 'a principled, human rights-based approach to the issue of refugee law and policy in Australia by feeding high-quality research into public policy debates and legislative reform.' McAdam writes, 'Relative to the rest of the world, Australia receives an extremely small proportion of asylum-seekers: only 2 per cent of the industrialised world.' But, is three per cent, or four per cent, better? The law cannot determine that number. Human rights provide no guide: except apparently that more is better.[63]

Paul Collier's study, *Exodus: Immigration and Multiculturalism in the 21st century*, suggests that, left ungoverned, as has occurred in Europe,

---

62 David Marr, *ABC FM Radio Classical* interview, 24 January 2014.

63 University of NSW, http://newsroom.unsw.edu.au/news/law/launch-andrew-renata-kaldor-centre-international-refugee-law accessed 30 January 2014.

migration will accelerate and become excessive. This is why migration controls, far from being an 'embarrassing vestige of nationalism and racism', are important tools of social policy. He makes plain what is obvious to almost all Australians, that a national identity and a clear set of rules that all citizens obey are the price of liberty. More powerfully, he argues, 'nations are important and legitimate moral units' (Collier, 2013, 292). In other words, an apparently straightforward public benefit, when taken to extremes, becomes a public 'bad', and yet the charitable purpose is not challenged.

4

Government pays to lobby itself

In *On Politics*, Alan Ryan, poses a key question: 'how can human beings best govern themselves?' (Ryan, 2012, xxxiii). This is a disarmingly simple question, yet the answers have confounded most societies. Clearly, democracy is the key, but Ryan notes 'the discrepancy in political effectiveness in modern industrial societies is between the organized and the unorganized.' He asks, 'can democracies protect the public at large – unorganized – against well-organized special interests?' (Ryan, 2012, xiv).

More realistically, 'If we are persuaded that in all societies only a small number of people will actually play a role in governing the society, it makes all the difference just *how* the elite secures and retains the allegiance of the many … Unillusioned commentators on modern democracies describe democracy as ruled by competing elites' (Ryan, 2012, xvi). Participation in the political process takes place through organisations, and charities are, first and foremost, organisations. They may raise funds for charitable purposes, but many apply their orgnisational wealth, much of it taxpayer-funded, to politics. Not only do some regard participation as the key to healthy democracy, but their right to publicly subsidised participation. But 'is it really necessary to subsidize the exercise of liberty to produce a vibrant civil society? (Reich, 2013, 190). How did revolutionaries ever survive before publicly subsidised political participation came along? In short, very nicely thank you. Paying people to lobby government produces more politics and more government, not necessarily better societies.

Most 'organised' citizens want something from taxpayers. There is no rule about how many, or how few, citizens should participate in order for a democracy to be vibrant, let alone viable. The desire for participation of all citizens in a democracy is noble. It is a noble trap into which judges and political activists have fallen.

Polite fiction – charities do not lobby

Charities argue that they advocate, not lobby. The 2008 Federal Lobbying Code of Conduct defines 'lobbying activities' as communications with a government representative in an effort to influence government decision-making. It does not, however, include communications with a parliamentary committee, or a 'grassroots campaign', or responses to requests by government for information. A lobbyist is defined as any person, company or organisation that conducts lobbying activities on behalf of a third party client. The definition specifically excludes DGR charities.[1] Charities are not lobbyists, in the same way that trade unions and business associations are not lobbyists, but that does not mean that they do not lobby. Nor does the fact that submissions to government, but not the minister, unless requested, are not lobbying. These are distinctions without a difference.

It has long been the advice that charities can lobby, as long as it is in pursuit of a charitable purpose (Falkiner-Rose, 2007, 5). How much lobbying charities can undertake, however, that is how much charitable resource they devote to politics, is a moot point. Historically, a 'trust for the attainment of political objects' was invalid because courts had 'no means of judging whether a proposed change in the law would or would not be for the public benefit' (Halsbury, 2013, 75(290)). The High Court

1 Department of the Prime Minister and Cabinet, http://lobbyists.pmc.gov.au/conduct_code.cfm accessed 6 March 2014.

overlooked this matter in *Aid/ Watch Incorporated v Commissioner of Taxation* and decided that an association engaged in researching, monitoring, and campaigning on delivery of overseas aid should maintain charitable status.[2]

The Court ruled that, in Australia, there is no general doctrine that excludes political objects from charitable purposes. Although the Court indicated that certain forms of advocacy would not be denied charitable status, it did not align the objects of political parties with charity, and so it remains a non-charitable object to promote education in and promulgation of the views of a political party. The High Court failed to notice, however, that *Aid/ Watch* did no charity work whatsoever, and that there was no restriction on its free speech, only that it was subsidised by the public purse to pursue its political objectives. The Gillard Government embedded the High Court decision into a statutory definition of charity, which, for the first time, licenses lobbying without constraint, allowing 'promoting or opposing a change to any matter established by law, policy or practice in the Commonwealth, a State, a Territory or another country, if … the change is in furtherance or in aid of one or more of the [charitable] purposes.'[3]

Charities that have 'a political element' do not necessarily lose their charitable status merely because the promotion of any viewpoint may at some stage involve a political or legislative aspect. The issue is one of degree; where the activities of an association 'directed at political change' demonstrate an effective abandonment of its charitable objects (Halsbury, 2013, 75(295)), the Tax Commissioner would come calling. Australian law is now very liberal; indeed, it could be argued that the taxpayer has no defence against organised and subsidised lobbying by charitable interests. Participation in political campaigns is forbidden in name only, as almost all charities want more government support for their

2 Aid/Watch Incorporated v Commissioner of Taxation [2010] HCA 42 (1 December 2010).

3 *Charities Act 2013*, Sect 12.

cause. Senator Christine Milne, leader of the Greens, blamed an anti-Greens backlash in key states at the 2013 Federal election 'on the failure of environmental groups [most of whom are charities] to prosecute their agenda.'[4] She understands better than most that charities lobby.

Charities lobby government because they reckon it pays dividends. The results of a recent US study of not-for-profits (charities) indicate that a 10 per cent increase in lobbying expenditures produces a 0.5 per cent increase in contributions (Nicholson-Crotty, 2011, 599). But contributions are not the only gains from lobbying; it can bring money and favourable rule changes to the cause. That does not hold necessarily for every other cause. Lobbying, just as every other activity, has opportunity cost. It requires resources that otherwise could have been put to productive use. It may have a negative impact on economic activity. A recent study suggests that 'the higher the quality of economic institutions, the more costly is lobbying with respect to growth.' It depends on 'whether pressure enhances or inhibits institutions that foster economic freedom' (Heckelman, 2013, 360).

There are those who believe, fancifully, that Conservative governments use their powers to 'silence dissent' (Hamilton, 2007) among charities and others, on the basis that they have been forbidden to criticise government about specific matters when under contract to deliver government services. That matter has been put to rest with the passage of the *Not-for-profit Sector Freedom to Advocate Act 2013* (Cth), which prohibits Commonwealth agreements from restricting or preventing not-for-profit entities from commenting on, advocating support for or opposing changes to Commonwealth law, policy or practice.[5] Those same believers, however, seem untroubled by Leftist governments wooing charities to work with government to advance partisan causes. As always, wrong is in the eye of the beholder.

---

4 John Ferguson and Mark Coultan, 'We Paid for ALP Battles: Milne', *The Australian* 9 September 2013.

5 *Not-for-profit Sector Freedom to Advocate Act 2013.*

Charity leaders have attended Labor conferences in Australia for many years,[6] though possibly not as in as bold a fashion as in the UK. In the UK in 2012, more than 30 charities sponsored at least one fringe event at the Labour or Conservative party conference, and at least a dozen had stands in the events' exhibition halls.[7] The question remains, do the privileges provided by government, charity status (which includes charitable foundations (Jung, 2014)) and a seat at the government table, deny others?

Lobbying – by other names

The *Mental Health Council of Australia* is a HPC. It boasts, among its achievements, a number of changes in mental health policy 'as a consequence of MHCA action and advocacy'.[8] These include increases in mental health research, policy and service provision. Its revenue was $4 million in 2013 and it engaged 37 staff. In 2012 the revenue was $3.1 million; $2.7 million came from 'grants', presumably government grants, and $3,973 came from donations.[9]

Another HPC, *HearKids Australia*, advocates on behalf of children with heart disease. It recently released what it called a white paper. It cautioned, however, that 'Just like a government White Paper, this is a discussion document with suggestions for consideration and adoption. It is not intended as a list of lobbying demands.'[10] And yet, predictably, the first recommendation of the white paper was to 'develop a proposal for

---

6 As a national organiser for the Australian Labor Party, the author observed any number of 'charity activists' as early as the 1980s attending the ALP national conference.

7 Dan Corry, 'Charities at Party Conferences: Worth it?' *New Philanthropy Capital*, http://www.thinknpc.org accessed 2 October 2013.

8 Mental Health Council of Australia, *Annual Report 2012-13*, page 7.

9 Mental Health Council of Australia, *Financial Statements 2012* (published June 2013), page 21.

10 HeartKids Australia, http://www.heartkids.org.au/our-work/advocacy/ accessed 2 December 2013.

funding assistance from government(s) to resource a national congenital heart disease register' (Leggat, 2011, 41).

The *Foundation for Alcohol Research and Education* (FARE) is a HPC, which declared an income of $5.6 million in 2013. In fact, it draws on the funding that the Australian Parliament, with a $115 million grant, used to establish FARE in 2001. The *Foundation* was set up to distribute funding for programs and research that aimed to prevent the harms caused by alcohol and licit substance misuse.[11] The *Foundation* can fairly be characterised as part of the 'public health' lobby who are proponents of the 'availability hypothesis', that restriction on availability will solve overuse problems.[12] In 2011, the CEO attended a regional tax forum, organised by MPs Tony Windsor and Rob Oakeshott, 'to argue the case for alcohol's inclusion at the Tax Summit held in October 2011'.[13] The CEO stated that *FARE* has 'moved from a grant making body, to becoming a proactive and strategic leader, funding key alcohol-related research upon which to base significant policy change, and a leader, advocate and organiser of the efforts to reduce alcohol misuse in Australia.'[14] *FARE* was involved in the 2013 election campaign (*FARE*, 2013) with 10 policy prescriptions to reduce alcohol harm.

The charity, *Uniting Care Harrison*, informed its supporters that, 'Sadly, the State Government has decided to cut the funding to *Social Housing Advocacy & Support Program*, a successful homeless program run by organisations across Victoria, by up to 40 per cent.' *Uniting Care Harrison* advocated that the State Government review the decision, as they believed 'preventative homelessness programs like SHASP' saved the government money in the long term.[15] No proof of claim was furnished.

Carers Australia is a PBI that advocates and lobbies on a wide range

11 FARE, http://aerf.com.au accessed 30 November 2013.

12 Mike Keane, 'Don't Blame the Booze, It's Zero Tolerance of Violence That's Needed', *The Australian* 8 January 2014.

13 FARE, *Annual Report 2011-12*, page 3.

14 As above, page 1.

15 Uniting Care Harrison, *Annual Report 2012*, page 12.

of issues that affect carers. It 'also' manages the delivery of national programs, support and services for carers across Australia. It claims to 'work in collaboration with carers, Carers Associations, government and peak bodies to develop policy, advocacy, programs and events to improve the lives of Australia's 2.6 million carers.'[16]

The *Aboriginal Legal Service NSW/ACT* is a PBI with an income of $20 million in 2012, almost all of which is from government. It spends a considerable amount of its resources advocating changes to the law. 'At ALS, we advocate for the protection of the rights of Aboriginal people … We write submissions to Federal and State Governments to try and make change there. We lobby pressure groups and stakeholders to try and make change.' It is currently 'aiming to influence the NSW Government' in a campaign for 'Justice Reinvestment', which is 'to shift spending away from corrections and detention and towards programs that identify and support young Aboriginal people in need.'[17]

The CI, *Social Ventures Australia*, has 'learnt through engagement and advisory roles with the Federal and State Governments, that SVA has the capacity to build the relationships needed to influence policy and funding shifts.'[18]

The *Endeavour Foundation* is a PBI. Its income in 2012 was $164 million, of which government subsidies constituted $99 million.[19] The *Foundation* produces an advocacy manual for its employees and clients and supporters. It describes its advocacy as 'about influencing and changing the "system" (legislation, policies and practices) in ways that will benefit people with a disability as a group within society. Systems advocacy encourages changes to the law, government and service policies, and community attitudes' (Endeavour, 2011, 5).

---

16 Carers Australia, http://www.carersaustralia.com.au/how-we-work/accessed 25 November 2013.

17 Aboriginal Legal Service NSW/ACT, *Annual Report 2012*, page 37.

18 Social Ventures Australia, *A Fair Go 2011-12 Annual Review*, page 2.

19 Endeavour Foundation, *Annual Report 2011-12*, page 69.

Baptist Care is a PBI. It declares that it 'will put our values of courage and justice into action by showing leadership in the way we speak up on behalf of those who are vulnerable or marginalised by mainstream society.'[20] The institution's 2012-13 income was $95 million, of which 73 per cent came from the government and 15 per cent from paying clients. It not clear from its financial statement how much is from donors who presumably share its values. And yet the CEO argues:

> we, as a society, … reject those who might have a call on our time and resources. We settle for grudgingly negotiated rights, and justice is too hard to believe in … Evasion, manipulation and compromise are normalised in business and personal relationships. As each one of us comes to believe we can grab what we want at any cost to achieve our own personal desires, our world shifts a little more into alienation and we blame everyone except ourselves.[21]

This sermon is subsidised by taxpayers.

The *National Trust* makes two intriguing statements. One is on its website; 'We rely heavily on community support generated through membership subscriptions, sponsorship, donations and bequests, property admissions and retail sales. Of the collective total operational revenue generated by the organisation less than 10 per cent is sourced from government.'[22] The other is in a submission to government on Sustainable Population Strategy, under the name of its patron, the Governor-General, in which it advised, 'There is no doubt that population change (changes in demographic profiles and numbers) adds pressures to a wide range of social and environmental values … there is something to be said for reducing the velocity of city growth and directing planning

---

20 Baptist Care, http://baptistcare.com.au/community/advocacy/accessed 26 November 2013.

21 Baptist Care, *Annual Report 2012-13*, pages 7 and 36.

22 National Trust, http://www.nationaltrust.org.au/our-organisation accessed 6 March 2014.

concepts to setting up new growth centres. There is no need for cities to get bigger.'[23] The submission provides no proof, or even evidence, for its claims.

Queensland Advocacy Incorporated is a PBI which has a responsibility to deliver direct services. Instead, it sees itself as an advocacy organisation for the disabled, and is almost entirely funded by government. 'A particularly effective way of motivating change is through advocating for the reform of parliamentary legislation and government policy.'[24] It may be effective, but is that what the taxpayer wants?

The *Lowitja Institute* claims to 'work with Australia's leading health research institutions, policy makers and community organisations to commission and invest in targeted, world-class health research that will improve the health and lives of Aboriginal and Torres Strait Islander people.'[25] It commissioned a research discussion paper, 'Legally Invisible – How Australian Laws Impede Stewardship and Governance for Aboriginal and Torres Strait Islander Health'. This paper argued 'in favour of constitutional recognition of the health needs of Aboriginal and Torres Strait Islander people.' This Institute claims that the 'paper has made a significant contribution to the ongoing debate over reforming the Constitution to recognise Australia's First Peoples.'[26] The paper provides no proof for the conclusion on Aboriginal recognition in the Constitution.

Surf Life Saving NSW had an income of $20 million in 2012, 35 per cent of which came from government grants. 'In further recognition of

---

23 Australian Council of National Trusts, 'Sustainable Population Strategy', Submission to the Department of Sustainability, Environment, Water, Population and Communities. 2011, paragraph 3.1.5.

24 Queensland Advocacy Incorporated, http://www.qai.org.au/index.php?option=com_content&view=article&id=35&Itemid=9 accessed 21 November 2013.

25 National Institute for Aboriginal and Torres Strait Islander Health Research Limited is a PBI and trades as the Lowitja Institute.

26 The Lowitja Institute, http://www.lowitja.org.au/legally-invisible-constitutional-recognition-and-health-law-reform accessed 20 November 2013.

the importance of Surf Life Saving in the NSW community, this year marked a significant gain for *Surf Life Saving NSW* politically with the establishment of the Parliamentary Friends of Surf Life Saving, which will advocate for the Surf Life Saving movement. Our sincere thanks go to Mr Darren Webber MP, Member for Wyong, for his initiative in putting forward a motion in [the] NSW Parliament to set up this Parliamentary Friends of Surf Life Saving group.'[27] The author has supported *Surf Live Saving* (Australia) for many years but, based on this information, is having second thoughts.

One Health is a PBI whose message is simply incomprehensible. It seeks to achieve participatory democracy in the public sector. 'To achieve this outcome we have created *The Human Movement Scheme*. Guided by the primary value of "Holism", the scheme engages individuals, communities, businesses and policy makers to co-create positive political change.'[28]

These many, many examples are the very stuff of redistributive politics. Charities, in these roles, are not acting in a charitable manner. They are using taxpayer resources to seek further taxpayer resources based of their own conception of the general welfare.

Policy heavy, service light charities: hardly incidental purposes

It is not as if governments are not sensitive to the use of government funds for political lobbying. The Australian Livestock Export Corporation Ltd (LiveCorp), for example, is a not-for-profit industry service provider (not a charity) with approximately 45 members and associate members involved in export of Australian livestock. It is funded by a statutory levy of its members. The Australian Government has legislated for it to receive government funds and specifies that 'LiveCorp must not engage in or use the funds for agri-political activity', which does not include the

27 Surf Lifesaving NSW, *Annual Report 2011-12*, page 37.

28 One Health Organisation, http://onehealthorganisation.org/about-one-health/our-approach/ accessed 22 November 2013.

LiveCorp board or an individual director recommending a candidate for election, or a candidate funding his or her own campaign activities.[29]

Except during election periods, there are relatively few staff employed by the major political parties in Australia (Johns, 2006, 48). Arguably, charities have the greatest number of staff devoted to advocacy and lobbying of any sector, including political parties. Table 4.1 lists the larger charities whose 'service delivery' is heavily weighted towards advocacy, research, campaigning and lobbying. Although the data from each charity does not allow a breakdown of staff responsibilities, each charity employs large numbers, many of whom appear to be engaged in advocacy.

It may surprise donors and taxpayers to know that Tim Costello, CEO of *World Vision* Australia, Don Henry, CEO of the *Australian Conservation Foundation* (until very recently), and Claire Mallinson, Director of *Amnesty International Australia*, have four things in common. They have all been in their job longer than almost any senior politician. They command more policy resources than any political party. They are in the public debate more than any backbencher. They also head charities. This is as it should be in a healthy and vigorous democracy with competing interests and conceptions of the good. But how much of their work is government funded? Are their donors aware of what they do in the name of the donations? Are they doing good? And how much of their time is spent lobbying? Is that charity work?

Donors wholly fund *Amnesty International* in Australia, so there is less concern that direct government funds are at risk. *Amnesty* is explicitly an advocacy organisation and makes claims to influencing government policy. For example, 'We've got a long-term commitment from Commonwealth and Northern Territory governments to support homelands ... This week they announced $221 million dollars in funding over 10 years for

29 *Funding Agreement 2010-14* between the Commonwealth of Australia represented by the Commonwealth Department of Agriculture, Fisheries and Forestry and Australian Livestock Export Corporation Limited, paragraphs 8.4 and 8.5.

homelands communities in the Northern Territory.'[30] Whether *Amnesty* had any influence is dubious and, indeed, the outcome was probably not beneficial to Aborignes, but they were highly explicit about the political nature of their aims with their donors, and the spending of government money.

A large US survey of charities, professional associations and mutual benefit societies, labor unions, advocacy groups, and religious congregations and advocacy in the state of Indiana found that the odds of participating in advocacy increased as non-profits increased in size. The study found no relationship, between government funding and participation in advocacy, except that the odds of doing 'core' advocacy compared to 'peripheral' advocacy decrease with substantial amounts of government funding.[31] One of the most interesting findings is that a considerable proportion of non-profits that participate in advocacy do not devote many resources to it. For instance, about one-fifth does not devote any staff time or financial resources to advocacy. This suggests that, for the most part, when non-profits engage in advocacy, they do so in a way that is ancillary to higher-priority activities (Child, 2007, 276).

The situation in the US is that there are more severe restrictions on lobbying and far more disclosure of activities required among charities than is the case in Australia, which is consistent with the findings of the Indiana study. There is no comparable data about Australian charities, but the small sample for this book suggests that a great deal of lobbying takes place and, for some types of charity, considerable resources are devoted to lobbying. Further research may prove enlightening.

---

30 Amnesty International (Australia), http://www.amnesty.org.au/indigenous-rights/comments/28287/ accessed 20 November 2013.

31 Core advocacy includes those that devote most of at least one type of resource (volunteer, human, or financial) to advocacy; peripheral advocacy non-profits include all others involved in some form of advocacy activity.

Table 4.1: Significant 'policy research, advocacy, lobbying' charities, 2011

Charity	Income	Staffing	Campaigns
Greenpeace Australia Pacific	$17M	90	Climate Change; Forests; Anti-GM food; Oceans; Whaling; Anti-nuclear
Australian Conservation Foundation	$12M	70	Climate change; energy; Sustainable living; Anti-nuclear
WWF Australia	$19M	Unknown	Climate change, biodiversity, forests
Wilderness Society	$12M	90	Forestry; Wild Rivers; Coal Seam Gas, Kimberly, Coast and Marine …
The Climate Institute	$3M	12	Emissions trading; Australia's international climate diplomacy
Environment Victoria	$2M	20	No new coal power; Save the Murray; Putting a Price on Pollution
Conservation Council Of WA	$2.7M	20	Anti-CSG; anti-nuclear; anti-mining; marine; anti-forestry; Kimberley
Conservation Council South Australia	$1.1M	20	Biodiversity; Coast & Marine; Water; Planning and Development
Environmental Defenders Office NSW	$2.3M	16	Natural Resource Management; CSR; Climate Change
The Australia Institute	Unknown	8	Climate change; Economy; Society (media regulation); Government
Union Aid Abroad	$7.7M	Unknown	Burma Campaign; Zimbabwe; Ban Asbestos; Palestine
Australian Council for Internat'l Development	$2.5M	21	Make Poverty History; Aid effectiveness; Increasing aid budget
St Vincent De Paul (National Office)	$800,000	8	More resources for social welfare
Public Interest Advocacy Centre	$2.4M	25	Access to Justice; Freedom of Information; Human Rights
Amnesty International Australia	$23M	Unknown	Death penalty, indigenous rights, refugees, weapons, torture, violence
Public Health Association of Australia	$2.15M	8	Population health approach; social determinants of health
Oxfam Australia	$9M	65	Make trade fair; Climate change; Make Poverty History; Anti-mining

Sources: Annual reports and websites of organisations, and thanks to Don D'Cruz for assistance in assembling this data.

Democratic participation is an elite activity

Participation does not of itself ensure better decision-making. As a process, it can suffer problems of inequality, legitimacy, corruption and co-option. In the film, *The Rise and Rise of Michael Rimmer* (1970), English comedian Peter Cook starred as the political anti-hero, a prime minister intent on holding power by any means. His vehicle was participatory democracy. He had Her Majesty's Post deliver to voters, daily, ballots for them to decide on all manner of problems. There were scenes of working-class semi-detached bungalows and middle-class rural cottages being inundated by posties. In the face of the assault, the masses gave up and pleaded with the prime minister to do the job he was paid to do — make decisions. Cook gleefully acceded to their demands.

It was a delightful illustration that there are real limits to the extent to which people can take, or want, the responsibility of making collective decisions. This is not to argue that governance is best left to government and public servants or, indeed, to a corporatist model of collective interests — big business and trade unions, and big charities — to rule in conjunction with government. There is a need, however, to ensure that the enthusiasm for engagement is not merely an opportunity to privilege some interests at the expense of others or, indeed, for government-funded political activism.

The practice of paying charities to lobby hides behind an argument that political 'participation' is a good thing. Participation is not widespread in Australia and tends to fall to small groups of players. The electorate at large passes judgment on the performance of political parties in mollifying these groups at the same time as satisfying the broader needs of the non-organised constituencies. The idea that governments should encourage participation is pregnant with assumptions about the role of government. Participation assumes an enthusiasm on the part of many to be involved in politics. It assumes that the 'proper' course is for people to be self-governing in a direct sense. It eschews the alternative course, which is for people to elect representatives to govern on their behalf, leaving the citizen free to pursue other matters. Participation entails collective decisions, and collective decisions require answers to basic questions such as, who are to decide? In other words, it is a political issue that involves the difficult task of representation.

Whole classes of decisions about public issues are made collectively, but at a level vastly removed from the intended recipient. The reasons for this are to ensure the objective and equitable application of agreed rules and programs. Participation also implies that the community is inherently better placed to decide what is good. It confounds participation with knowledge. While participation may increase knowledge of events, it usually leads to having to choose between options. The issues are whether the options are any different to those that officials have to choose, and whether the sense of ownership, which participation is meant to enhance, makes the options more likely to be successful.

Participation does not solve fundamental problems of governance, such as defining the general interest or the allocation of benefits and costs of any decision or program (Sunstein, 2002, introduction). By contrast, the bureaucratic state brings certainty, expertise, low decision-making costs and powerful enforcement to questions of governance. Even if the community is engaged in establishing norms and standards, these matters are never made by a continuous application of participation. As interesting is the propensity for individuals and communities not to be involved: to be relieved of the costs of decision-making so that they may proceed with their lives.

The role of government in stimulating engagement is particularly elusive. For example, it is sometimes claimed that government action can help to build social capital. In this regard the conclusion reached by the Productivity Commission was pessimistic: 'Whereas devising policies to create new social capital generally is problematic, governments should at least consider the scope for modifying policies that damage social capital' (PC, 2003, 68). Essentially, the Commission concluded that government can destroy social capital by substituting government provision for individual and group initiative, but government does not build it.

A democracy of active citizens is held to be superior to a democracy of politically apathetic citizens. On close reflection, it may not be so. A consensus of activists is a process-oriented policy; it sets a premium on a saleable outcome. It does not ensure a least cost or public interest outcome. It also lends itself to interventionist outcomes because it promises to involve further the participants. Participants begin to own the policy and want to implement it, monitor it and meet again, in endless iterations. The consensus method is very different to the inquiry method, for example, which allows for voice, but then allows for reflection and analysis, and an opportunity to study the situation without the filter of groups of policy apparatchiks. While advocacy democracy values knowledge and expertise in the citizenry, it devalues those same characteristics among policy-makers (Dalton, 2004, 136).

Figure 4.1 illustrates the level of participation in various political activities in Australia. As at September 2013 there were almost 16 million Australians eligible to vote, but only 14.7 million were enrolled, or 93 per cent of those eligible.[32] A further seven per cent who were enrolled failed to vote,[33] and a further five per cent voted informally.[34] Around 45 per cent were involved in some form of campaign activity, which consists of those people 'who were working with people of the same concern, or boycotted or bought a product as a form of political statement, or contacted a politician or government official.'[35] The purchase of newspapers is some indication of those who take politics sufficiently seriously to want to be kept informed at a reasonably high level. Many receive their news of politics from radio and television, but in terms of

---

32 Australian Electoral Commission, http://www.aec.gov.au/Enrolling_to_vote/Enrolment_stats/index.htm accessed 25 July 2013.

33 Australian Electoral Commission, 'Election 2010 – turnout.' http://results.aec.gov.au/15508/Website/HouseDownloadsMenu-15508-csv.htm accessed 25 October 2013.

34 Australian Electoral Commission, "2010 Federal Election - Informal voting at House of Representatives.' http://www.aec.gov.au/About_AEC/research/paper12/hor.htm accessed 25 October 2013.

35 *Australian Survey of Social Attitudes*, from the analysis discussed below and in appendix 5.

the argument about participation it may be reasonable that those actively involved would, in addition to other sources of news, read newspapers. At the July-September 2012 audit, there were 2.16 million printed newspapers circulating on a weekday in Australia and approximately double that number at the weekend, which is about 12 per cent and 25 per cent respectively of those eligible to enroll to vote.[36] In addition, journals that carry political argument of some sophistication to a non-academic readership such as *Quadrant* have a circulation of 5,500 and *Griffith Review* of 1,000.[37]

Figure 4.1: Participation in political activities, per cent of Australians eligible to vote

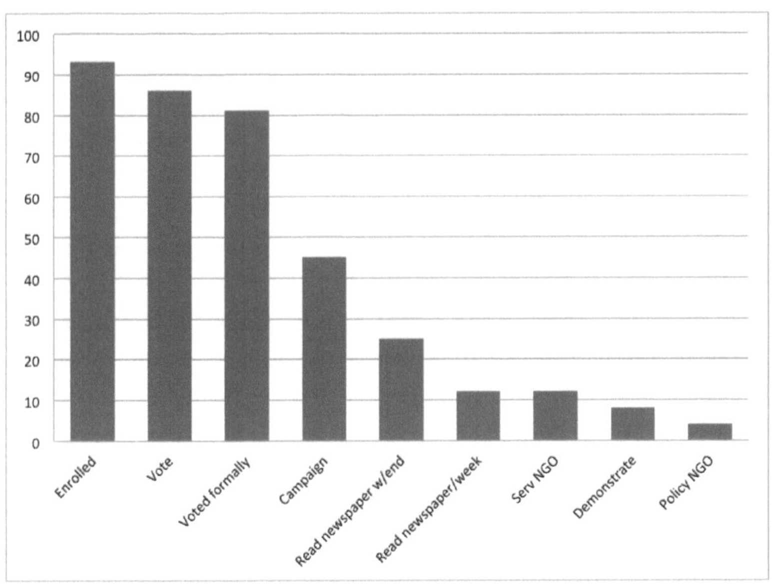

Sources: various as indicated in the discussion.

36 Audit Bureau of Circulations, http://www.thenewspaperworks.com.au/go/news/circulation-over-time/title/993b00df-5056-887e-a646cf9c733a304d accessed 25 July 2013.

37 Letter to members from Keith Windschuttle, editor of *Quadrant*, 12 December 2013.

Figure 4.1 also indicates the membership of non-government organisations, many of which are charities. These were divided into two classes; service NGOs and policy NGOs. Service NGOs consist of those people who joined a self-help/consumer health, special needs, neighbourhood or community-based group. Participation was low at 12 per cent. The demonstration category – protest, march or demonstration – showed very low levels of participation at eight per cent. Policy NGOs consist of those people who were members of a political party, or a lobby group to change specific government policies, or a group working to improve the environment, or an environmental or aid organisations, or a group that promotes rights. These groups showed the lowest level of participation of all activities at four per cent.

The Australian data show that, as the requirements of greater commitment on the part of the citizen increase, the overall level of participation declines and, incidentally, the inequality in participation rises in favour of the more highly educated.[38] These results place in doubt claims made by charities that they represent civil society and clearly show that advocacy or participatory democracy suffers from the problem of very unequal use. It also seems to suggest that increased public access to political activity places greater demands on citizens. Clearly, there are limits to the extent to which citizens can participate in ruling themselves. When these limits are reached, as they are in any activity more extensive than voting or seeking out the help of a politician or a local group, questions arise about the representative nature of those prepared to make the sacrifices required for higher order participation.

A recent study of the internal democracy of a selection of Australian advocacy NGOs, for example, found that 'in most [NGOs] policy is initiated by a small group that includes CEOs and some board members, including the chairperson' (Dalton, 2005, 38). Charities are policy communities, people who share a viewpoint. Whether their viewpoint

---

38 *Australian Survey of Social Attitudes*, from the analysis discussed below and in appendix 5.

should be granted privileges above others is an essential question for governments who wish to engage with these communities.

Those involved in charities are different

By the very nature of their volunteering for the job, activists form an elite. This is as true of the local activist as the national politician. There is good evidence that those who support a charity are different to the remainder of the electorate. They are better educated, of a higher class, more politically active and are politically placed among those who are more willing to pay taxes, although with only a mild bias to the Left overall. The results here outlined analyse these four independent variables – education, class, political activity, political ideology – relating to membership of charitable organisations taken from the 2005 and 2007 *Australian Survey of Social Attitudes*, the details of which are available in appendix 5.

Demographic characteristics of charity members

The 2007 socioeconomic data show that, both active and inactive members of a charity organisation perceived themselves as being significantly higher on the social group scale compared to people who did not belong to a charity. However, only those people who were inactive members actually earned more than people who did not belong to a charity.

The 2005 socioeconomic data show that membership of an aid organisation was the only independent variable that explained significant variance in actual personal income and perceived family income. In this case, members of an aid organisation accurately perceived their income to be higher in comparison to people who did not belong to a charity. Although the personal income of active charity members did not differ significantly from either members or non-members, they perceived their family income to be less than members and on par with non-members.

The 2007 education achievement data show that inactive members of a charity were more educated than people who did not belong to a charity. Inactive charity members were more likely to have completed year 12 and to have either a bachelor or postgraduate degree. In contrast, non-members were more likely to finish high school before year 10 or only complete up to year 10. They were less likely to have post-high school qualification; where they did, this qualification was more likely to be a trade or apprenticeship. Active members of a charity exhibited fewer deviations from the expected distributions, although they were less likely to have a trade qualification or apprenticeship.

The 2005 education achievement data show that similar trends in explained variance were exhibited across the three independent variables of 'rights group', 'environmental group' and 'aid organisation'. Members of these groups were more likely to have completed year 12, and were less likely to have finished high school prior to year 10 or at year 10. In contrast, people who did not belong to a charity exhibited the opposite trend; they were more likely to have finished high school prior to year 10 or to have only completed year 10, and they were less likely to have gone on to complete year 12. Active members of these three types of organisations exhibited no significant deviations from expected distributions.

Although the trends in post-high school qualifications were not identical for all the three independent variables, there were some similarities. Generally, members were more highly educated whilst non-members were less educated. Members were more likely to hold bachelor or postgraduate degrees whilst non-members were likely to have no post-high school qualification or a trade or apprenticeship. Active members were less likely to have no post-high school qualification.

Attitudes towards government provision, taxes and services

The 2007 data showed that people who did not belong to a charity were more unsure about paying taxes to protect the environment (local, national and global environment) whilst members and active members of a charity tended to be more in favour.

The 2005 data showed that members of all three types of groups (rights, environmental and aid) were more in favour of increasing social spending over reducing personal income taxes in comparison to people who did not belong to any of these groups. Interestingly, active members of the three groups did not differ significantly from either members or people who did not belong.

Members of an environmental group or aid organisation, in comparison with people who did not belong to these two groups, tended to disagree with the statement that privatisation of government services has more benefits than costs. Active members of these two groups (environmental and aid) did not differ significantly from members or people who did not belong. In contrast, active members of a rights group (in comparison to people who did not belong) tended to disagree with privatisation of government enterprises. Members of a rights group, in this case, did not differ significantly from active members or people who did not belong.

Finally, active members of a rights group tended to agree with government redistribution of income from the better-off to those who are less well-off. The other two groups (environmental and aid) did not exhibit meaningful differences between different types of membership.

Although the specific trends are not clear across all survey questions regarding government provision, taxes and services, there was a general trend whereby members[39] and active members of the four groups (charities, rights groups, environmental groups and aid organisations) tended to have stronger opinions regarding these questions in comparison to people who did not belong.

Political attitudes and behaviours

In regards to political ideology, inactive members of a charity identified as more left wing in comparison with active members and people who

39 'Members' in this instance is intended to encompass 'inactive members' of charities (2007 survey) and 'members' of rights, environmental and aid groups (2005 survey).

did not belong to a charity. Active members of a rights group identified as more left wing, as did members, whilst people who did not belong identified as more right wing. Members of an environmental organisation identified as more left wing in comparison with people who did not belong who identified as more right wing. Finally, active members of an aid organisation identified as more left wing than people who did not belong.

The 2007 data show that these respective political ideologies were reflected in the results regarding preferred political party, whereby inactive members of a charity preferred to support the Greens whilst active members were more likely to support the Liberal and National parties. In contrast, people who did not belong to a charity were less likely to support the Greens and less likely to have chosen to support a party. Active and inactive members also demonstrated greater support for their preferred party in comparison with people who did not belong to a charity. These findings are consistent with the previous section in which, generally, active and inactive members of a charity appeared to exhibit stronger opinions regarding an issue (in this case, preferring a particular political party and degree of support for this party).

In terms of broad trends in the 2005 data, members of a rights, environmental or aid group were all more likely to support the Greens compared to active members and people who did not belong. Active members of a rights group or an environmental group were also more likely to support the Greens. In contrast, active members of an aid organisation were more likely to support the National Party; however, the small counts in each cell for active members of these three types of groups should be kept in mind. Lastly, people who did not belong to any of the three types of groups were universally less likely to support the Greens.

Results from the 2007 survey indicated that there were only marginal differences exhibited in political interest and activity, whereby people who did not belong to a charity tended to be less interested in politics and less active in regards to politics compared to active and inactive members of a charity. Differences in this respect, however, were fairly minimal.

Finally, members and active members of a rights group, environmental group or aid organisation universally exhibited more political activism in comparison to those people who did not belong to these organisations. Both members and active members were more likely, over the past two years, to have contacted a politician or government official, taken part in a march, protest or demonstration, and to have worked together with people who shared the same concern.

Aid/Watch Incorporated v Commissioner of Taxation

Charity activists are more politically active than others, and favour greater government intervention. Just as well for them, and the taxpayer, that they have always been free to lobby, so long as they maintained charity work as their dominant purpose. Thanks to the decision in *Aid/Watch* charities are now free to lobby and do no charity work whatsoever. The implications of the High Court decision are far reaching. The quid pro quo for taxpayer-funded political activity will require the Australian Government to restore the status quo in the charity sector, either through an explicit set of restrictions on lobbying, or through a regime of disclosure similar to the corporate sector, or by assisting in arming the donor with better information about charities' activities.

The charity sector will rue the day if it allows the decision in *Aid/Watch* to determine the future of the sector. On the surface, the decision is a dream for the sector's advocates. The implication, however, is that charities are in direct competition with political parties and politicians for power and policy. Policy competition is a good thing, but the purpose of charity is different. A taxpayer subsidy to political lobbying by charities is different again. The apolitical or 'clean skin' nature of charities provides a distinct advantage over parties and business. The clean skin will tarnish as charities become more involved in politics.

Justice Heydon remarked of *Aid/Watch*'s 'demand' for a complete phase-out of support for extractive industries, 'these industries often damage the environment, but they also often bring wealth to many who would otherwise be poor.' Similarly, 'the connection between opposing the Free Trade Agreement between Australia and the US and relieving poverty was obscure.'[40] In other words, *Aid/Watch* may be doing as much harm as good.

The fundamental misconception of the decision in *Aid/Watch* is that the High Court mistook charities' freedom to play politics with their freedom to play taxpayer-subsidised politics. Charitable works are by and large accepted as in the public interest. They are rarely questioned. Charitable lobbying should not be afforded the same luxury. The ATO was quite right in seeking to remove *Aid/Watch*'s charitable status on the basis that its dominant purpose was not charitable. *Aid/Watch*'s dominant purpose was to lobby. They never helped a soul on the ground.

Public benefit

The High Court decided that a charity engaged in 'lawful means of public debate concerning the efficiency of foreign aid directed to the relief of poverty is a purpose beneficial to the community.'[41] Were a charity, set up to cut foreign aid, arguably a public benefit, to come before the Court, as argued earlier, it is probable that the judges would have run a mile.

Public benefit is a very difficult concept, and it has always been the accepted interpretation that courts have no way of knowing what is publicly beneficial. The question has nothing to do with whether an organisation could retain its charitable status and tax benefits while engaging in political debate. Tim Costello of *World Vision*, a tax-supported charity, never ceases being involved in political debate. But Costello never made the mistake of making politics the dominant purpose of *World Vision*. Now, thanks to the Court, he can. Donors may withdraw

40 *Aid/Watch Incorporated v Commissioner of Taxation* [2010] HCA 42 (1 December 2010), [60].

41 See footnote 40.

their support if they judge that a charity strays too far from its purpose, but given the taxpayer encouragement to donate, this is less likely than would otherwise be so.

The law firm, Maurice Blackburn, which represented *Aid/Watch*, was, naturally, overjoyed at the decision. But their representative was nevertheless cautious, stating that the High Court decision 'overturns 90 years of Australian law swinging the pendulum quite to the other end, in that it recognises that engaging in public debate is a public benefit in itself.'[42] That caution is well-placed. The decision raises a host of questions. Since 1917 charities in Australia have been required to be circumspect about their political activities. Charities have had to ensure that political activity is secondary to charitable purposes. To what extent is that restriction now lifted? What does this mean for existing charities? And what about civil society organisations previously deemed 'too political' to be recognised as charities? What are the implications for Australia's political system, and for wider political culture? Imagine if the 'corporate social responsibility' critique, which is applied to corporations, was applied to charities. What contribution does the charity make? What is its social licence to operate?

Justice Heydon later commented that the *Aid/Watch* decision was an example of the High Court 'constitutionalising private law' and queried whether the law now referred to 'free speech at large or just the four heads of charity?'[43] Or, as another commented, *Aid/Watch* may actually only apply to charitable purposes that involve the relief of poverty (Chevalier-Watts, 2011, 157). Others worry about the implications of *Aid/Watch* on the basis that the Court did not make any reference to the issue of non-charitable objects being ancillary. Instead, it appeared

42 Maurice Blackburn Lawyers, http://www.mauriceblackburn.com.au/areas-of-practice/social-justice-practice.aspx accessed 6 March 2014.

43 'The Charity Ball: CIS Roundtable' with Gary Johns, Robert McLean and Dyson Heydon, Centre for Independent Studies, Sydney 25 June 2013. http://www.youtube.com/watch?v=RdswL4ni7T4#at=19 accessed 6 July 2013.

to broaden the established notion generally that political objects 'may not defeat a charitable trust, even if they form a more than ancillary role within the charitable trust'. The Court has undermined the status quo 'without any clarification on the relevance of the issue of ancillary', and opens up the possibility of a number of organisations now obtaining charitable status where once the law would have determined that their overt political activity should defeat their charitable status as the public benefit could not be determined (Chevalier-Watts, 2011, 155). Some argue that, despite the decision being a 'surprise', it was, nevertheless, a case of 'judicial generosity' (Harding, 2011, 45) and a 'good outcome for democracy' because charities were no longer in fear of being 'muzzled' (Williams, 2011, 7). There should be 'robust protections' for charities who want to dip into politics (Barnden, 2011, 19). But charities were never muzzled. They were always free to speak out but, as with any other citizen, they should not expect to be above criticism simply because they claim to be doing good, and they should not use government money to prosecute their case to government.

Labor Governments especially have invited charities into the policy process. The recent AusAid review panel, assessing program evaluation, saw 'scope to engage Australian, international and local NGOs more systematically in policy development.' It noted, however, that 'Policy development is a core function of government and government will, legitimately, sometimes have vastly differing perspectives from NGOs. But policy is generally improved through engagement with informed stakeholders.' The panel concluded that, 'The partnership agreements with the six NGOs with the greatest Australian community support (*World Vision*, *Oxfam*, *Caritas*, *PLAN* (Australia), *ChildFund*, and *Christian Blind Mission*) are working well and have facilitated greater policy engagement' (Hollway, 2011, 213).

The Abbott Government appears to disagree and has dissolved AusAid and moved its operations into the Department of Foreign Affairs and Trade, a key reason being the overly close relationship between AusAid and charities. It was no coincidence that *Aid/Watch* was a foreign aid charity or that its defenders were extensively engaged not only in that field but were, more generally, high advocacy charities such as *World Vision* and the *Australian Conservation Foundation.*

UK and US decisions on charities and politics

In other jurisdictions, such as the UK, it is well established that charities may 'not have a political purpose as their main object and may only undertake political activities (such as responding to consultations, presenting petitions, campaigning for changes in policy or regulation) where those activities explicitly further the organisation's main charitable purpose, are subsidiary to it, and are presented in a non-partisan manner independent of a political party or favoured political solution' (Dunn, 2008, 259). The trouble is, and this is the flaw in the High Court decision, there is no clear-cut demarcation between subsidiary and core activities in the law.

The Charity Commission of England and Wales set out guidance on the demarcation (Charity Commission, 2008), but, in some opinions, has failed to rein in clearly political activities. Complaints have been made about the political activities of the *RSPCA* and the *League Trust*, the charitable arm of the *League Against Cruel Sports.* In another example, the purposes of the *Sheila McKechnie Foundation* are 'to train individuals to engage in campaigning to achieve political ends, that is to say political agitation financed by the general body of taxpayers.' The *Unite Foundation* is a registered charity set up by the Unite trade union. One of the purposes of the *Foundation* is said to be to 'provide support for Trade Unions and Trade Union development'(Brodie, 2010, 13). That would appear to be political; yet the Charity Commission has found itself able to register the *Unite Foundation* as a charity, thus enabling it to finance its activities at taxpayers' expense. The Charity Commission seems to take a benevolent approach to politically acceptable charities and organisations on the Left; but when it comes to independent schools the full force of charity law (as misinterpreted by the Commission) is brought down upon them (Brodie, 2010, 13).

In the US, the law offers a way for charities to lobby without limit, which is to create an affiliated, non-charity that, while not eligible to receive tax deductible contributions also, is not subject to the lobbying limits imposed on charities (Mayer, 2011, 410). The issue has been reignited recently in the US Supreme Court's decision in *Citizens United v FEC* which seems to cast doubt on the speech-related restrictions federal tax law imposes on charities, including the limits on lobbying.

The Supreme Court canvassed government subsidy to charities in the form of tax benefits and, separately, concluded that a charity's rights are sufficiently 'vindicated' by the ability to speak through the alternate channel of a non-charitable affiliate. At issue is the ability of the US Government to restrict the relationships between charities and their non-charitable affiliates that engage in lobbying, as well as affecting other contexts where the government places speech-related conditions on provision of government subsidies. The US Court explicitly rejected the argument that the prohibition on corporate electioneering should be upheld because corporations have the alternative of engaging in election-related speech through a separately segregated fund, commonly known as a political action committee or PAC (Mayer, 2011, 416). Issues arise about the separation of the charity and the entity for lobbying and also limits to speech in the use of their private funds for those organisations receiving direct government funds. The practice of the public cross subsidy to lobbying is a very sensitive subject in the US, apparently less so in Australia.

5

Drumming up trade

'Moral entrepreneurs' who rely on alarming the public about threats to their health and safety have an incentive to exaggerate the peril in the short term and find new fears to exploit in the long term. (Snowdon, 2012, 7)

In a wealthy nation, where average wages and salaries have increased 52 per cent, and government pensions and allowances have increased 24 per cent in real terms between 1994 and 2012 (ABS (b), 2013), and where social mobility is not overly class bound (Leigh, 2007, 15), it is difficult to explain why charities, particularly those in the welfare sectors, continue to grow. In the seven years prior to 2007 (PC, 2010, 63), not-for-profits (largely charities) grew more than double the real growth rate of the economy. While there has been considerable growth in the fields in which charities abound – health, education, and the environment – the charity growth trend seems strong in all sectors. In 2007, there were 51,000 tax concession charities and 24,000 were eligible DGR charities (ATO, 2007, 196). In 2011, there were 55,000 tax concession charities and 28,000 DGRs (ATO, 2013, 101). Need, it seems, is in endless supply.

There are a number of possible reasons for growth. New charitable fields such as the natural environment and human rights expand as incomes rise and appeal to a new generation of activists. Professional as well as patient interests drive some of the older fields such as health, and yet others, welfare for example, are kept in business because poverty is measured in relative terms. Most importantly, the charity sector has discovered that spending more on fundraising increases donations (Omura, 2010; Pallotta, 2008). An important part of fundraising consists of making claims about the problem a charity seeks to solve, which requires the public provision of information, marketing and promotion to potential donors (Omura, 2010, i).

Awareness campaigns

If a major motivation for donors is awareness of need, the media facilitates it. A survey of donations to relief appeals – often advertised on television – reveals that the amount of time spent watching television is positively related to relief donations (Bekkers, 2010, 930). More extended media coverage of an earthquake has a strong positive relationship with private contributions supporting those affected. In turn, the amount of attention the media pays to beneficiaries' needs depends on, among others, the number of beneficiaries (or those affected in the case of disasters), and the demographic and psychological distance between potential donors and beneficiaries.

Awareness expresses itself in many forms. Charities use readily identifiable symbols such as coloured awareness ribbons to attract donors (figure 5.1). A recent count identified 45 different ribbons to advertise 200 charitable causes, ranging from a variety of cancers to bullying awareness.[1]

1 http://en.wikipedia.org/wiki/List_of_awareness_ribbons accessed 20 July 2013.

Figure 5.1: Awareness ribbons proliferate

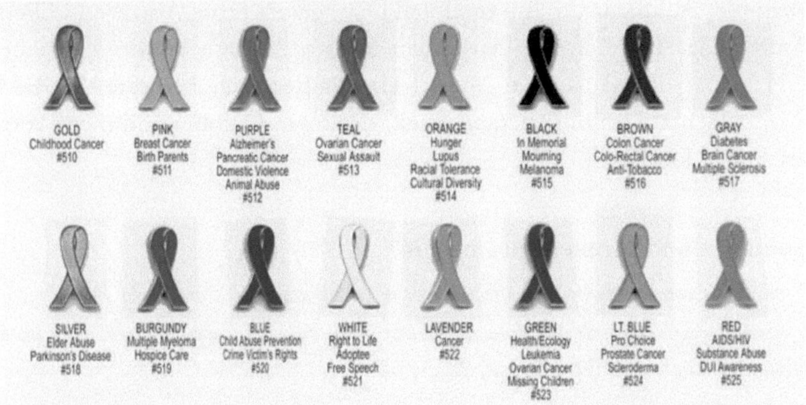

Source: *Spiked online*, 17 July 2013.

Attracting attention also comes in the form of date claimers. Claims on the donating public's time appear to be increasing, as the calendar of events fills to capacity. There is a day, a week, a month, a year, indeed, a decade, for every occasion. The calendar is almost full with awareness for, mostly charitable, causes (days and weeks are listed in appendix 2). While there are few awareness days in January of each year (charity fundraisers are no doubt aware that donors are busy with Christmas and New Year and holidays), beginning in February, the calendar fills. Every day of February signals a day of awareness about a cause that someone has deemed sufficiently important to be named. Mostly, the causes are medical, and the date is claimed to allow time to reflect and hopefully raise funds for research into a cure for various diseases such as ovarian cancer or heart disease.

Some causes are overtly political such as the UN World Day of Social Justice, around which many charitable causes are built. The UN, in fact, seems to be the chief instigator of days, weeks, months, years and decades of awareness and 'consciousness raising' (UN dates are set out in appendix 3). Local charities use the opportunity to raise funds for their cause on the back of UN-designated awareness periods. For example, 26 June is the International Day against Drug Abuse and Illicit Trafficking. The *GiveNow* Australian website 'donate button' links the UN day to the Australian Mental Health Research Institute Appeal.[2] World Mental Health Day (and week) occurs in October and these, too, are linked locally.

Statistics and problem promoters

Nonprofits could enhance the effectiveness of their donation appeals by framing the message consistently with the donor's emotional state … (discontinuity, recovery from grief, and loneliness). (Merchant, 2011, 615)

Creating awareness of social problems through campaigns is the sine qua non of charitable activism, and a powerful weapon in the armoury is statistics. When social problems arise they often do so based on the 'evidence by some combination of *problem promoters* – activists, reporters, experts, officials, all private organizations – who have worked to create the sense that this is an important problem, one that deserves our attention' (Best, 2012, 282). Charities are not alone in using statistics to expand the market for their services; sometimes charities are assisted by official sources of social statistics that exaggerate the extent of a problem. Whether charity-generated or official, there are many examples among Australian, or universal, causes where statistics are bulked-up to suit the problem promoters.

Template exaggeration (insert favourite cause here)

A recent plea, by an eminent 'high-profile' Australian, may serve as a template for promoting any number of causes, in this case, blindness.

> Experts have long warned us of the impending 'grey tsunami' that growing cohort of ageing Australians, largely spearheaded

---

2 Givenow, http://www.givenow.com.au/australiandrugfoundation accessed 29 July 2013.

> by the nation's 5.5 million baby boomers, who will place unforeseen pressures on our health, social services and pension systems.
>
> One of the consequences of an ageing population is a marked increase in age-related health conditions and diseases: Alzheimer's and other forms of dementia, diabetes, stroke, heart disease and cancer. But something we hear less often about is the debilitating impact of blindness and vision loss that often come with ageing.
>
> It is estimated that by 2020 close to one million Australians will be vision impaired, and 100,000 people blind, if preventive action is not taken … This translates to billions of dollars of public expenditure each year.
>
> Vision 2020 Australia works with governments and partner organisations to prevent avoidable vision loss and blindness in Australia and globally …[3]

At a broad level, every cause will build the numbers of possible sufferers and future costs, as if these cannot be paid for out of the pockets of the 'sufferer' or in the normal course of medical services, and as if advances in medical science are not a help rather than a burden. Indeed, all of the costs are foreseen. They simply have to be paid.

Indicators of nothing much at all

Community Indicators Victoria, initially funded by the Victorian Department of Health and now also in conjunction with the University of Melbourne, is an example of an organisation that has created a measure in search of a problem. Its measure, Feeling Part of the Community, is a case in point. The 'Indicator Rationale' is that 'community strength is found in the human relations that people draw upon for identity, interaction and support. A strong community is one where people understand and work towards sustainability and is inclusive of their most disadvantaged

3 Barry Jones, 'Grey Tsunami Threatens Blindness on Unprecedented Scale', *The Australian* 11 October 2013.

groups. To do this people need to be involved, feel capable of working through issues, and feel supported by their fellow citizens.'[4]

The indicator, 'Feeling Part of the Community', is a construction that contains numerous assumptions about the conditions under which a person may feel well. It could be argued that one may feel perfectly well by not being part of the community. That some researcher or public servant believes that a person should be connected in order to feel well is no surety that it is so. Any relationship between being well and feeling part of the community has to be proven by other means and indicators, which begs the question of connectedness as a valid indicator of wellness.

Cost of costs

An example of inflated estimates comes from the HPC *Foundation for Alcohol Research and Education (FARE)*. According to *FARE*, every year around 10 million Australians are negatively affected by another person's drinking. There are some 367 deaths, 14,000 hospitalisations, 70,000 victims of alcohol-related violence, 24,000 victims of domestic violence, and almost 20,000 children who are victims of substantiated alcohol-related child abuse every year.[5] These findings come from *The Range and Magnitude of Alcohol's Harm to Others* (Laslett, 2010), commissioned by FARE, and used to justify its recommendations to tighten alcohol restrictions and increase taxation.

Access Economics, which was commissioned by the National Alcohol Beverages Industries Council, to review the *FARE* report, found many serious errors. Access Economics concluded that the claims that the social cost of alcohol was as high as $36 billion a year were grossly exaggerated and based on flawed research. Access Economics found, among others, four major problems with the report. [6]

4 Community Indicators Victoria, http://www.communityindicators.net.au/metadata_items/feeling_part_of_the_community accessed 27 November 2013.

5 FARE, *Annual Report 2012-13*, page 8.

6 A copy of Access Economics report could not be sourced, other than a report of it at http://www.theshout.com.au/2010/10/11/article/36b-Alcohol-Harm-Figure-Grossly-Overstated/RDVJMNLNEI.html accessed 30 November 2013.

First, the research relied on the perceptions of a non-representative surveyed group of infrequent drinkers who have high rates of anxiety and depression and low rates of employment. An infrequent drinker may perceive another's drinking as heavy or sporadic even if it is within healthy levels. There is also substantial doubt that this skewed group can accurately assess whether strangers' behaviour is due to alcohol or to something else, especially when survey questions relate to harm caused by 'being woken up' or other events where the stranger is not even sighted by the respondent.

Second, in health economics it is very important to attribute the cost of events, such as road crashes, to all contributing factors. The report ignored other risk factors, such as fatigue, speed, illicit drugs and road conditions, which can also be involved, and instead attributed all the costs of any crash where an operator has illegal blood alcohol to that cause alone. This error is made for other costs also, not only crashes, and so overstates harms many times.

Third, measures used to estimate the cost of lost 'wellbeing' are double-counted, and any detriment to healthy life is ascribed to alcohol – when it might well be due to the higher levels of anxiety and depression in the group or, indeed, any other health condition, none of which was controlled for in the analysis. The $8.5 billion estimated cost component is thus invalid.

Fourth, it treated people who are not employed as though they were, and ascribed productivity losses to them. Access Economics argued that research must include cost-benefit analysis that weighs up the impact of alcohol abuse by some in the community with the benefits from responsible drinking by most Australians. Alcohol consumption provides enjoyment value for many Australians, which is measured by the amount consumers are prepared to pay, which is tens of billions of dollars. *FARE* has responded to these criticisms in the literature by seeking further research into the relevant costs of alcohol policy (ACIL Allen, 2014).

In a similar critique of publicly-funded cost of illness studies, other research has shown that headline cost estimates depend on an incorrect procedure for incorporating real world imperfections in consumer information and rationality, producing a substantial over-estimate of costs. Other errors further inflate these estimates, resulting in headline costs that are unrelated either to total economic welfare or to GDP and therefore of no policy relevance. Counting only external, policy-relevant costs deflates overall figures substantially. Cost of illness studies appear effective in mobilising public opinion towards increased regulation and taxation that is not justified under more sensible assumptions (Crampton, 2011).

Racism and Aboriginal health

Aborigines have enough problems without problem promoters creating more. A recent report instigated and promoted by the *Lowitja Institute*, a PBI, attempts to attribute Aboriginal psychological problems to racism. The *Experiences of Racism* survey among Victorian Aborigines linked 'self-reported' racism to 'self-reported' measures of psychological distress (Ferdinand, 2013, 4). Participants were asked, 'How often have you seen people being treated unfairly because of their race, ethnicity, culture or religion?' This question is biased. A positive response may indicate that the participant is prejudiced, not the 'perpetrator', or that the treatment may have been among non-Aboriginal groups, or that the unfairness was not unfair, or that there may have been a good reason for the perceived unfair behaviour.

On the measures of psychological distress there is no theoretical justification to suggest that the alleged racial discrimination causes psychological distress. It is simply assumed. In short, the survey prompted participants to look for racism as the cause of a problem, which the participant was able to define, after it was suggested that they should look for one. Where, under prompting from the survey, fault was found, they were corralled to conclude that racism was the cause. Having been sent in search of racism, they were bound to attribute whatever stress they were experiencing to racism, and, moreover, to assume that if there were racism, they would have to be suffering from it. Circularity is a fatal weakness in the research.

Aboriginal workers were recruited to administer the surveys and 'community workers' distributed surveys through their personal and professional contacts as well as at local community events and functions. Surveys were administered face-to-face in group or individual sessions. There is a distinct possibility that the survey was an exercise searching for racism as an explanation for any and all problems that the participants were suffering. The group context may have reinforced the group solidarity and enhanced the feeling of prejudice by the 'outside' world and, as well, aggravated the level of perceived suffering. There would have been an incentive to mark-up the hurt felt as a sign of group solidarity.

Forty per cent of participants indicated that they had experienced racism 'within the justice system', which presumably means that at least 40 per cent had dealings with the justice system. So, a group of Aborigines, who are highly likely to be attending an Aboriginal-run centre for those who have problems, are asked if they feel good about being Aboriginal. When they answer 'no', it is inferred that racism is the cause. The survey noted, however, that the most frequent difficulties reported by community workers in conducting surveys were low levels of literacy and numeracy in the communities. These factors may be a plausible explanation for the perceived problems reported.

Participants were asked, 'Has your property been vandalized because you are Aboriginal?' The result reported was that 55 per cent of the participants reported having property vandalized. How would a person know whether their property was vandalized because they were Aboriginal? Presumably there are many other possible explanations, not all of them complimentary to the victim. The survey concluded that 'rates of vandalism experienced by Aboriginal people are much higher than would be expected based on the overall rate of property destruction in the local government areas studied' (Ferdinand, 2013, 19). This is an ill-advised comparison. It could readily be concluded that the figures are higher because of inter-Aboriginal rivalry or Aboriginal disregard for property. These would be uncomfortable, but equally plausible conclusions to the one that the reader is invited to draw.

One reason a charity may design a survey that sets out to discover behaviour that it can attribute to racism is that Aborigines in Victoria are not physically distinguishable from any groups in what is an ethnically highly diverse community. The survey was undertaken in two rural and two metropolitan local government areas. The degree to which Aborigines in Victoria marry outside of their community is very high – 82 per cent for men and women in Melbourne and 72 per cent for men and 75 per cent for women in the remainder of Victoria (Heard, 2009, 3). Moreover, the marrying out of Aborigines in Victoria has been of many generations standing. They are a far less identifiable people than, for example, full blood Aborigines in remote Australia.

The question of light skin colour of Aborigines is sensitive. As the report suggests, 'someone who can be visibly identified as belonging to an ethnic minority group is likely to have higher exposure to racism than someone who is not visibly identifiable' (Ferdinand, 2013, 7). However, this survey does not take the 'visibility status' of Aborigines into account as there is no accepted way of assessing visibility for Aboriginal people and 'questions to this effect were likely to be highly offensive to communities.' Which poses the question, how would a person know that an Aborigine was an Aborigine in order to display prejudice? If, however, an Aborigine interpreted an adverse reaction to their behaviour as racist rather than disapproving of bad behaviour, for example, then the explanation would be predetermined by the offended when the offence may have been quite valid. A person could also be offended because they were not identified as an Aborigine.

The survey is not scientific and suffers from sampling, pre-judgment, self-interpretation, suggestibility and invalid comparison errors. The survey not only promotes a cause, it also runs the risk of promoting highly suspect solutions by attributing all problems to a pre-determined cause.

Butterfly Foundation and eating disorders

The *Butterfly Foundation* represents all people affected by eating disorders – sufferers, their families and their friends. The *Foundation* claims that there were more than 913,986 people in Australia with eating disorders and that the total socio-economic cost of eating disorders was $69.7 billion in 2012. Further, the *Foundation* projects that there will be more than a million people with eating disorders in 2022 (Butterfly, 2012, 90). These are alarming claims and of very recent origin.

The *Foundation* reported that the last official estimate by the Australian Institute for Health and Welfare in 2003 was that there were 23,464 people with eating disorders in Australia. A search could find no such data in the AIHW study, but there were other estimates attributable to eating disorder from the same study. For example, two measures of the extent of the illness was that it caused the loss of 6,062 'disability-adjusted life years' out of 350,000 for all mental disorders and 5,921 'years lived with disability' compared to 327,391 for all mental disabilities (Begg, 2003, 217 and 250). Further, the ABS reported only 12 deaths in 2010 from eating disorders (ABS (c), 2012, 5). Although the disease affects the very young and can be of long duration, the figures indicate a very small number of people affected.

The *Foundation* argues that the AIHW figures were an underestimate as they were not based on Australian data and only covered two eating disorders, anorexia nervosa and bulimia nervosa. No estimates were made for Binge Eating Disorder or Eating Disorder Not Otherwise Specified, which have higher prevalence than AN and BN. The Foundation relied on 'the latest meta-analysis of epidemiological studies from the published literature', which were projected on to population figures. On the basis of the new studies, the *Foundation* estimated that 1,829 deaths were attributable to eating disorders in 2012 (Butterfly, 2012, 9).

The prevalence of eating disorders of 913,986 people in 2012 was constructed as follows:

- Anorexia nervosa –26,052
- Bulimia nervosa –107,915
- Binge Eating Disorder – 428,833
- Eating Disorders Not Otherwise Specified – 351,485.

Fortunately, the less damaging disorders are more prevalent, although BED and EDNOS carry risk of more serious illness. These figures jar, nevertheless, with earlier estimates and another, which is that in a recent Australia-wide health survey, 700,000 Australians rate their health status as poor: a much smaller number than is supposed to suffer from an eating disorder among countless other causes of illness from which Australians suffer.[7]

Not only has the *Foundation* managed to arrive at a very large number of sufferers, to illustrate the importance of its cause it also added very big economic numbers. The impact of eating disorders on productivity was estimated to be $15 billion in 2012: of this cost, $2 billion is due to lost lifetime earnings for young people who die. Eating disorders also have lengthy duration – an average of around 15 years in survey respondents – which can mean long lasting productivity impacts for those living with eating disorders, including lower employment participation ($6 billion), greater absenteeism ($1.8 billion) and presenteeism (attending work while sick) ($5.3 billion) until, bingo, 'the 'burden of disease' from eating disorders is estimated as $52.6 billion.

In addition to the possibility of the type of error related in the alcohol and cost of illness studies above, there are two others. First, costs are estimated throughout a lifetime but they are the same costs that many other illnesses share and could readily cite as costs that may

7 Australian Bureau of Statistics, *Australian Health Survey: Updated Results, 2011-2012*, table 1 'Selected Health Characteristics - 2001 to 2011-12 – Australia.'

be avoided. People are unable to work for many reasons, including many illnesses. Second, despite the attempt to lift the status of eating disorders, what will it take to solve the problem? The recommendations are to 'medicalise' the problem and seek government funds for monitoring and research. The big numbers do not provide a guide to the likelihood, or cost, of effective remedies, which in the race for a place in the charity sun, is very important.

Beyondblue and anxiety

Allied to eating disorders are mental conditions such as depression. Sometimes, however, in order to win a place in the sun, charities will drum up trade on the basis of more prevalent but far less dangerous ailments. Mental health has lagged other medical issues in the charity field, but is making up for lost ground in the marketing of anxiety, in this case by a charity that advocates for those concerned with depression.

In 2012, the charity *beyondblue* had an annual income of $48 million, $33 million from governments and $14 million from donations.[8] In May 2013, it launched a $2 million 'national awareness campaign' to help Australians recognise the most common symptoms of anxiety conditions. *Beyondblue* claimed as part of the campaign that two million Australians do not recognise that they have anxiety symptoms. Roy Morgan Research showed that the proportion of Australians aged 18 and over who reported experiencing an 'anxiety condition' in the last 12 months had grown by almost 40 per cent in the last four years. The research showed 13.8 per cent, an estimated 2.44 million Australians, experienced an anxiety condition in the year to December 2012, compared to 9.9 per cent in 2008.

The Morgan Research differed from that of the ABS. In 2007 ABS found that, while 2.3 million Australians had 'self-diagnosed' anxiety disorders (ABS, 2008, 8), affective disorders, including depression, were 6.2 per cent of the population, or fewer than 1.5 million. The interesting

---

8 Beyondblue, *Annual Report 2011-12*, page 86.

issue is why *beyondblue* opted for a lesser form of mental disability when the numbers suffering depression and other affective disorders were more than enough to keep such a charity busy. The answer may be that anxiety is some sort of flag to the more severe condition, or that anxiety undiagnosed and untreated may lead to greater problems. No information was forthcoming from *beyondblue* to prove this argument. Instead, they reported that '12 per cent of Australians view anxiety as a major mental health problem, compared with 58 per cent who view depression as one.'[9] While people increasingly identify as having anxiety, they do not see it as a major mental health problem. Two questions arise. Is *beyondblue* suggesting a link between anxiety and depression and, second, why raise awareness if there is no link?

Kate Carnell, CEO of *beyondblue*, observed that while the campaign aimed to raise awareness of anxiety 'in the same way *beyondblue* had raised awareness of depression over the last 12 years', it did not need to 'raise awareness of anxiety … [as this] had already happened, probably because of other such launches.'[10] This suggests a question: does reported anxiety rise because charity advocates keep talking about it? Is there merely a word recognition factor, rather than a real condition in the community, at work? Google Trends reflect how many searches have been undertaken for a particular term, relative to the total number of searches on Google over time. The number 100 represents the peak search interest. The figures that Carnell used were from a Roy Morgan survey. 19,000 respondents ticked a box of various medical 'conditions'. It is clear from the number of mentions of the term, 'symptoms of anxiety', has become more frequent in the media in the past few years, strongly so in the last two years (figure 5.2).

9 Beyondblue press release May 2013, http://www.beyondblue.org.au/media/media-releases/media-releases/national-anxiety-campaign accessed 14 May 2013.

10 As above.

Figure 5.2: Web search, 'symptoms of anxiety', Australia, 2005-13

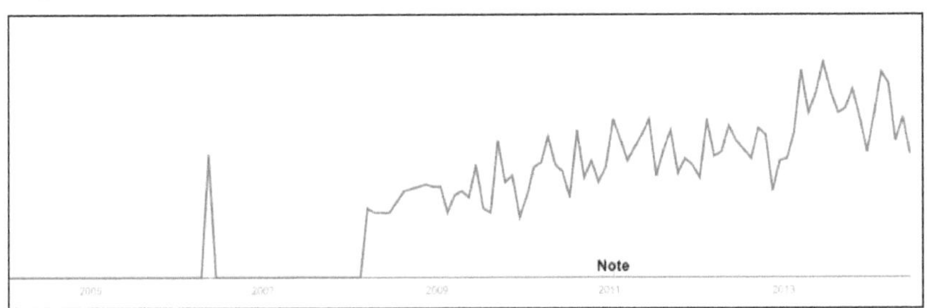

Source: author and http://www.google.com.au/trends.

Perhaps the Roy Morgan data do not suggest 'a growing problem', just a growth in recognition of a term that is well recognised. Anxiety was called a condition when in fact it was the respondent's perception that they had experienced 'anxiety' in the last 12 months. Calling it an anxiety condition gave the impression that it was more than a perception; rather it was a medical condition. The response to the Morgan survey was a 'self-report' of incidence of health-related categories, so that respondents were asked, 'what have you had in the last 12 months', one of which was a category called 'anxiety'. It is not a medical category and the Roy Morgan representative volunteered that the self-report was 'not sufficiently tight' to have a 'scientific base' or 'sufficient predictive qualifications'.[11]

Explosion in official statistics

The business of drumming up charity trade is mightily assisted by production of official statistics, especially where these inflate problems. Statistics which give the impression that there are no trade-offs in the nation's aspirations, or that all problems may be equally solved, or at the same time, do no favours to taxpayers or donors.

11 Author interviewed Nick Williams of Roy Morgan 14 May 2013.

Australian Bureau of Statistics measures homelessness

The Australian Census is unique in estimating the level of homelessness. No other national census has attempted to do so, as measures are usually estimated from other sources such as field surveys. The census in 1996 was the first to estimate Australia's homeless population with a special enumeration strategy, labelled Counting the Homeless (CTH), using a 'cultural' definition of homelessness. The cultural definition distinguishes primary, secondary and tertiary categories of homelessness on census night.

Primary homelessness includes all people without conventional accommodation. These include people living on the streets, sleeping in parks, squatting in derelict buildings, or using cars or railway carriages for temporary shelter.

Secondary homelessness includes people who move frequently from one form of temporary shelter to another. On census night, it includes all people staying in emergency or transitional accommodation provided under the Supported Accommodation Assistance Program (SAAP). Secondary homelessness also includes people residing temporarily with other households because they have no accommodation of their own, and people staying in boarding houses on a short-term basis.

Tertiary homelessness refers to people who live in boarding houses on a medium to long-term basis. They are homeless because their accommodation situation is below the minimum community standard of a small self-contained flat.

The original (1996) estimates of the homeless population using the cultural method estimated the homeless at 105,304. The same definitions and methods were then applied to the 2001 and 2006 Census. It estimated the homeless at 99,900 in 2001 (Chamberlain, 2003, 2), and 104,676 in 2006 (Chamberlain, 2008, viii).

Then reality hit. The rate of homelessness had not declined despite strong economic growth and housing construction in the preceding decade. These were sufficient reasons to arouse suspicion about the validity of the estimation exercise. The ABS ordered a revision. The reasons for the revisions are many; but, in short, the ABS estimated homelessness using the Census when it did not include a homeless indicator. This meant that while some groups of homeless people were unobservable in the Census data, several other groups who were observable, but not homeless, were counted as homeless. For example, construction crews and owner-builders, young professionals travelling overseas, and people following mobile employment opportunities were counted as homeless. Making inferences about the observable – indeed, searching for the homeless in nonsensical categories – brought the count into grave error (Johns, 2012, 46).

As well as counting the wrong people, the ABS estimates had two major credibility problems. The first was acceptance of a 'cultural' definition of homelessness. The second was that a large part of the so-called homeless were in supported accommodation, which is the 'solution' for homelessness, for example, for women (in the main) escaping violent relationships. How can the solution be added as the estimate of homelessness?

As shown in table 5.1, the common definition of homelessness as those without shelter yielded an estimate of a mere 16,375, which was then revised down to 7,764 (plus 1,970) in 2006, and 14,158 and 8,943 (plus 1,395) respectively in 2001. In a population of 23 million 9,000-10,000 homeless seems manageable. How many women would be expected to run from violent husbands or children away from home on any one night in such a population?

Table 5.1: Homeless estimates, 2001, 2006 and 2011

Type of Accommodation	2001 CTH estimate	2001 ABS review estimate	2006 CTH estimate	2006 ABS review estimate	2011 Census
Boarding houses	22,877	23,749	21,596	16,828	17,721
Supported accommodation	14,251	13,420	19,849	17,331	21,258
Friends and relatives	48,614	17,877	46,856	19,579	17,369
Improvised dwellings, sleepers out	14,158	8,943	16,375	7,764	6,813
Persons in other temporary lodgings	...	1,395	...	1,970	686
Severely crowded dwellings	...	...	...	...	41,390
Total	99,900	65,384	104,676	63,472	105,237

Sources: (ABS (a), 2012, 6; ABS, 2011, 4).

The ABS worked up the definition in conjunction with the 'homeless' sector, that is, charities, including the *Salvation Army*, who were lobbying for a large number as a means of impressing upon policy-makers the importance of 'their' issue. The revision of the headline figure of 104,676 down to 63,472 for 2006 was a severe blow, coming on top of the revelation that the actual number of homeless was only 9,734 for 2006. Following the revision, the homelessness charities continued to claim the early 105,000 (rounded up) figure, refusing to place the revised figure on their websites.

Not to be defeated by the embarrassment of the massive write-down, the ABS and the sector struck back by further broadening the definition of homelessness. The ABS decided to add those living in severely crowded dwellings. The headline figure for all homeless persons for the 2011 Census was 105,237, back to where the sector had it for 2006, and 1996 under the CTH estimates. The figure without the 'crowded' definition was just 63,847, only slightly more than the 2006 review estimate. Only 6,813 were actual sleepers out (ABS, 2012, 6). These broader definitions of those in housing stress or, indeed, in supported accommodation, for which no other solutions seem plausible, may be of real concern, but they could not be called homeless.

Australian Human Rights Commission and sexual violence

In April 2012, the Australian Human Rights Commission (AHRC) invited Ms Rashida Manjoo, the UN Special Rapporteur on violence against women, to conduct a study tour of Australia (AHRC, 2008). The Rapporteur was shown four statistics, among others, suggesting that Australia was a violent place for women:

- One in three women has experienced *physical violence* since reaching the age of 15
- Almost one in five women has experienced *sexual assault* since reaching the age of 15
- 22 per cent of women and five per cent of men aged between 18 and 64 years have experienced *sexual harassment in the workplace* in their lifetime
- Approximately one in three women aged 18-64 years had experienced *sexual harassment* in their lifetime.

The first two statistics were derived from an ABS survey in 2005 (ABS, 2006). Interestingly, the women's component of the 2005 survey was funded by the Australian Government's Office for the Status of Women, while the male component was funded by the ABS. The latter two statistics were derived from a 2008 survey conducted for the AHRC (AHRC, 2008).

The first statistic showed that one in three women in Australia has experienced *physical violence* since reaching the age of 15. The AHRC could also have informed the Rapporteur that almost half of all men in Australia has experienced *physical violence* since reaching the age of 15 (ABS, 2006, 17), and that women were responsible for 22 per cent of all *physical assault*. In addition, while almost one in five women in Australia has experienced *sexual assault* since reaching the age of 15, one in 20 men in Australia has experienced *sexual assault* since reaching the age of 15.

It is important to appreciate the source of violence. There is a strong inference that most violence against women is by their partners. Partners are a source of threat, but the greatest threat was from strangers and family and friends. These different sources of violence bespeak very different issues for public policy. Some violence may, in fact, be between siblings, for example, or parents and young adults, where the young adult may be the aggressor, which may be an altogether different concern to that by strangers and partners.

While violence is abhorrent at any time, a lifetime measure is likely to provide an unrealistic result. A life without a single incident of violence would certainly be fortunate. The ABS also provides measures of violence in a 12-month period (figure 5.3). These are more revealing about the scale of the 'problem'.

Of physical assaults on females, police were informed in 87,000, or about 33 per cent of cases, with the result that about one per cent of all women in a twelve-month period are subject to physical assault that results in the police being informed. Women perform about 20 per cent of these. The data for police reports were not made available in the other categories of assault and threat of assault.

The survey on sexual harassment in the workplace found that of those who experienced sexual harassment in the workplace, 84 per cent did not make a formal report. The most common reason (43 per cent) for respondents not making a complaint was their perception that the behaviour was not sufficiently serious. Around 29 per cent of respondents took care of the problem themselves.

Figure 5.3: Women's experience of violence during the last 12 months, 2005

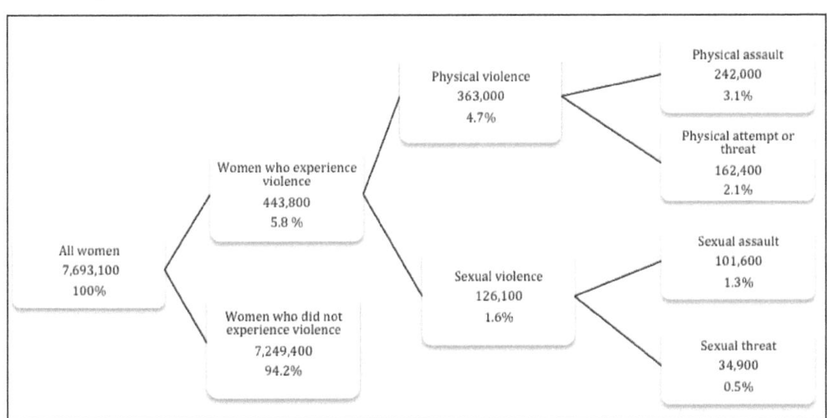

Source: (ABS, 2006, 5).

It is important to understand that shame or embarrassment, cultural reasons or distrust of police may have caused the low incidence of reports. It is nevertheless clear that the problem of the assault of women is not accurately portrayed by the headline generated for the Rapporteur tour. The Rapporteur may also reflect that much of her time would be spent in less civilised countries, where the 'better angels of our nature' are less in evidence.

White Ribbon Australia, a CI, appears eager to promote the biggest numbers on female assault and violence. A study sponsored by *White Ribbon Australia* of the statistics of male violence against women concluded that 'statistics would be highest and more accurate when a broad definition was used and reporting was based on lifetime experiences' (Chung, 2013, 10). It repeats the figures given to the Rapporteur and others: 'Anywhere from one-quarter to one-third, and even up to one-half, of Australian women will experience physical or sexual violence by a man at some point in their lives.[12] While there is no explanation why the larger figure

12 White Ribbon Australia, http://www.whiteribbon.org.au/uploads/media/updated_factsheets_Nov_13/Factsheet_5_Facts_and_figures.pdf accessed 10 January 2014.

would be more accurate, there is an explanation why it has been chosen. It brings in charity, and government dollars.

Australian Bureau of Statistics – what progress?

In 2002, the ABS started to measure Australia's progress beyond the economic and social indicators that were its standard brief. Following the first release of *Measures of Australia's Progress* (MAP), the ABS asserted that 'international and national interest in measuring societal progress in this integrated way has accelerated.' During 2009, the G20 Summit (of which Australia is a member) encouraged its member countries to develop measures that take into account the social and environmental dimensions of economic development. In Australia, a 2020 Summit in 2008, organised and sponsored by the Australian Government reinforced the need for improved, broad indicators of progress. Nationally, there has also been a surge of interest in broader measures of societal progress with many Australian communities and regions becoming interested in assessing the progress of their local area in this way (ABS (b), 2012, 10).

Figure 5.4: Measures of Australia's Progress

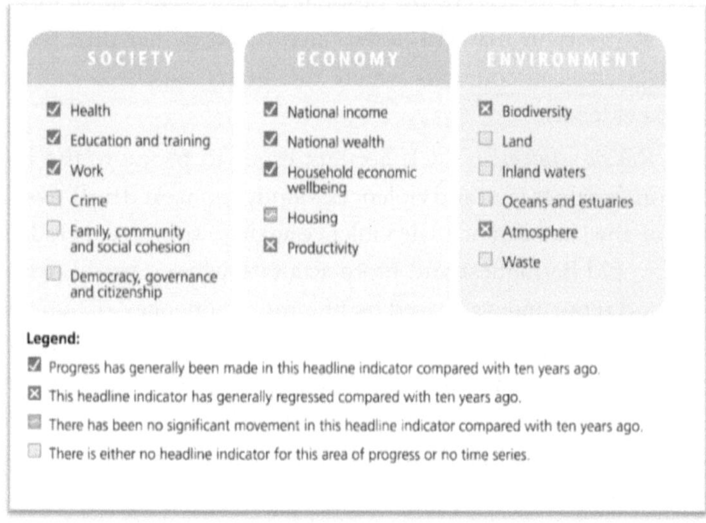

Source: (ABS (b), 2012).

The publication, *Measures of Australia's Progress*, is designed to help Australians address the question, 'Is life in Australia getting better?' The range of statistical measures that MAP presents demonstrates change under three broad headings: the society, the economy and the environment, as shown in figure 5.4. Within these domains, several dimensions are addressed, such as health and work within the social domain, national income within the economic domain, and biodiversity within the environmental domain. Within most of these dimensions, a headline indicator, which directly addresses the notion of progress, is used to tell a story about the extent of progress within that dimension. Within each dimension there are also contextual measures and these provide context to support the progress indicators.

Despite the overt enthusiasm of the Statistician to measure a wide variety of matters, after more than 10 years the ABS has no measures much beyond the standard fare of economic and social statistics. Although the ABS and the Australian Institute of Health and Welfare publish a great deal of other material, for example, on levels of violence, analysed above, these have not been successfully incorporated into the larger measures indicated in the figure 5.4.

Consider two matters on the environment scorecard, atmosphere and biodiversity. The report indicates that levels of carbon monoxide, nitrogen dioxide, sulphur dioxide and lead in urban air have decreased during the past two decades, but ozone and particle levels have not declined. It also reports that greenhouse gas emissions are very high and that the temperature has risen. So, some good, some bad, but the report suggests regression by marking the box with a cross, which is not the truth across atmospheric matters.

Biodiversity is another that measures as regression compared to a decade ago. There is nothing wrong with attempting to measure biodiversity. The problem is that one person's biodiversity is not another's. It can be argued that 'it is not biodiversity that matters, in the sense of the maximum variety on Earth'. What matters is 'revealed biodiversity

… the parts of nature people can afford to consume' (Jones, 2013, 67). Revealed diversity is rising. In the developed world, opportunities to consume nature have been expanding by leaps and bounds.

Experimental economics shows that people regret losses more than they relish gains, and so it is with ecology. Retreating species are lamented, even though their numbers may be overflowing in other countries so that measures of loss may be offset with gains elsewhere, and by other types of gain. These are not, however, revealed in the measures of progress. Remaining ignorant of losses and gains is not useful but, then again, nor are measures that imply that there are no trade-offs or that there are shared values about what is progress.

Treasury and Wellbeing

The Australian Treasury is responsible for another set of statistics where apparently innocent measures in fact create a misleading sense that all manner of things are possible and that life is but a shopping list to be ticked off. For some years it has presented a strategic framework, part of which is a section entitled, *The Wellbeing of the Australian People* (TWOTAP). The Treasury takes a view of wellbeing as reflecting a person's substantive freedom to lead a life they have reason to value.

This view encompasses more than is directly captured by commonly used measures of economic activity. It gives prominence to respecting the informed preferences of individuals, while allowing scope for broader social actions and choices. Treasury identifies five dimensions that directly or indirectly have important implications for wellbeing. These dimensions are the:

- Set of opportunities available to people
- Distribution of those opportunities across Australian people
- Sustainability of those opportunities available over time
- Level and allocation of risk borne by individuals and the community

- Complexity of the choices facing individuals and the community, including concerns about the costs of dealing with unwanted complexity.

A critique by J.J. Pincus of the (2011-12) framework, which the discussion below follows closely, raised substantial problems, the likes of which are evident in the charitable sector. The Treasury argues that the checklist 'reinforce our conviction that trade-offs matter deeply, both between and within dimensions'.[13] The Pincus critique is that, 'by offering a checklist only, but no clues as to how Treasury deals with trade-offs, Treasury has abrogated its responsibility to provide a useful guide to its decisions and advice' (Pincus, 2013, 1).

The checklist provides no means of weighting or ordering the importance of each dimension. Businesses, for example, are urged to use the triple bottom line of people, planet, and profit, yet if profits are persistently absent or low, the business may be taken over or go broke. Thus profit ranks above the other two. Viable businesses must be willing to consider trade-offs between the items in the 3P checklist. Neither ordering nor weights is found in TWOTAP.

It is impossible to show that wellbeing has improved, unless there is an improvement in every single dimension of the checklist. When some items improve and some worsen, no summary statement about wellbeing can be made, as was true in the ABS Measures of Australia's Progress. Furthermore, TWOTAP does not provide a basis upon which to choose between different improvements even in an overall improvement. Without ordering or a set of weights, there is no way to tell if wellbeing has improved in any one of the five 'dimensions'. Using only a checklist, it is logically impossible to justify the choice of one situation over another, without employing some weighting system or rank ordering of

---

13 Australian Treasury, 'Treasury's Strategic Framework 2012-13'. http://www.treasury.gov.au/About-Treasury/OurDepartment/Treasury-Strategic-Framework accessed 2 August 2013.

the 'lexicographic' kind: for example, filter first by opportunity; then by distribution; then by sustainability; and so on.

Pincus analysed each of the five points. For present purposes, one will suffice. Conventionally, changes in the 'set of opportunities' are measured using an economic aggregate like consumption, with the components valued at willingness-to-pay or cost; and with the valued bundle encompassing non-marketed as well as marketed goods and services. Every item mentioned in TWOTAP, except 'political rights and freedoms', can be accommodated in the extension of the national accounting framework by, for example, supplementing the national aggregate for consumption, by accounting for leisure, for non-market activities, for health and longevity, and for externalities, including environmental damage. The weights given to the various items are the valuations of the individuals concerned, whether revealed in market transactions or inferred from objective evidence about subjective valuations. If there is 'market failure', for example, if pollutants are being poured into the atmosphere without any charge or adequate charge, then the approach is to include the cost of the pollution as a deduction from the aggregate of goods and services consumed. In arriving at the cost of pollution, the approach is to use estimates of the values that individuals place on clearer air or on the cost of abatement. The essential aspect is that the valuations of the individuals affected are taken at face value.

In contrast, in TWOTAP, Treasury indicates that it will be 'respecting the informed preferences of individuals' and, presumably, not be respecting uninformed preferences. TWOTAP refers to things that Australians have 'reason to value'. As Pincus wrote, 'this is to distinguish them, presumably, from things that Treasury officials believe Australians value for no good reason' (Pincus, 2013, 6).

Productivity Commission and relative deprivation: a moving famine

Many charities deal in disadvantage but, strange as it may seem, there is no ready measure of disadvantage. On the contrary, there are many measures, as a recent Productivity Commission paper has explained.

Disadvantage was traditionally understood as poverty, and poverty as inadequate income. But inadequate income, while easy to measure, does not necessarily establish disadvantage. The test for disadvantage has been interpreted as 'insufficient outcomes'. As Sen argued, 'while income has an "enormous influence" on lives, it is "impoverished lives, and not just depleted wallets" that matter' (Sen quoted in McLachlan, 2013, 5). The concept of poverty has not only become more complex, it has been defined in relative terms and therefore cannot be eliminated. Moreover, it has also become multifaceted. Those who suffer multifaceted poverty may be fewer, but their problems may be more intractable.

Estimates based on broad proxies of poverty – deprivation, disadvantage, and exclusion – indicate that:

- Between 10 and 13 per cent of Australians were estimated to be income poor (households below 50 per cent of median income) in 2010
- 17 per cent of adults were estimated to be experiencing multiple deprivation in 2010 – the main indicator is going without dental services
- A quarter aged 15 years plus experienced some degree of 'social exclusion' in 2010. Included people who were marginally excluded, as well as people who experienced deeper forms of exclusion.

A much smaller proportion of Australians are estimated to be experiencing deeper or multiple forms of disadvantage:

- Three per cent of Australians experienced a combination of low income, low consumption and low net wealth in 2007
- Five per cent of those aged 15 years or more experienced deep social exclusion and nearly one per cent very deep social exclusion in 2010

- Ten per cent experienced relative income poverty for at least five years, five per cent for seven years or more and just over one per cent for all nine years
- Three per cent of Australians aged 15 years or more experienced deep social exclusion for five or more years, and less than one per cent for seven years or more (McLachlan, 2013, 8).

Most disconcerting was the finding that sustained economic growth between 2001 and 2010 had little impact on the estimated proportion of Australians who were experiencing relative income poverty. It seems that as the actual level of poverty declines, new ways of expanding the numbers arise. The exception is the concentration on those who suffer 'very deep exclusion', which is around one per cent.

Australia may have anywhere between a one per cent problem and a 25 per cent problem depending on the measure. Estimating the cost of disadvantage is complex. But it is more important to understand what are the most effective investments for reducing and preventing disadvantage; and what are the costs and benefits. These are matters that charities (and governments) need to address. Selling the need for charity on the basis of the biggest number is not helpful, but the official statistics are not making it any easier.

6

What donors want

The 'don't ask, don't tell' mentality of reporting is understandable but it evades the duty of care to the clients.
Michael Traill, *Social Ventures Australia*[14]

There is plenty of research to prove need for charity, but how much is there either to disprove it, or to prove the effectiveness or otherwise of remedies? *Dunn & Lewis*, a harm prevention charity, is not the only Australian charity to have received a significant government grant, but not only does this fact not appear prominently on its website, it has no annual report and no report on its performance.[15] In the UK, some authorities argue that government should collect 'better evidence on the impact of [tax] reliefs on donor behaviour' (C and AG, 2013, 13). This is well and good, but only one half of the equation. Governments and donors should also be asking for better evidence on the impact of the work undertaken with donations. In Australia, although many charities report in exemplary ways for most aspects of their operations, few report on the impact of their work.

14 Interview with author and Cassandra Wilkinson, 3 July 2012.

15 Dunn & Lewis, http://www.dunnlewisfoundation.org.au accessed 11 January 2014.

Whether to report performance

Large pools of philanthropic capital in the US are driving debate on the concept of perhaps the ultimate in charity markets, a stock market (Husock, 2007, 21), including a predictive market (Goldberg, 2009) where analysts, much as in the stock market for corporations, make judgments about the performance of charities and advise about buying and selling stocks (or donations). David Crosbie of the Community Council of Australia wants an alternative to the Australian stock exchange for investors who want 'social returns'.[1] But how an investor knows whether a program works or, of several programs, which is the most cost-effective, is moot. Enthusiasm for capital, not lack of government funding, is stimulating the exploration for proof of charity effectiveness. These are dreams at present, because many in the sector struggle to report at all, much less in a way that informs donors.

Whether charities are the agents of the public and therefore to be treated as fully public assets (Bryce, 2012), or their duties are in a narrower band of stakeholders such as donors and trustees (Van Puyvelde, 2011), or to the recipient and wary of powerful donors (Ostrander, 2007) is subject of considerable and engaging debate. What is unambiguously clear is that the motivations of charity managers as agents of donors and trustees may vary from those of donors and trustees. Managers may perceive their interests in growth of the organisation through maximising donation income. Trustees may guard charity reputation and purpose; donors may want the greatest social benefit for their 'investment'.

Unless all of the donors are sitting on the board of trustees, the charity needs to report its performance to a wider audience. Charities are aware that not reporting what they do with moneys granted to them by government or philanthropic donors runs the risk that the money may stop. Reporting is costly, and comparing the performance of charities, even rating them one against others, can be unfair. Then again, reports

1 David Crosbie, 'Booming Charity Sector Could Deliver Stock Market For Good Purpose.' *The Sunday Mail (Qld)* 27 May 2013.

can be used by charities as marketing tools and mislead donors about the public benefit of their deeds. It is always necessary to align this mix of motivations and obligations. One way to do so is to report results so that each interest is aware of the outcomes, and the charity's performance.

Recent debate in the US, the world's largest and most mature charity market, between the CEO of the charity rating agency, *Charity Navigator*, and the director of the Bradley Center for Philanthropy and Civic Renewal is a possible pointer to the future for Australian charity reporting.[2] The latter is sceptical of the influence of charity rating because, he argues, most donors give on the basis of 'heart' not 'head'. *Charity Navigator* does not demur, but contends that reporting does not preclude the necessity for rational assessment of benefit in charitable activity.

Charity Navigator, one of several charity rating agencies in the US, recorded more than six million site visits in 2012. Clearly, a considerable number of donors are looking for evidence of charity performance. *Charity Navigator* only evaluates charities with $1 million or more in annual revenues, which is only six per cent of US charities, but these collect 86 per cent of revenues. In terms of influencing the vast bulk of funds, it is therefore necessary to influence only the large charities. Sample research in Australia suggests that industry concentration levels are low, with the four largest players in the industry accounting for well under 10 per cent of industry revenue so that donor switching among alternative charities may influence fewer funds than is the case in the US.[3]

Some have found that donors do not care about the use of funds (Berman, 2003, 428). Others consider that because the majority of donors rely on local knowledge or trust, charity ratings do not affect donor contribution (Szper, 2009, 37). Nevertheless, a number of studies have found that donor behaviour is influenced by charities' performance and

---

2 Non-profit Quarterly, http://www.nonprofitquarterly.org/philanthropy/22083-debating-the-realities-of-ranking-charities.html accessed 13 May 2013.

3 IbisWorld, *Charities and Not-for-profit Organisations in Australia: Market Research Report.* http://www.ibisworld.com.au/industry/default.aspx?indid=1950 accessed 25 May 2013.

its disclosure (Bowman, 2006; Trussel, 2007; Chen, 2009; Kitching, 2009; Sloan, 2009; Petrovits, 2011). More particularly, while the overwhelming majority of donors do not consult online raters when making donations, those who do are likely donors who give large sums of money or donors who are engaged in advocacy (Cnaan, 2011) so that their donations may be influential.

A recent US survey found that while nine out of ten donors say that charity performance is important, only three out of 100 undertake research to find the 'most effective' charity (Hope, 2011, 5). The research also suggested, however, that 'effectiveness and impact data are the areas where users say the information is important and is not meeting their needs' (Hope, 2011, 19). One reason for lack of donor research is that 'the vast majority of nonprofits [in the US] do not publicly report on the results of their work.'[4] In perhaps the most information-rich charity market, the US, relevant and reliable information is not widely available to help donors make decisions about charity performance (Chen, 2009, 350). Nevertheless, there is ample evidence that charities readily accede to measures on spending and fundraising that they may not feel comfortable with but are readily used by donors (Bhattacharya, 2008, 468).

Australia is less information-rich but, it is arguable better data may drive better performance and conceivably attract more dollars to the charity market. It is not as if charities are not already used to performance criteria. The business of winning tenders from government and competing for funds from charitable trusts often requires detailed reporting.

Social investment/social capital markets

Social investment is a concept that suggests that it is possible to receive a measurable return on donor 'investment' in a charity (Bernholz, 2012). Motivating the social investment industry is charities' desire to

4 Non-profit Quarterly, http://www.nonprofitquarterly.org/philanthropy/22083-debating-the-realities-of-ranking-charities.html accessed 13 May 2013.

gain access to income, somewhat more sophisticated than 'give and forget'. It implies that there is a measurable return on investment and should, therefore, be a predisposition to report performance, probably financial performance. Social investment models ask for a lower return on investment by those who want to see a social as well as a financial return. The search has brought new players with finance experience into the charitable sector seeking to use their skills and expand the source of funds available to charities. If social investment attempts to treat philanthropy as investment, the implied rate of return should be the measure of impact. Instead, it tends to be the measure of forgiveness, or a black box.

Three examples of social investment are *Midnight Basketball*, *Social Enterprise Finance*, and *Social Ventures Australia. Midnight Basketball* (a charity for troubled youth) is, arguably, the most market-oriented. For example, 'capitalist solutions will deliver a model that's better able to Incentivise problem solving for clients.' *Midnight Basketball* wants results to generate dollars. They argue that governments do not provide money for meaningful research, but only pay for activity and branding.[5] The metrics and proof of return as a reliable measure of impact are, however, underdeveloped.

Social Enterprise Finance is a 'business' funded by the Australian Government's Social Enterprise Development and Investment Fund. A consortium of equity investors and lenders has invested $10 million, matching the government's $10 million funding.[6] Its preferred measurement tool is 'the quality of the service', which does not fit well with measuring a return on capital.[7]

Social Ventures Australia is in two parts; the *Social Impact Fund*, created

---

5 Author and Cassandra Wilkinson interviewed Jonathon Wolfe, *Midnight Basketball*, 4 July 2012.

6 Social Enterprise Finance, http://sefa.com.au accessed 4 June 2013.

7 Author and Cassandra Wilkinson interviewed Duncan Power, *Social Enterprise Finance Australia*, 3 July 2012.

with a $4 million Commonwealth loan; and a consultancy to charities. The purpose of the fund is to invest in social enterprises with a financial and social return. The consultancy side is closely allied. It purports to analyse the efficiency and effectiveness of charities and social enterprises, using various cost and benefit techniques. *SVA* has undertaken around 50 social return on investment (SROI) analyses, similar to cost-benefit analyses, but with more 'self analysis and stakeholder analysis'. The important *SVA* insight is that the groups they analysed 'just wanted the relationship with us in case it led to funding'.[8]

Naming donations 'capital' does not alter the fact that charities want money. The essential difficulty is to prove a return on what are essentially soft loans, or gifts. The danger is that, unless performance measurement is published so that donors can be better informed, measurement consultants may simply soak up charity capital without any good effect.

Social impact bonds

The social impact or performance bond is a further attempt to access a more secure or new stream of funding. In this model, governments agree to pay on results to non-government, often, not-for-profit providers (CSI, 2012; Hems, 2011). The first such bond was the Peterborough Social Impact Bond for Peterborough prison, UK, in 2010. The bond hopes to cut reoffending rates. The financing body, Social Finance, raised £5 million from social investors, which allowed for organisations to be paid in advance for their work. It is the responsibility of the Social Impact Bond manager to ensure that the outcomes are achieved and the investors receive a return on their initial investment. They are not paid until the minimum reduction in reconviction events is achieved. Investors, not the providers or the taxpayer, hold the risk of failure. Results are not due until 2014. An interim evaluation was too preliminary to draw conclusions (Disley, 2011).

---

8 Author and Cassandra Wilkinson interviewed Michael Traill, *Social Ventures Australia*, 3 July 2012.

In March 2012, the NSW Government announced two pilot Social Benefit Bonds. *Mission Australia* and partners are developing a Recidivism pilot while the *Benevolent Society*, Westpac, the Commonwealth Bank and *Uniting Care Burnside* are planning two Out of Home Care related pilots.[9] Neither is close to reporting. A simpler technique is Output Based Aid, a form of results-based financing that is designed to enhance access to and delivery of infrastructure and social services through use of performance-based incentives, rewards or subsidies. Output Based Aid links payment of aid to delivery of specific services or 'outputs'. These can include, for example, connection of poor households to electricity grids or water supply systems, installation of solar heating systems, or delivery of basic healthcare services (GPOBA, 2012).

What to report – analytic techniques

Demonstrating effectiveness is difficult, and key funders … will demand efficiencies, accountability and transparency … This will create new challenges in how non-profit organisations … demonstrate the impact of their outcomes. (JB Were, 2011, 2)

What to report is a more difficult problem to solve than whether to report. A whole world of assessment is opening up. It has the potential to engulf the sector. Key policy questions facing the sector include which techniques will prove to be of use, to charities and donors, and who will pay for such work.[10] There are many potential uses for evaluation data: program improvement, publicity, mission consideration, fundraising, volunteer and staff motivation, expenditure review, and more. The choice of method may vary with the charity's role, whether it is service provision, civic engagement, social entrepreneurship, or political advocacy (Eckerd, 2011, 101). Charities will also distinguish measures of

9 NSW Treasury, http://www.treasury.nsw.gov.au/__data/assets/pdf_file/0005/21794/SBB_-_Request_for_proposal_outcome.pdf accessed 16 May 2013.

10 Tools and Resources for Assessing Social Impact, http://trasi.foundationcenter.org accessed 16 May 2013.

internal efficiency and/or external effectiveness and whether these are to be published (Iwaarden, 2009, 5). Almost certainly, financial reporting will be central to any technique.

Financial reporting

Financial reporting should be straightforward so long as measures are comparable so that results may be compared (PC, 2010, 100). Recent headlines in a leading newspaper told the story: 'Analysis of the performance of 15 well-known charities shows some are spending up to 40¢ in every donated dollar on fundraising, while others are spending less than 5¢.'[11] Unfortunately, as there is no standard of accounts for the charity sector, the 'analysis' may have been highly misleading. Financial ratios on matters such as efficiency, stability and capacity are generated by some Australian charities. Many boards use them to monitor the health of their organisation, but wider application for comparative purposes awaits national standards (Ryan & Irvine, 2012, 33). There has been considerable progress on the financial side with the National Standard Chart of Accounts for charities circulating as part of the public consultation for the 2014 Annual Information Statement (ACNC (c), 2013). Use of the NSCOA is, however, optional.[12] One good example of strong reporting in financial ratios is that required of charities operating in South Australia. Table 6.1 provides a case study of a small charity annual return. Donors may use the data to calculate a ratio of funds raised to funds distributed.

---

11 Rachel Browne and Michaela Whitbourn, 'Charities' Fund-Raising Costs Swallow Millions in Donations.' *The Age* 21 December 2013.

12 ACNC Commissioner, Susan Pascoe, http://www.probonoaustralia.com.au/news/2013/06/deal-standardise-nfp-accounting accessed 13 June 2013.

Table 6.1: South Australian fundraising income and expenditure statement

	Money collected $	Costs associated with collection $	Available for Charitable Purposes (A) - (B) $	Amount distributed for charitable purposes in the financial year $
Section 6 Licence	121,214	55,607	65,607	50,000

Source: South Australia Attorney General's Department Consumer and Business Services, http://www.charities.sa.gov.au/default.asp?action=charities_details&licenceNo=CCP1670 accessed 19 April 2014.

The CPA has recently published, *Charities – A guide to financial reporting and assurance requirements*, to inform charities and their advisers on their financial reporting and assurance obligations under the new *Australian Charities and Not-for-profits Commission Act 2012* (Cth) (CPA, 2013, 3). There are also guidelines issued by State governments of a financial nature, for example, in fundraising. The issue, at present, is how many charities have taken up any standard. In the sample of 200 charity annual reports for this study, only one reported as follows. The *ANZ Breast Cancer Trials Group* fundraising costs are 'calculated using fundraising income (excluding bequests) as per the *Charitable Fundraising Act 1991* (NSW) and the Best Practice Guidelines of the Office of Charities, NSW Office of Liquor, Gaming and Racing.'[13] The business of comparable data has a long way to run.

The *Kids' Cancer Project*, for example, is a HPC raising funds for cancer research and awareness. The results are reported in table 6.2.

13 ANZ Breast Cancer Trials Group Ltd, *ANZ Breast Cancer Trials Group/ Breast Cancer Institute of Australia Annual Report 2012-13*, page 42.

Table 6.2: *Kids' Cancer Project* raising funds for cancer research and awareness

Source of funds	Gross revenue	Surplus	Per cent for charity
Raffles	$7,832,612	$2,314,207	30 per cent
Merchandise	$194,203	$22,347	12 per cent
Donations	$3,990,140	$3,449,453	86 per cent

Source: The Kids' Cancer Project, *Audited Accounts 2012-13*, pages 28-30.

These cost of fundraising figures, especially the return from raffles, appear poor. Some charities, however, use raffles as a means of gathering names and addresses to commence a direct mail campaign for donations, knowing that the rate of response is likely higher among those that purchased a raffle ticket, than others of the public. To judge the fundraising ratio on a single incidence could be misleading. Whether or not an agreed standard of reporting eventuates, it is best for donors to review ratios across a number of years and for all sources of income.

It is also true that charities fundraising ratios may be affected by 'strategic positioning in the market' and not a reflection on efficiency. Charities may be revenue maximisers or cost minimisers; they may use professional fundraisers; they may have few large donors or many small donors; their costs may be higher. Each will have a great impact on results (Baber, 2001, 331). Moreover, financial statements do not necessarily reveal whether managers spend on meaningful projects, or whether spending is efficient or effective (Baber, 2002, 680). In the *Kids' Cancer Project*, for example, the Project spent $2,858,657on funding research and $655,849 on 'awareness raising'. Spending money on awareness rather than research for cures for cancer may seem difficult to justify. It may be justified as a fundraising expense.

The figures displayed in figure 6.1, for example, show results for *Care Australia*, a foreign aid charity, on three efficiency measures. The program expenditure ratio, which is the total amount spent on overseas programs, and includes program support costs and community education campaigns, expressed as a percentage of total expenditure, is 85 per cent. The cost of fundraising ratio, which is the total amount spent on public fundraising expressed as a percentage of total revenue from the Australian public, rather than total revenue (excludes funding and associated costs related to grant funding from AusAID and other organisations), is 35 per cent. The cost of administration ratio, which is the total amount spent on administration and accountability expressed as a percentage of total expenditure, is five per cent. Each of these seems admirable, but compared to what?

Care Australia seems to have very low cost of administration. This may reflect genuine efficiencies, or be the result of a long-established brand. There is, however, danger in chasing low administrative costs for its own sake. A low administrative cost may not be an unqualified good and the impact of administrative costs is unevenly distributed among organisations. Low administrative costs are much easier to achieve in large organisations which, although the sector may not agree, is an argument for charity consolidation (Lohmann, 2007, 441).

Figure 6.1: Care Australia – exemplary ratios

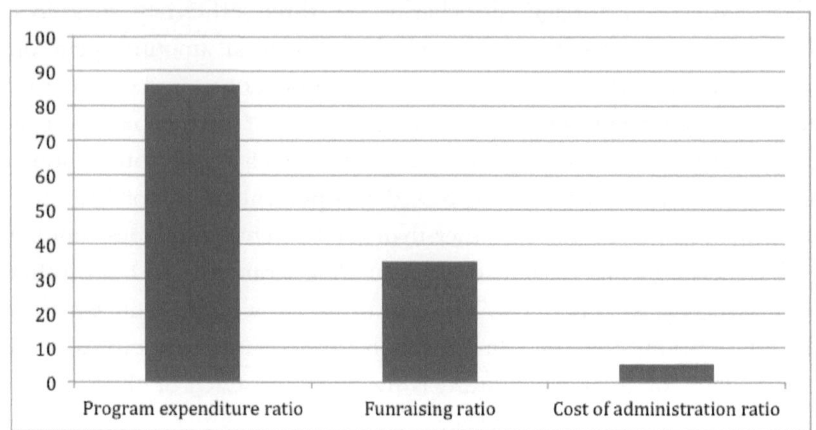

Source: Care Australia, *Annual Report 2013*, page 33.

The US charity rating agencies, which incidentally are run as charities and funded by philanthropy, have set financial standards for charities. They often recommend a particular standard and measure, for example, that program expenses should not exceed 65 per cent of total expenses. This replaced a previous standard, which required that program expenses not exceed 50 per cent of revenues. Some doubt the validity of judging charity performance by using such ratios to evaluate widely different organisations, or of compliance with them. There is a suspicion that a 'standards' approach can lead charities to bend or shift 'cost allocations', although others find no such evidence (Bhattacharya, 2008, 486). Motivations to 'game' measurements are a feature of all measurement and reward systems.

A recent study noted that donors accessing charity comparison websites are increasingly able to evaluate accounting information of several competing charities before they make a donation. The study presented an experiment where individuals adjust their donations after studying the program-spending ratios of the charities. The results indicate a flight to extremes – accounting information affects donations to charities at the extreme ends of the shortlist, but charities that are in the middle do not benefit. Threshold information (information whether each charity meets generally accepted guidelines for program-spending ratios) affects donation adjustments only if this information influences the positions of the charities at the top and bottom of the shortlist (van der Heijden, 2013).

Benefit or impact analyses

Financial reports are one part of the charity performance equation. Another is to report the benefit or impact that charities generate. The donor may not find healthy financial ratios sufficient evidence of the effectiveness of their donation. There is no reason, for example, to assume that charities with higher fundraising costs are 'worse buys', or that, because a charity may be an efficient fundraiser, it effectively directs resources to the causes it serves (Berber, 2011, 2; Steinberg, 1986, 348). The donor needs to know about fundraising and program costs in conjunction with program delivery. Together, these provide powerful information for improving performance.

The difficulty is that there is no single or clear benchmark for evaluating charity benefits. The *Gates Foundation* has reviewed a number of approaches to integrating cost in estimating what it describes as 'social value creation'. These include cost-effectiveness analysis and cost-benefit analysis, and social return on investment, which has been developed by philanthropic and non-profit organisations (Tuan, 2008). The terminology used to describe benefit varies, the terms 'impact', and 'social value' seemingly interchangeable. In turn, these are not to be confused with intermediary measures of program output and outcomes. Benefit (impact/social value) refers to a wider concept than outputs or outcomes and means outcomes minus what would have happened anyway to the beneficiaries of a charity. The real or 'net benefits' of a program are those effects that can be attributed to the program and not to any other factors.

Cost-Effectiveness Analysis

Cost-effectiveness analysis involves calculation of a ratio of cost to a non-monetary benefit or outcome, for example, cost per high school graduate, cost per child cured of malaria. CEA is used in situations where 'monetising' the benefits of a program or intervention is not possible or appropriate. The purpose of CEA is to combine appropriate measures of outcomes with costs so that program and policy alternatives within the same domain can be ranked according to their effectiveness relative to their results; and to side-step uncertainties about how to value different aspects of program benefits by looking at the ratio of benefits to costs without reducing them to common units (e.g. monetary units). CEA is widely used in health care where costs of intervention are compared to their impact on an individual's quality-adjusted life years or disability-adjusted life years (Tuan, 2008, 10).

Cost-Benefit Analysis

Cost-benefit analysis (CBA) monetises the benefits and costs associated with an intervention and then compares them to see which one is greater. CBA is the most demanding approach to analysing costs and outcomes as it requires a comprehensive measurement of costs and program impacts, for example, primary and secondary, direct and indirect, tangible and intangible impacts, and the ability to place a dollar value on program impacts across stakeholders. CBA provides a full accounting of the net benefits to society as a whole, as well as various stakeholders (Tuan, 2008, 10; WSIPP, 2013).

The purpose of CBA is to help the decision-maker to decide whether a program or intervention is of value, and to compare the program to alternatives and choose the one with the greatest measure of merit. The output from cost-benefit analysis can be measures of net benefits, also known as the net present value; the ratio of benefits to cost; or, the internal rate of return, which is the rate of growth a project is expected to generate. There is only one example of a cost-benefit analysis in the sample of charities, the *Fred Hollows Foundation* (PWC, 2013), which was 'at large' rather than a specific evaluation of its own programs. The technique is used in business to help decision-makers prioritise or choose among various uses of funds for programs and projects. This is precisely what the charity market needs. The question is, who would fund such work?

Social Return on Investment

The social return on investment (SROI) method seeks to document the impact of a charity's effort in a less formal manner than CEA or CBA. The developers and promoters of the SROI caution users that results are based on different judgments of social return and that it is not appropriate to compare the social return ratios alone. A charity is encouraged to compare changes in its own social return over time and examine the reasons for changes (Nicholls, 2012, 8).

Nevertheless, SROI may provide several ways of assessing whether the outcomes of a charity result from the charity's activities, i.e., net benefit. These methods provide a way of estimating how much of the outcome would have happened anyway and what proportion of the outcome can be identified as being added by the charity's activities. SROI uses the language of impact, but the meaning is net benefit. It is quite explicit that SROI evaluations should account for deadweight – measure outcomes that would have happened anyway – and displacement – how much of the outcome displaced other outcomes. At the same time SROI seeks to account for attribution – how much of the outcome was caused by other factors – and drop-off – how long the outcomes last. SROI also reminds users that measuring impact reduces the risk of over-claiming benefit. The risk of not measuring and accounting for all of the factors involved in an outcome is that donors may 'invest' in initiatives that do not work, or do not work as well as intended (Nicholls, 2012, 55).

There are instances, however, where SROI is misapplied and used as a marketing tool, for example, by overstating impact. Appendix 6 contains a critique, prepared by John Humphreys, of common errors found in some SROI analyses.

Reputation

There are amalgam measures. Reputation is one such measure. It is not clear, however, whether reputation is the same as performance. AMR surveys Australians to measure the reputation of the country's top 40 charities on a range of dimensions including innovation, workplace, citizenship, governance, leadership and cost management, and ranks them accordingly. As part of the research, 2,217 Australians were surveyed. Australia's *Royal Flying Doctor Service*, for example, was named Australia's most reputable charity, ranking highest in the 2013 AMR Charity Reputation Index.

The *McGrath Foundation* was ranked second. The charity was also viewed as having the strongest leadership and demonstrating the most outstanding citizenship among the individual charity attributes measured. Other charities which rate well included the *Guide Dogs*, *National Breast Cancer Foundation*, *Fred Hollows Foundation*, *Starlight Children's Foundation*, *beyondblue*, the *RSPCA* and the *Salvation Army*.

AMR's Managing Director, Oliver Freedman, explains that 'organisations also need to be innovative, strong community leaders, demonstrate appropriate cost management, be transparent in their governance and provide a good workplace for employees.' The *Royal Flying Doctor Service* scored 'well in all these dimensions, and their overall reputation ranking reflects this community view.'[14] This is a lot to take in, but does reputation, an amalgam of other measures, cause donors to shift donations from one charity to another? Some research suggests that there are four main reporting factors related to donations: efficiency in allocating resources to programs; financial stability; information available

---

14 Pro Bono Australia News, 'Australia's Most Reputable Charity Revealed.' http://www.probonoaustralia.com.au/news/2013/12/australia's-most-reputable-charity-revealed accessed 21 December 2013.

to donors; and reputation (Trussel, 2007). Reputation is but one piece of information on which donors may rely.

Difficulty and limitations of reporting

The Productivity Commission argued that 'there has been an increasing willingness for [charities], particularly those which deliver services to clients, to embrace evaluation', but warned that 'improperly applied, evaluation can lead to poor outcomes' (PC, 2010, 99). There is considerable debate about how and when evaluation of charity performance should be used. Some argue that data should be used to make funding allocation decisions across program areas; others within program areas; and still others that data should be used only to promote the work of individual charities (Tuan, 2008, 8).

Charities and researchers can argue the toss, but donors will want evaluations that suit their purposes. Some may wish to shop between charitable fields to find an agent for their donation, for example, cancer treatments or foreign aid, or planting trees. Others will know the field, but not the charity, and others will know only the charity in their preferred field, and may not need to compare, even if they would benefit from doing so.

There is evidence that a substantial number of people are seeking across-program information; for example, there are more than 170 online giving websites in the US. Donors in these cases needs to consider the program or field of charity best suited to their interests. If they want their donation to be of most benefit, they face a complex allocation decision. They need data setting out priorities. There are no Australian sites that provide such guidance.

Online giving websites in Australia – *Karma Currency Foundation, GiveNow, GiveEasy, Donate Planet* and *Connecting Up* – each facilitate the payment of donations to a range of charities. None provides data for assisting prioritising decisions to program areas and none provides assistance in choosing a charity to donate for a specific program.[15] The emergence of these sites indicates a growing market in donors at large, that is, those not attached to an organisation or cause. There are also a number of charity lists at various websites – *Australian Charities, Australian Charity Guide, Charities Aid Foundation, Everyday Hero, Philanthropy Australia, Pro Bono Australia* and *Remember Me* – that collect charity links under subject headings. None is comprehensive and none provides guidance on choice or ratings or recommendations.[16] Each carries some form of advertising from charities or allied businesses.

There are numerous other barriers that stand in the way of gaining information that would help donors decide the best use of their money. The first of these is the nature of the relationship between the donor and the charity.

The relationship

Funding simply isn't based on performance, but on relationships nonprofits cultivate with funders and the inspiring stories and anecdotes nonprofits tell about their admirable mission. (Goldberg, 2009, 2117)

Charities cosy up to donors, whether philanthropists, philanthropic trusts, government or the anonymous small donor tossing a coin into the tin. Charities have relationship managers whose task is to keep the conversation going: 'it is about the relationship, charity people stick close to their donors',[17] they get in close and hug them (Waters, 2011). There can be a cost to the relationship. Donors' demands can be significant and sometimes they come with strings attached (Barman, 2007, 51). This

---

15 http://www.karmacurrency.com.au, http://www.givenow.com.au, http://giveeasy.org, https://donateplanet.com and http://www.connectingup.org accessed 4 June 2013.

16 http://www.auscharity.org, http://www.australiancharityguide.com, https://www.cafonline.org, http://www.everydayhero.com.au, http://www.philanthropy.org.au, http://www.probonoaustralia.com.au/directory, http://www.rememberme.com.au accessed 1 June 2013.

17 Author interview with charity manager, observation of disabled youth charities, 9 May 2013.

almost always applies to government grants, but also to philanthropic donations. Charitable transfers in many different forms have come to require recipients to undertake some 'donor-specified action' as a precondition for receiving the transfer (Bougheas, 2007, 561). Charities may be aware that recipients are no longer simply given charity, but are required to undertake some donor-specified activity in order to qualify, or 'tough love'. These conditions may be costly and impose unnecessary costs on some of the more productive recipients. There can be false economy in donor demands, but charities could respond by, for example, encouraging donor competition, asking for less stringent conditions, or agreeing to joint monitoring (Bougheas, 2007, 579). The question for the charity is to decide whether the strings are worth the money.

Cherry-picking

The *Australian Indigenous Education Foundation* claims it 'has found a way to make the best education available to the most marginalised children in [Australia] by offering scholarships which cover their school or university fees.'[18] The founder, Andrew Penfold, has stated that, 'Our program is not about cherry-picking the best and brightest kids; it's about giving opportunity to kids of all walks of life who want to make the most of those opportunities, irrespective of where they come from.'[19] Clearly, it is sensitive to the claim that such programs of assistance can appear to be successful by selecting people who would otherwise have succeeded without such assistance.

According to their own measure, however, the target that they are tackling is 'the most marginalised', meaning disadvantaged. The *AIEF* is looking for students who are 'tapped into the idea they could achieve more …'[20] Selecting those who want to succeed is an important element

---

18 Australian Indigenous Education Foundation, http://www.aief.com.au/home.aspx accessed 4 June 2013.

19 Andrew Penfold, 'From Locked up, to Looking up.' *The Weekend Australian* 9-10 February 2013.

20 Rick Morton, 'A $100 million Plan to Deliver a Better Future.' *The Australian* 7 May 2013.

in success, but presumably among those who show promise, they would choose the most marginalised. The two case studies that *AIEF* allowed to be featured in their recent extensive press coverage were students who appeared to be not at all marginalised. Thanasi Tiliakos, a 14-year-old student from Darwin, wanted to attend a boarding school outside of Darwin. He received a scholarship worth $50,000 to attend Scots College, Sydney. Avea and Siale Sabatino attend Presbyterian Ladies College, Sydney. Their parents work in the Western Australian mines.[21]

The most marginalised students are those who live in remote Aboriginal communities. About 20,000 children on Aboriginal lands attend Aboriginal schools. 'These students had by far the worst results, with failure rates often exceeding 90 per cent' (Craven et al, 2013, 14). The case studies promoted by *AIEF* appear not to satisfy their goal. In addition, it is highly likely that scholarships could have been applied to less expensive schools, possibly in the region in which the students lived. All charities are susceptible to singing the praises of their performance, and picking easy marks is a cheap way to perform.

A better target, arguably, for *AIEF* was a student from Cherbourg in southeast Queensland. Miranda Fisher reflected on her community, 'twelve-year-olds smoking cigarettes, 15-year-olds drinking alcohol and smoking marijuana, 18-year-olds pushing needles in their arms while men in my community abuse their partners on a daily basis … five years ago, I was given the opportunity to leave Cherbourg to study at boarding school in Toowoomba.' Fisher also retold the views of those remaining in Cherbourg, 'Miranda, don't come back here after you finish school! Cherbourg is no good for you. Go and live outside and make a good life for yourself.'[22]

---

21 Patricia Karvelas and Justine Ferrari, 'Funds Secure Lifetime of Opportunity.' *The Weekend Australian* 11-12 May 2013.

22 Miranda Fisher, 'Not 'Just' School, It's a Lesson for Life." *The Weekend Australian* 17 November 2013.

Data manipulation and verification

Charity managers may have incentives to manipulate their reported program-spending ratios, the percentage of expenses allocated to programs rather than to administrative or fundraising functions, because donors use them in determining contribution decisions (Trussel, 2003). Charities, for example, that use direct mailings or other activities that combine a public education effort with fundraising appeals must allocate the joint costs related to these activities to programs, fundraising, and administration. A large study found that charities use joint-cost allocations 'to mitigate changes in the program ratio … between 16 percent and 28 percent of changes in direct programs are counteracted by changes in ratio of all spending related to joint costs and the share of joint costs allocated to programs' (Jones, 2006, 176).

Charity: Water, for example, is a charity that digs wells to supply clean, safe drinking water to people in developing countries. The charity claims that '100 per cent of all public donations directly fund water projects, and we prove every dollar using photos and GPS coordinates on a map.'[23] This claim is misleading. Private donors, companies and foundations that support the organisation through unrestricted donations and gifts in-kind underwrite *Charity: Water's* operating costs.

Attached to the *Charity: Water* website is a link to *Charity Navigator*, a charity rating agency, which indicates that the administrative and fundraising expenses are in fact 13 per cent of the program.[24] Further, in 2012, *Charity: Water* received a $5 million Google Global Impact Award to pilot remote sensors on 4,000 projects.

Unwilling to report

The UK Institute of Fundraising sampled the top 500 charities in the UK in 2007 and found a rather disturbing result. It seems that 61.5 per

---

23 Charity Water, http://www.charitywater.org/about/charitywater_auditreport_2012.pdf accessed 1 June 2013 at page 13.

24 Charity Navigator, http://www.charitynavigator.org accessed 1 June 2013.

cent of the UK's largest charities have no indirect costs associated with their fundraising, including one with voluntary income of more than £4.8 million. The suggestion is that charities are hiding the true cost of fundraising. The Institute argued a case for a further toughening of the Institute of Fundraising code of practice on accountability and transparency in fundraising and for the new fundraising regulator, the Fundraising Standards Board, to form a view on this matter (Sargeant, 2008, 340). The sample of Australian charities for this book noted widespread unwillingness to report although, with some strong exceptions, two being *Kids Cancer* and *Care Australia* (table 6.2 and figure 6.1) among others.

Unwilling to pay for information

While charities may be reluctant to be as open as need be in order to have an informed donor market, donors, too, have to bear some responsibility, or cost. A recent field experiment, in which more than 200 donors participated, suggested that donors are often unwilling to pay for information to improve programs. Half of the subjects in the experiment were unwilling to pay for information that could have increased the social benefit of their gifts. Those who made larger gifts were no more likely to purchase information. The experiment suggests that subjects focused on the fixed cost of acquiring information rather than the benefits of knowing which programs are most effective. The experiment sheds light on the reasons why there are so few evaluations of foreign aid projects, namely, they are costly to charities and largely ignored by donors (Null, 2011, 464). A better-informed donor market will persuade only some to seek better answers. As in any market, these may be sufficient to start a trend towards better reporting. Sharing evaluations of similar programs may be sufficient to guide better donor decisions, a role which a charity rating donor-informing agency could perform.

Who asks what?

For information-based policies to be effective, external interested parties must be provided relevant information. They must act upon it in ways to change their beliefs about specific charities, and act on these beliefs (Szper, 2011, 134). If no one uses data, then it is of no use. So, who asks what?

While nearly five million Australians claim deductible gifts, few are likely to spend time asking about performance: unless it is very accessible and digestible. However, the 40,000 individuals who claim gifts of greater than $5,000, the many who claim franking credits (146 claim more than $500,000), and the greater number who support charities but do not claim, are likely candidates to seek better information on charity performance (ATO, 2013, 102; PMCBP, 2005, vii).

A recent review of charity accounting standards and regulation in the UK during the last 25 years concluded that the creation by government of a climate of greater accountability and 'the widespread adoption of appropriate accounting and reporting practices', has the potential to provide greater confidence in a more accountable and more legitimate sector (Hyndman & McMahon, 2011, 172). Whether that drives better charities is moot. The report found, however, that there was no pressure to ensure that information was updated. The quality of the information was not sufficient to inform the donor in a way that would have them decide how their monies would be best used.

A 2006 survey of 73 of the UK's largest charities reporting on *GuideStar* concluded:

> charities more readily provide descriptive information … than information about performance and future plans … stakeholders have little indication of the effectiveness and efficiency with which charities are operating (Dhanani, 2009, 186).

The study suggested that increased use by government of charities as service providers has forced charities to do better 'to themselves and to other stakeholders', although 'better' was mainly confined to financial reporting (Hyndman & McMahon, 2011, 173).

Foundations

Researchers in trusts and foundations are the most likely to seek out evidence of impact (Hope, 2011, 61).The lack of mandatory reporting makes it impossible to give accurate data on these in Australia, but *Philanthropy Australia* estimates that there are approximately 5,000 foundations giving between $500 million and $1 billion dollars per annum. This includes PAFs and approximately 2,000 charitable trusts and foundations administered by trustee companies.[25] This list includes only Australian foundations whose primary purpose is to make grants and who provided *Philanthropy Australia* with an annual report or distribution report. It does not include foundations whose income is derived from legislated levies or from fundraising.[26]

For this book, the 10 largest Australian foundations were asked for evidence that they required some form of evaluation of impact in charities they supported. These included the *Macquarie Group Foundation*, the *Ian Potter Foundation*, the *Sydney Myer Fund* and the *Myer Foundation*, *Lord Mayor's Charitable Foundation*, *Geoffrey Gardiner Dairy Foundation*, *AMP Foundation*, *Colonial Foundation*, *Helen Macpherson Smith Trust*, *R.E. Ross Trust*, and the *William Buckland Foundation*. Although these foundations seem to be comfortable with surveys seeking information about where their funds are directed (Anderson, 2013), few were forthcoming in response to the request for information about the ways in which they choose the charitable cause and charity to receive their funds.

The *AMP Foundation* was helpful. While it was not able to disclose a particular technique, it indicated that *AMP* uses a number of factors. These include reporting against mutually agreed program Key Performance Indicators, understanding how *AMP* partners are funded and whether they are seeking diversified funding streams, how they are managing governance, advocacy, communications, mission drift,

---

25 Philanthropy Australia, http://www.philanthropy.org.au/research/fast.html accessed 6 June 2013.

26 Philanthropy Australia, http://www.philanthropy.org.au/research/factsheets/PA_factsausfdns.pdf accessed 6 June 2013.

employee turn-over, and assessing whether the organisation's strategy is in line with its purpose. *AMP* does not have a rigorous way of measuring these, but the evaluation is formed through progress reports, discussion with community partners and understanding the sector more broadly.[27]

The *Macquarie Group Foundation* was also helpful. Staff interests, particularly those closely involved with the *Foundation*, drive its choice of cause. There are no standard tools or specific themes, except that they fund a number of start-up charities and provide some infrastructure for these start-ups. In terms of acquittal, they require outputs, outcomes and milestones. They also ask questions of the organisation, for example, any significant changes to the board and what parts of a program did not work.[28]

The survey of foundations, weak as the response was, does seem to indicate a paucity of technique in evaluation, or at least in sharing such techniques. A 2011 survey of 173 grant-making foundations in the US suggests that while CEOs claim that assessment of a foundation's effectiveness is important, few board members are involved or understand the need to measure effectiveness. Too many relied on anecdotal feedback, and too few on either beneficiary surveys or cost-benefit analysis (Buteau, 2011, 8). There are some exceptions and these rely on serious research. The *Edna McConnell Clark Foundation*, for example, invests in sophisticated evaluations of all programs, including using methods such as randomised controlled trials, longitudinal matched comparison group studies, quasi-experimental studies, 'matched-pair' studies and cost-benefit analysis (EMC, 2012, 4).

Community foundations

There are 27 active Community Foundations in Australia with total grants of $12 million per year.[29] These foundations are independent philanthropic organisations that work in a specific geographic area to

27 Personal communication with AMP Foundation representative, 13 June 2013.

28 Interview with a Macquarie Foundation representative, by telephone 28 June 2013.

29 Wings, http://wings-community-foundation-report.com/gsr_2010/gsr_theme_facts/assets-and-grants.cfm accessed 11 June 2013.

build endowed funds from multiple donors. They provide services to the community and its donors, make grants and are a vehicle for local donors who wish to contribute their cash, trusts, bequests or real property to create permanent endowments.

A search of the annual reports of each suggests that most of the grants are very small and associated with many sub-funds, each with specific goals. The largest foundation is the *Australian Communities Foundation* (formerly *Melbourne Community Foundation*). Donors establish a named sub-fund under the *Foundation*'s legal structure and all contributions are pooled and invested. The *Foundation* works with donors to make grants to the causes, organisations and issues they want to support. The *Foundation* approved 410 grants totalling $3.8 million in every State and Territory as well as internationally (ACF, 2012, 16). Commitment to 'social, economic and environmental justice' appears to be a unifying theme in the programs, but the annual report consists of stories without evaluations or reference to evaluations (ACF, 2012, 3).

The *Foundation*'s annual conference in Mackay in 2012 offered 14 papers, only one of which mentioned impact evaluation, and it reported on the situation in the US (Brown, 2012). There is little evidence that community foundations have embraced the concept of evaluating the impact of their charity programs.

Trustee companies

There are nine trustee companies. They administer charitable trusts and foundations, including for general charitable purposes. These manage about 2,000 charitable trusts and foundations with assets of about $3.9 billion. During 2006-07, trustee companies distributed about $280 million to charities as grants from those trusts and foundations or directly as part of deceased estate administrations (PA, 2009, 14).

The largest is *The Trust Company* (TTC). It is trustee to 850 charitable trusts distributing more than $40 million income per year from a combined corpus of around $1 billion. Most of these are testamentary;

there are particular beneficiaries and no discretion in their grant. Some are broad discretionary trusts. For these *TTC* has created a granting model called 'Engaged Philanthropy'. In all, 57 grants worth $5 million were distributed in 2012; these aim to achieve 'a discernible social impact' (TTC (b), 2012, 4).

Figure 6.2: Theory of change checklist

Assumptions
What is the problem you want to address?
What are the underlying causes?
What impact do you want to achieve?
What would the solution look like?
Target group
Who would be impacted?
How could you reach/influence the identified groups?
What vehicles would you use?
Strategies
What tools or process would you need to influence the groups?
What resources would you need to influence the groups?
Who else is working in the field?
Outcomes
How will you know when you have succeeded?
What counts as success?
What indicators will you use to measure your achievements?

Source: Based on *TTC* (TTC (a), 2012, 27).

Most charities have a belief about what works best in their field, sometimes termed 'a theory of change'. A theory requires an understanding of the change being sought, clarifying the change process required and assessing the impact of the work being undertaken. *TTC* is beginning to employ a theory of change evaluation framework (TTC,

2012, 10), which is set out in figure 6.2. It seems to be seeking three things: engagement with philanthropists, collaboration between charities for improved impact, and evaluation for improved impact. At this stage the programs appear to be working on engagement and coming to grips with the 'theory of change' that projects embrace. The questions are simple, yet testing. It is a planning tool, a guide to exploring effectiveness rather than a technique for measuring it. *TTC* reports that its various programs 'had no issue in outlining the outputs that they had achieved … However, few were able to provide data in regard to outcomes and then use this insight to guide strategies and actions over the next 12 months' (TTC(a), 2012, 27).

Other trustees profess to seek 'evidence of realistic, measurable and achievable goals and outcomes, including societal impact' from their charities, but there is no evidence of the techniques involved.[30] There are many statements of good intention on behalf of grant-makers, for example, that 'Good grant making contributes in meaningful ways to the creation of a fair, just, democratic and prosperous society … by serving the public good, while catalysing economic and social reforms' (AIGM, 2011, 3). Worthy as these aspirations are, there is little evidence to suggest that trustees press charities for information about the desired outcomes. The statements are a mixture of assertion, wishful thinking and self-affirmation.

Private ancillary funds

A PAF is a type of trust. It was previously known as a prescribed private fund to which taxpayers could make tax-deductible donations. The fund may make distributions only to other DGRs that have either been endorsed by the ATO or are listed by name in the income tax law. During each financial year, a PAF must distribute at least five per cent of the market value of the fund's net assets as at the end of the previous financial year (AT, 2009, 5).

30 Perpetual, *Philanthropy Australia Seminar*, 'How Australia Gives.' 26 October 2012, Sydney, page 31.

Trustee companies manage some PAFs; others are managed by the individual who established them and/or their nominated trustees. Apart from ensuring that monies have been properly accounted for, *Philanthropy Australia* has encouraged trustees to accept responsibility to evaluate whether grants for significant projects have been effective. This would require the inclusion of evaluation as part of projects and, where appropriate, using external independent parties (Ward, 2008, 17). There is no evidence available, however, of the measures that PAF trustees ask of charities to which they make a distribution or, indeed, of their own programs (distribution of monies was canvassed at figure 3.1, page 69).

Government

Governments profess to want to know the impact of their policies and to use evidence as the basis for their policy choices. Unfortunately, it is rare that governments use evidence well; when it is available they frequently ignore it. Industry assistance is decried by the Productivity Commission but remains solidly supported by both sides of politics because constituencies rely on the subsidy. To politicians, votes are evidence. Unfortunately, governments often produce poor-quality evaluations that are not, in the end, very informative. These are often conducted within the government agencies responsible for the program. When external evaluators are used, it is common for government to insist that the results not be published. In short, the results of evaluations are typically not independent, transparent or widely distributed. All of this is inconsistent with 'evidence-based policy and undermines the ability to deliver on [various proposals, such as] closing the Indigenous gap, raising educational achievement, and reducing social exclusion' (Cobb-Clark, 2013, 90).

Foreign aid is one of the most contested parts of government and charity policy. Australian Government agencies have long sought to understand the effectiveness of aid but, even here, the record is not good. A recent review of AusAID programs found that AusAID managers rated projects themselves, though at design stage they were subject to independent input and review. The individual assessments are not made public. AusAID, and to some extent the broader aid program, is also subject to a variety of external performance reviews, from the Australian National Audit Office, peer reviews by the OECD, parliamentary scrutiny and government-commissioned reviews (Hollway, 2011, 288).

Independent evaluations of AusAID's 'completion' and 'progress' reports are another key part of its evaluation policy. Under current guidelines, a report must be completed for an activity every four years, either during its implementation or upon completion. Reports are required for projects above $3 million and are to be independent and made public.

A study of AusAID evaluation reports commissioned by the Review Panel, however, found that implementation of AusAID's evaluation policy is patchy: of 547 projects that should have had a completion or progress report in 2006–10, only 170 were recorded as having been done. Of the 170, only 118 could be found. About 26 per cent of the completion and progress reports were assessed to be of insufficient quality to publish. Only about 20 have been published on the AusAID website. None of the 118 completion or progress reports reviewed provided an unsatisfactory rating, which questions the credibility of the reviews (Hollway, 2011, 289). The creation in 2006 of the Office of Development Effectiveness and its Annual Review of Development Effectiveness were designed to help to prioritise aid effectiveness. No other bilateral donor has an equivalent to the ARDE. Overall, however, the ARDE has only been a limited success; there is increasing delay in its release (Hollway, 2011, 31).

Corporate foundations

Corporations funnel most of their community support through their foundations (PA, 2009, 25). Corporations control their trusts, so charities are not involved. Only shareholders or employees have rights to enquire. Corporates are as reluctant as government to disclose the benefit of their giving. Such reporting as is disclosed must be regarded cautiously as so much of it is opaque. Reportedly, and encouragingly, Westpac requires a log-frame approach to reporting from any applicant and requires that grantees participate in a program evaluation workshop at the commencement of funding to enable them to measure the social outcomes of their programs.[31]

Case studies on 'shared value'

Corporate support for charities suffers from an extraordinary lack of clarity of language. The language changes on an almost annual basis, so it is important to decipher what a corporate is actually achieving for a charity. Two recent examples demonstrate the difficulties.

Westpac was seeking to finance the *Leukaemia Foundation of Queensland* to accommodate patients who have visitations to Brisbane hospitals for treatment. The arrangement had come about as a result of the Queensland Government's desire to redevelop the Brisbane Royal National Association showgrounds. The developer, as a condition of the tender, had to devote some moneys to charity. The developer approached the hospital because it had previously worked on the hospital development. The hospital was aware of the needs promoted by the *Foundation*.[32] The conditions forced on the developer resulted in a possible windfall for the *Foundation* by arranging for extra accommodation at favourable rents. Had the Queensland Government not placed the condition on the development, would the taxpayer have received a better social return by other means? Would another partner have brought a better return?

PwC have invested in a mobile telephone application where 50 per cent of profits are to be shared with designated charities. The claim is that the 'app' is more likely to be used because of the charity label.

31 Westpac, http://www.westpac.com.au/about-westpac/westpac-foundation/grants/approach/accessed 7 July 2013.

32 Sandy Blackburn-Wright, Social Innovation Wesptac and Bill Petch CEO Leukaemia Foundation, *Social Impacts and Outcomes Forum* 31 May 2013, Brisbane.

In other words, the company is using charity as inducement to sell the product.[33] The return on the bait, above and beyond the success of the app, would be difficult to know. Shared value brings business thinking to charity. The concept may be fruitful and experimentation is encouraging, but it does not necessarily guarantee a more effective outcome.

Who reports what?

Simply going through the motions of providing inputs and resources is no longer sufficient in itself: we need to ask 'are we obtaining outcomes desired by our clients?' Mallee Accommodation and Support Program.[34]

The desire for evaluation of charity programs and the completion and publication of evaluation programs are two very different things. The number of evaluations reported among the charities in the 200-sample drawn for this book were few and the rigour poor. Those on record were, *Boystown*'s Young Parenting Program, *Youth and Family Services Logan City*, *Grow*, *Annecto*, *ACT for Kids*, *The Alannah and Madeline Foundation*, and *Anglicare Victoria*. There must be many more, but these have not been published on the website or within the annual report of the sample of 200. Of course, thousands of other charities exist, but from this sample, the pickings were slim indeed.

The *Boystown*'s Young Parenting Program was a self-report of those who participated in the research; in other words, it was a biased sample. While the majority reported positive changes since starting the program, and the young parents reported 'positive feelings around employment and education prospects', there was no data to validate any actual outcomes in terms of employment or better parenting, and no control group to measure net impact.[35]

---

33 Mark Reading, Corporate Responsibility Partner PwC Australia, *Social Impacts and Outcomes Forum* 31 May 2013, Brisbane.

34 Mallee Accommodation and Support Program Inc., *Annual Report 2012*, page 33.

35 Boystown, http://www.boystown.com.au/downloads/rep/BT-Glugor-House-Evaluation.pdf accessed 16 January 2014.

The *Youth and Family Services Logan City* reflected on the fact that 'Like many service organisations, *YFS* finds it challenging to measure and report on the outcomes', instead only reporting on 'outputs' such as the number of participants, the hours of service undertaken or the number of training sessions run. The *YFS* service, Next Step, is an intensive case management program, which purports to assess each client's progress. The aim is to develop an assessment tool that strengthens measures of client progress but, as yet, no results are available.[36]

Grow surveys members every year regarding the impact of their participation in the program on their mental health. They report those in reciept of professional help and/or hospitalisation prior to and following the program. The data which, if collected year on year, can be a valuable guide to the service's impact. The service reported that 95 per cent of respondents 'stated they would refer others to Grow.'[37] This may be a useful marketing tool, but it is not an evaulation of impact.

Annecto is a PBI with multiple objectives mainly working with people with disabilities, although these are difficult to fathom or identify. It had an income of $27 million in 2013, of which 90 per cent came from government, much of the remainder from fees. It is attempting to develop measures of impact by using Community Indicators from the McCaughey Centre at the School of Population Health, Melbourne University. These include subjective measures of well-being, including 'the Principles of Inclusion through the United Nations Convention on the Rights of People with Disability.[38]

Act for Kids (preventing and treating child abuse and neglect) 'is committed to evaluating the outcomes families experience after working with us.' The 2013 evaluation showed that there was a 15 to 21 per cent improvement in 'family functioning', 'child safety' and 'wellbeing' for all families, and for those most at risk of abuse and neglect, a 26 to 30

---

36 Youth and Family Services (Logan City), *Annual Report 2013*, section 2, page 3.

37 Grow, *Annual Report 2012*, page 8.

38 Annecto, *Annual Report 2012-13*, page 15.

per cent improvement.[39] The measures would need to be verified as having had a positive impact on the abused child. Nevertheless, a year on year measure of outcomes is a valuable tool for the charity and the donor.[40]

The Alannah and Madeline Foundation has a program to prevent bullying and has studied the impact on the time teachers spend managing such behaviour in schools. The research reports that '98 per cent of principals perceive that the hours spent engaged in bullying issues has decreased for teachers and themselves since implementing *Better Buddies*.'[41] The program may be valuable, although measures of school principals' perceptions about the success of a program may not satisfy donors. Principals may be grateful for any help, so long as their resources are not used. Evidence about this was not provided in the report.

Anglicare Victoria has a research program based on its work with parents with complex needs, such as financial difficulty, mental health disorders, homelessness, substance abuse, intellectual disability and family violence. It seeks to understand how professional support services can assist parents to deal with their adverse circumstances. It also seeks to understand how such pressures affect children. *Anglicare Victoria* supports a number of external research and evaluation projects. These are projects relevant to the work of *Anglicare Victoria* initiated by external researchers such as government departments, academics and students.[42] There are no results available, but the intentions are solid, albeit government-funded.

---

39 ACT for Kids, *Annual Report 2012-13*, page 6.

40 ACT for Kids, https://www.actforkids.com.au/centre-of-excellence.html accessed 28 November 2013.

41 The Alannah and Madeline Foundation, *Chairman's Brief 2011-12*, page 22.

42 Anglicare Victoria, http://www.anglicarevic.org.au/index.php?pageID=7894 accessed 28 November 2013.

7

DonorInform Limited

Establish a national Registrar for Community and Charitable Purpose ... to make it easier for donors to identify and access information about NFP organisations [and to] improve confidence in NFP organisations' governance, accountability and performance. (Philanthropy Australia, 2011, 7)

To grow the proportion of giving that is planned will require [inter alia] an extensive web-based listing of the variety of organisations that a person wishing to make a decision about where to place a gift to best support a particular cause ... could search. (PMCBP, 2005, 41)

Governments tend to concentrate on lowering the price of charity, either by lowering the price of giving by subsiding donors through taxation concessions, or by lowering the price of delivering charity by taxation concessions or direct subsidy to charities. Governments, less commonly, subsidise the cost of information. The New Zealand Charities Commission, for example, was established to create a more efficient charity market by increasing information available to donors. A criticism was that charities 'gamed' the information requirements in an attempt to 'look poor', and that the information they provided to the market was likely to be flawed (Cordery, 2013, 848). Attempts to have charities report their performance are fraught. These matters are not easy and, in present circumstances in Australia, some charities have convinced government that information is a burden: the less required the better.

Charity does not exist in a vacuum; it relies on the support of government, representing taxpayers, and donors. Government could help the availability of information for the donor, not by setting standards of reporting, but by lowering the cost of information. It could set standards of accounting in the sector and subsidise charity conformity with those standards; failing that, it could collect basic information and let the sector make these available to donors. Such disclosure is not, as the New Zealand case suggests, the ultimate in effective oversight of charity, but it can be a useful tool if there 'exists a receptive audience with the necessary resources to react to the information released' (Breen, 2013, 876). There are enough donors who, by their own inquiries and persistence and desire for a modicum of good information, can create a charity market that does more good.

Policy

Public register is a minimum

Ideally, charities should not receive assistance from government. In return, they would be entitled to be free of government interference. Because charities are heavily reliant on government, however, the question is not one of whether to regulate charities, but how and how much. The so-called Right, as demonstrated in the views of, for example, the *IPA* and the *CIS*, want little or no scrutiny of charities, as if there were no obligations in the privilege afforded by government. On the other hand, the so-called Left, as demonstrated by those charities who supported *Aid/Watch*, appear to support disclosure, but have no qualms about supporting non-charity work, especially subsidised free speech. There are holes in the arguments of both sides.

The Abbott Government has vowed to abolish the ACNC on the basis that it wants to relieve the burden of regulation on charities. And yet the charity sector agreed to the Commission and its requirements of greater transparency on the basis that it would lighten the regulatory burden. The ACNC has undertaken work to develop 'report once, use often' formats to minimise multiple and varied reporting requirements, which, other things being equal, should lower the reporting requirements. The ACNC requires from large charities only, a simple list of income and expenses. Far more, for example, is required of charities in the UK and the US, as shown in appendix 7. The ACNC requirements do not countenance scrutiny of charities' performance in any other sphere, such as program effectiveness.

During the 2013 election campaign, David Crosbie, the CEO of the Community Council for Australia representing the charity and not-for-profit sector, remarked, that the 'ACNC is already showing that for less than $15 million a year it can deliver real outcomes for much lower costs than was previously being provided by government officials for similar, but inferior services.' He claimed that less than six per cent of the sector support returning regulation of the charities sector to the ATO upon the abolition of the ACNC.[1] The real story is that some charities do not want the modest level of scrutiny that the ACNC was empowered to require of charities. Those charities, sensitive to the reactions of public knowledge of their assets, successfully lobbied to have the Abbott Government promise to abolish the ACNC on the grounds of over-regulation.

Should abolition proceed, what level of scrutiny of charities is possible without the ACNC? Under the Howard Government, advice from the Prime Minister's Community Business Partnership, quoted above, was to establish a searchable website of charities to assist the donor. More recently, *Philanthropy Australia*, which represents philanthropic interests, has suggested establishment of a community and charitable registry to allow members of the public access to information about charities. The public register is a perfectly simple request that either the ACNC, or

---

1 David Crosbie, CEO Community Council for Australia, http://www.probonoaustralia.com.au/news/2013/09/red-tape-charities-and-politics-curious-mix? accessed 3 September 2013.

the ATO, or a charity registrar, could achieve. Which organisations are included on the register, and the nature and extent of the information to be made available by compulsion on a register, are matters for debate.

A key contention is that donors should shape the charity market with their choices. Rating charities by means of objective performance is a worthy goal, but it can be very resource intensive and may not answer the donors' questions. Rather than establish a charity rating agency and website per se, it would be preferable to establish a donor guide on a website with links to charity information. The website would guide the donor to suitable charities in their field of interest. The website would seek to arm the donor with questions for charities, including how to interpret accounts, programs and charity effectiveness. The website may not list charities where donations are unlikely to make any difference, that is where they constitute a very minor percentage of income, or where a donor would be unlikely to consult any website. In choosing to donate to a school building fund, or a nursing home, for example, it is most unlikely that a donation will be made to other than one experienced directly by the donor or the family of the donor. Listing charities costs money, so it is better perhaps only to list charities that are most likely to prove useful to prospective donors.

A protocol for release of a charity list would need to be established to prevent commercial exploitation, for example, by advertisers. At present there is a capacity to search for a charity on the ACNC website by name only. This is insufficient to inform donors. Donors must be able to select from a suite of charities that they want to compare on various characteristics. A complete list needs to be made available to donor-service providers, DonorInform Limited being one, or other such donor-service provider under condition that only a small number of charities could be accumulated on a donor's list.

What donors and taxpayers want

Donors want a warm inner glow from giving and they have biases to which cause they may give. A donor's preferences may be, to some extent, shaped by the frequency of events or distorted by the prevalence and emotional intensity of the messages to which they are exposed (Kahneman, 2012, 2467). Charities want to find and solve problems; they identify needs; they have agendas; and they promote their cause. Satisfying donors and perhaps correcting their biases may be achieved by creating tools to allow donors to work out to whom they want to give and why.

Donors and taxpayers are likely to want different information from a charity register, even if there is considerable overlap. It should be possible, nevertheless, to satisfy basic information needs of both taxpayers and donors in a single organisation. Donors are most likely to want to know whether their donation is put to best use: they will want to know about efficiency and impact. An efficient and effective charity, which works on causes that are not otherwise supported by the taxpayer, however, is of little help to taxpayers. Taxpayers are most likely to be interested in why a charity has been granted privileges, whether it carries out its charter, acknowledges receipt of government monies, and whether its purposes and methods are controversial, for example, making ideological claims or devoting significant resources to lobbying government.

The taxpayers' means of reassurance in disclosure may rest in:

- Definition of a 'charity' and allowable purposes
- Nature of allowable activities
- Taxation advantages granted to a charity
- Disclosure of government payments to charities
- Evidence of evaluation required by government for a grant or contract.

The donors' means of reassurance in disclosure may rest in:

- Measures of fundraising costs
- Measures of administrative costs
- Measures of achievement of purpose
- Evidence of evaluation of impact.

Definition of 'charity'

The definition of charity continues to widen, either on the basis that what is regarded as a charitable purpose is wider, or that what is regarded as a public benefit is wider, than was once the case. Entitlement to charity tax favours is a task for parliament, not the courts (Turnour, 2012, 27). Parliament needs to reconsider what it is trying to achieve by allowing so many organisations to be granted charity status and, consequently, taxation benefits. At the very least, Parliament must reconsider the following.

Sole purpose

Since the passage of the *Charities Act 2006* (UK) those in England and Wales who seek charitable status for their purposes must satisfy a public benefit test by argument and proof, even if those purposes are within one of the Act's general descriptions of prima facie charitable purpose (Harding, 2011a, 21). This is sensible. No charitable purpose should be assumed to be for the public benefit. Neither should there be an assumption that some purposes are charitable. In addition, charities have been hiding behind a dominant purpose test. This in effect means that so long as their dominant purpose is charitable, notwithstanding how much, or little, charitable work they carry out, they are eligible for charitable status. The law should be amended in a way that demands that a charity has a sole purpose, that is to be charitable, and that the charity work is to be for the public benefit, that there is no element of private benefit, including self-regarding charity. A sole purpose test should ensure that a charity mostly undertakes direct charity work. Governments on behalf of taxpayers should reinstall some discipline in the definition of 'charity'.

Taxation

At present, for example, PBIs receive FBT exemption, for which it is required they undertake direct charitable work (although less so with recent judicial interpretations). Unfortunately, too many PBIs drift into policy and lobbying, which displaces direct work. In addition, most PBIs are not charities; they are government run, or heavily subsidised, businesses. FBT should be replaced by direct subsidy or charges to clients as a matter of service delivery policy, not a matter of charity.

Lobbying

Lobbying should be reinstated to its pre *Aid/Watch* status, that is, it is not a charitable purpose. All organisations and citizens are free to lobby, but they are not entitled to use public funds to do so. Lobbying is not a charitable purpose, but incidental only, so the key is to devise rules that either place a limit on lobbying or least require charities to inform donors has to how many resources they devote to lobbying.

In the UK there is disquiet about the extent of lobbying by charities. In responding to the Third Report of 2013-14 of the Public Administration Select Committee, the UK Government stated that charities should be more transparent about their political and campaigning activities. Clear information about how much a charity spends on political and campaigning activity would enable members of the public to make an informed choice about whether to donate based on an understanding of how an organisation uses their donation. The UK Government has recommended that the Charity Commission require charities to declare how much of their spending has been spent on political and communications work in their annual returns (UK Government, 2013, 18).

US charities are allowed to engage in political activity but, as in Australia and the UK, they are barred from endorsing specific candidates or parties. The US federal tax code explicitly allows charities to spend a nontrivial portion of their total revenue on policy-related activities. There are two approaches that charities wishing to engage policy-makers can take. They can declare 'an intention to influence policy' and spend up to 20 per cent of total revenue on lobbying activities up to $500,000. These expenditures are reported on the Form 990. All of that can be spent on direct lobbying, or contacting lawmakers, while only 20 per cent can be used for grassroots activities, or advocacy targeted at changing policy through public opinion.

Alternatively, charities can spend money on lobbying without nominating, so long as the level of expenditures does not become 'substantial'. While this added discretion may appeal, it brings regulatory uncertainty that most organisations wish to avoid. In 2000, only two per cent of organisations reported lobbying expenditures without taking the first option (Nicholson-Crotty, 2011, 592).

Commonwealth Governments are unlikely to set a limit on lobbying. Accordingly, these matters are best left to donors. Donors may wish to press charities to disclose what they spend on lobbying and then decide whether they wish their funds to be used to lobby government. Taxpayers would remain vulnerable to having their funds support causes they do not support (tightening the charity definition would help), and some lobbying would remain, but in the absence of government regulation, disclosure is a good 'second best' remedy.

Separation

One suggestion is that charity law be modified so that lobbying is done in non-charitable subsidiaries. *Greenpeace* and *Amnesty International* in the UK are precedents. Neither is a charity, but both have charitable arms which perform those purposes of the parent organisations that are charitable. *Amnesty International UK* comprises two legal entities: *Amnesty International UK Section Ltd* and *Amnesty International (UK Section) Charitable Trust*. The advantage of this structural arrangement is that it allows the public to choose whether to give to charitable purposes (which would be eligible for tax relief) or to influence public policy, which would not (Seddon, 2007, 93).

ASH Australia, Action on Smoking and Health (Australia) Ltd, is a HPC funded by the *Cancer Council of Australia* (the peak body of cancer councils, not *Cancer Australia*) and the *Heart Foundation*. Its work is entirely advocacy 'to reduce tobacco use through a range of effective measures such [as] … government regulation of all aspects of tobacco products, including disclosure and regulation of contents.'[2] This organisation may provide a model for the separation of charities from lobbyists.

The charitable status of think tanks is contestable. Think tanks do not fit the typical image of a charity, although as organisations they promote education in public policy. They are established for a charitable purpose and for the public benefit but are, by their very existence, lobbyists. The position in Australia is that, for example, the *IPA* has a trust into which research-only funds can be made and that these are tax deductible. Its other incomes, for example, membership, are not.

The UK Charity Commission has recently issued guidelines to help trustees of charitable think tanks, and those looking to set them up, understand their duties more clearly (UK, 2013, 19) but it is a clumsy solution to separate roles as per *Greenpeace* and *Amnesty* or, indeed, the *IPA*. There is nothing to stop the non-charitable or campaigning part of these organisations informing the work of the charitable (educative) arm. Again, governments are unlikely to take this option of separation, and informing the donor of these issues is a good second best.

Donor disclosure

There should not be any requirements to disclose the identity of donors. So long as donation is to a charity, it is deemed to be for a charitable purpose. The charitable purpose is the matter that requires disclosure, not the donor. Any move to disclose donors as, for example, with political donations, is misplaced, except when political work is undertaken in the name of charity. The risk in requiring identification of donors would be to freeze donations (arguably an underlying purpose of the political donations regime) and any hope that donations would shift to more acceptable or higher purposes as a result of disclosure would be harmed.

2 ASH, http://www.ashaust.org.au/default.htm accessed 30 November 2013.

Advice DonorInform Limited would provide

Priorities

Donors may wish to find a charity by cause or by locality. Then again, they may want to know which is the most effective intervention for charitable works across the spectrum of charitable fields. For more than a decade Bjorn Lomborg, a Danish statistician and political scientist, has brought together economists under the banner of the Copenhagen Consensus, to consider the world's most pressing problems. Their argument is that, each day, decisions are made about priorities. Governments and philanthropists, in particular, choose to support some worthy causes and disregard others. Donors are faced with a range of choices about causes to support. The Consensus attaches 'prices' and 'sizes' to each choice in order to inform the donors' choices. The most recent formulation of priorities was arrived at by answering the question: 'if you were to spend an additional $75 billion over the next four years to do good for humanity and the environment, where would you spend it first?' (Lomborg, 2013, 93).

Governments and international agencies often refuse to prioritise. They find it difficult to say no. In response to constituencies they try to please everyone, and fail to solve the most important problems in the most effective way. For example, the United Nations' Millennium Development Goals is no more than a shopping list of noble causes. There is little or no consideration given to relative costs or benefits of achieving each goal. When a charity declares that it has signed on to the MDG, it is really saying it has no idea what is the most important problem, or most effective intervention for a given problem. It is really saying that it will do what it has always done and use the MDG as a marketing tool. As Lomborg argues, 'relying on costs and benefits … is a transparent and practical way to establish whether spending is worthwhile or not' (Lomborg, 2013, 150). But charities rarely undertake cost-benefit analysis.

Lomborg and his panel of economists acknowledge the difficulties that cost-benefit analysis must overcome. But they argue the cost-benefit approach is an indispensable organising method and not without subtlety. The panel, for example, 'gave weight both to the institutional precondition for success and to the demands of ethical or humanitarian urgency' (Lomborg, 2013, 1466).

All charity works within a public policy context. That is, laws and programs of spending will have a major impact on the object of a donation, and affect its impact. No more so is this true than of foreign aid. A number of major recent studies argue that well-run political and economic institutions are fundamental to the well-being of a nation's people and that their absence renders any external intervention less likely to succeed (Acemoglu, 2012; Fukuyama, 2012; Pinker, 2012). A recent review of Australia's foreign aid concluded in similar terms: '[f]or most countries, in most times, it is their own policies and practices that are far more important than aid in determining whether or not they succeed' (Hollway, 2011, 4). Foreign aid development charities that do not take account of the political infrastructure in those countries where they intervene may be wasting their time and donors' money.

Program logic model with 'theory of change'

Donors may like to sort out their priorities first, but then, before dipping into the detail of a charity's accounts, ask some searching questions such as, what are you trying to do? Charities sometimes use what is known as a 'logic model' as an evaluation and planning tool to help track the logic of an intervention or program. Its most powerful contribution is the opportunity it affords to question the 'theory of change' implicit in any program (Ebrahim, 2010, 49).

When charity managers think about reporting performance to donors, they face a number of difficulties. It is difficult, for example, to know what can be reasonably measured in the logic chain — inputs, activities, outputs, outcomes, or impacts. Underlying this pragmatic question are two deeper questions:

1. Causality – understanding the relationship between cause and effect of an intervention
2. Control over results – exercising control over the results of interventions (Ebrahim, 2010, 18).

Charities that focus on measuring inputs and outputs risk being seen as failing to be accountable, failing to convince funders 'that they are making a difference'. Those that try to demonstrate broader societal outcomes and impacts risk taking credit for social changes beyond their control (Ebrahim, 2010, 13). These risks can be managed. A major part of any cost-benefit analysis, for example, is risk assessment. In any program risks may exist around fraud and efficiency, but also ineffectiveness. This is the risk that inputs will be delivered but few if any outputs and/or outcomes achieved. Fraud is likely to be very damaging to a charity's reputation and, where government is involved, a high political price. Inefficiencies may carry risk, and these can be presented in a dramatic manner, such as the wasteful travel budgets and high CEO wages. But, arguably, the greatest risk to taxpayers and donor dollars is program ineffectiveness (Hollway, 2011, 6).

The challenge for funders is to 'articulate a logic for achieving impacts (a theory of change), and then to put together a portfolio of nonprofits to achieve those impacts (an operational strategy)' (Ebrahim, 2010, 30). The challenge for charities is to articulate their theory of change and to justify to the donor why it is they intervene in some ways and not others.

In the foreign aid field, in particular, there is a history that each charity carries, some may say a burden, of ways of looking at problems such that the solutions offered are no solutions at all. The best way to cut through the pre-existing beliefs of a charity is to ask some simple questions. For example, does the aid charity ever advocate for free trade, as opposed to fair trade; does it advocate for minimum wages or no minimum; does it advocate for forestry and mining bans; does it support tariff reductions in competitor countries; does it advocate for property rights? The answer to each of these questions will reveal a great deal about a charity's theory of change, what it believes about how the world works. If the theory is wrong, then so is their charity. The efficiency of the spend will not save the program from its fundamental flaws.

Many advocacy groups proselytise on one side of the argument. *Oxfam* and *World Vision*, for example, claim that, while climate change is affecting everyone, it is affecting poor people in developing countries the most. It is true that the poor are most vulnerable to climate change, but what the best response is tends to be prejudged, rather than assessed according to the risks associated with all possible responses. These charities not only raise awareness of the problem of climate change for the poor, they also expressly lobby for carbon abatement, which is proving not only impossible to achieve, but costly for the poor.

It is important that DonorInform Limited arm donors with questions that would enable them to seek the charity theory of change. In this manner, charities and donors could learn to be more effective.

Social determinants of health and theory of change

The *Social Determinants of Health Alliance* is a problem promoter lobby group that uses the slogan, 'fair, just, right, equitable', and compiles a great deal of data that indicates a relationship between poor health and poverty. The *Alliance* asserts that inequality is a cause of poor health, and that, therefore, equality must be the solution.[3] Their intellectual leader is Michael Marmot who, in the introduction to a UN report, stated, 'Health [inequity] … is a matter of social justice and … social injustice is killing people on a grand scale' (CSDH, 2008, i). Unfortunately, Marmot and his Australian followers have no idea how to fix the problem other than 'tackle the inequitable distribution of power, money, and resources', which either means to lobby for further transfers of income from one group to another or for some kind of socialist revolution. Both have their shortcomings.

3 Social Determinants of Health Alliance, http://socialdeterminants.org.au accessed 13 August 2013.

The *Australian Alliance* is a self-described 'collaboration of like-minded organisations from the areas of health, social services and public policy established to work with governments to reduce health inequities in Australia.'[4] Australian charities and government agencies such as the Australian National Preventive Health Agency made copious submissions to a Senate committee considering the Australian Government's response to the UN report (CARC, 2013). Appendix 4 provides a list of members of the lobby who made a submission. Perhaps the most emblematic is the Health in All Policies Collaboration, a name that suggests that these medical professionals see all problems through medical lenses. Their skills are used to reinforce a pre-existing ideology, that is, that a more equal society is a more healthy society. Even if this is true, it would take a long time to achieve and many patients could die waiting.

The Australian Institute of Health and Welfare has a more sober view. It acknowledges the concept and that it can be used as a platform for interventions in some policy fields – transport, housing, environmental, educational, social and so on (AIHW, 2012, 13), but cautions that health determinants also vary in how modifiable they are. The more 'upstream' (social) determinants, such as education, employment, income and family structure, can be too difficult and complex to successfully modify. Modification for the more 'downstream' determinants can be more specific, for example, programs and policies aimed at influencing health behaviours – legislation against tobacco smoking in cars with children, restricting alcohol sales to young people, and enforcing the wearing of seat belts – help to reduce the burden of illness and injury.

The Institute noted that of all the ill-health, disability and premature death that occurred in Australia, almost one-third was attributed to the presence of health risk factors such as – tobacco use, alcohol consumption, lack of physical activity, poor dietary behaviour, use of illicit drugs, sexual risk-taking and violence. Many of these risk factors

4 As above.

have 'a strong social gradient', that is, the poor, however defined, have bad habits that are killing them. In 2010, the prevalence of tobacco smoking among people living in the lowest socioeconomic areas was twice the rate among people living in the highest socioeconomic areas (AIHW, 2012, 7).

The ability of governments to change behaviour is not great. The desire to change the conditions that may influence such behaviour, such as culture, is understandable. But opting to change the entire unequal structure of society in order to get a 'pay-off' in better health is frankly utopian. The UN report is utopian and misdirects resources. Donors may take these matters into consideration when looking for charities to support. Taxpayers should be appalled that public money is used in this controversial cause.

Advocacy disclosure

The difficulty with disclosing advocacy is that different charities can define it differently. In the absence of agreed standards of reporting, charities may be reluctant to disclose, quite apart from the ideological resistance to disclose among some, because they will be unfairly compared. No such reluctance has been shown by the *Nature Conservation Council of NSW*, which reports the percentage of its resources devoted to advocacy in its annual report.[5]

The *Nature Conservation Council of NSW* is a typical peak body organisation, an association of other environment groups. It is highly supported by government grants and spends much of its money on advocacy. The refreshing part is that it readily discloses this as shown in figure 7.1. Taxpayers should know how much of the charity resource is devoted to advocacy and lobbying, because they may well disagree with the purposes of the charity, that is asking governments for more money or changes to the law.

5 The Nature Conservation Council of NSW, *Annual Report 2012*, page 30.

Figure 7.1: The Nature Conservation Council of NSW, expenditure by category 2011-12

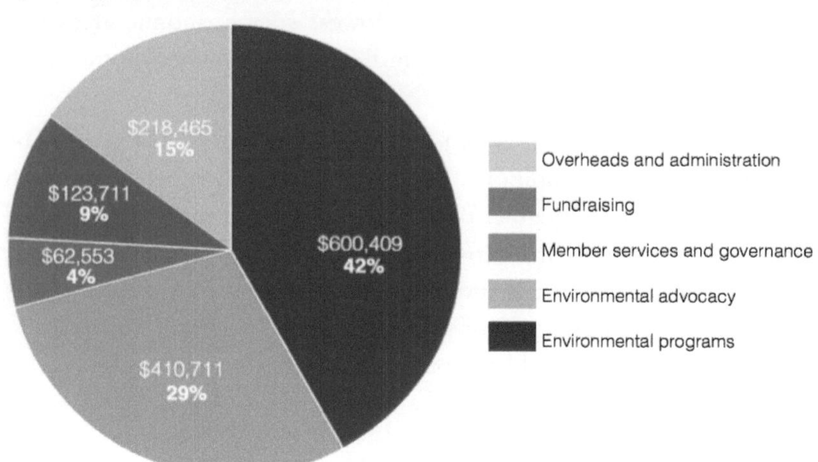

Source: Nature Conservation Council of NSW, *Annual Report 2012*, page 30.

Having governments write laws to define advocacy and lobbying and setting limits on the allowable amounts is, frankly, beyond Australian governments. In the absence of agreed rules, the best that can be achieved is to encourage donors to ask and cajole charities to report. Donors may like to have their preferred charity lobby, so in the practical world of politics, some knowledge is better than none. The *Council* is no doubt proud to lobby, and is an example of policy separation from charities it represents. Whether it is a charity, or whether their constituent charities also lobby, are relevant questions. In the liberal environment of charity regulation in Australia, beggars cannot be choosers. Donors asking questions will begin the process of disclosure. Charity reluctance can be overcome and, in time, they may lobby government to impose some standards of measurement in this area.

ACNC annual financial returns

Beyond donor priorities, charity theory of change, and lobbying disclosure, lie more detailed accounts of charity performance. For large charities with

Table 7.1: Large charities - income statement and balance sheet extract

	Gross Income
1	Government grants
2	Donations and bequests
3	All other revenue
	Total revenue
4	Other Income
	Total Gross Income
	Expenses
5	Employee expenses
6	Interest
7	Grants and donations made for use in Australia
8	Grants and donations made for use outside Australia
9	All other expenses
	Total expenses
	Net surplus/deficit
	Assets
10	Total current assets
11	Non-current loans
12	Other non-current assets
	Total non-current assets
	Total assets
	Liabilities
13	Total current liabilities
14	Non-current loans
15	Other non-current liabilities
	Total non-current liabilities
	Total liabilities
	Net Assets/Liabilities

Source: ACNC, 2014 Annual Information Statement: Guide to Requirements, Part C Financial Questions for Large Charities, http://www.acnc.gov.au/ACNC/Report/2014AISGuide.aspx#S4 accessed 6 March 2014.

an annual income in excess of $1 million, the ACNC requires a summary income statement and balance sheet extract that includes up to 15 pieces of information, in table 7.1. Typically this information will come from records already held by charities. In addition to the financial statement, there will be data required to describe the nature of the charities and their activities as well as the intended recipients in a tick-the-box format.

Efficiency measures

Data from the ACNC annual return could be used by donors to calculate various efficiency measures, many of which, incidentally, charities either publish or, at least, calculate for internal monitoring purposes. There exist a range of financial measures, expressed as ratios, which measure the financial health of charities. In general terms these provide measures of the financial efficiency of charities, but also the stability and capacity of charities. There are, for example:

- Administration Expense Ratio – an indication of expenses outlaid on administration and management
- Program Expense Ratio – an indication of expenses outlaid on program
- Fundraising Expense Ratio – an indication of expenses outlaid on fundraising
- Cost of Fundraising per cent – an indication of cost of raising each dollar of fundraising revenue.

There are other measures of financial health, which are mainly used for internal purposes, although they are good indicators of risk and shed light on the capacity of a charity to deliver programs. For example:

- Revenue Concentration – an indication of the dependence: contributions, grants, commercial revenue, investment revenue, other revenue

- Current Ratio – an indication of the ability to meet financial commitments in the next financial period (Ryan & Irvine, 2012, 33).

A number of US charity regulators have raised the over-reliance on such ratios as an indication of charity performance.[6] The three leading sources of information on US charities – *GuideStar*, *Charity Navigator*, and *BBB Wise Giving Alliance* – recently denounced the 'overhead ratio' as the sole measure of charity performance.[7] The organisations wished to correct the misconception that the percentage of charity's expenses that go to administrative and fundraising costs is an appropriate metric to evaluate when assessing a charity's worthiness and efficiency. The concern is that charities under pressure from donors may under-report overheads as a way of attracting funding, thus 'starving' themselves of future capacity (Goggins, 2009, 50). The same type of argument may, of course, be made of any firm in any competitive market.

DonorInform Limited would not create or gather overhead ratios. Instead, it would advise donors what to look for in these regards.

Impact measures

The Productivity Commission recommended that the Australian Government provide funding for establishment of a Centre for Community Service Effectiveness to promote 'best practice' approaches to evaluation, with an initial focus on the evaluation of government-funded community services (PC, 2010, 112). The Commission suggested the Centre should, among other things, provide a publicly available portal

---

6 Guide Star, http://www.guidestar.org/rxa/news/news-releases/2013/2013-06-17-overhead-myth.aspx accessed 3 July 2013.

7 The William and Flora Hewlett Foundation recently announced that it would cease support for groups like *Charity Navigator*, *GiveWell*, and *GuideStar* to provide publicly-accessible information about the financial performance and social impact of nonprofits. It is continuing to fund groups that provide research on philanthropic strategies that produce measurable results. Doug Donovan, 'Hewlett Ends Effort to Get Donors to Make Dispassionate Choices on Giving,' *The Chronicle of Philanthropy* 3 April, 2014.

for lodging and accessing evaluations and guidance for undertaking impact evaluations.

All charities and funders undertake some sort of analysis. This is implicit in the decisions that charities make about what activities to do, and the decisions that funders make about which charities to support. But the place that rigorous analysis could have in helping the charitable sector to improve is underplayed. Many charities and funders invest little in analysis, and do not understand how to approach it (Copps, 2010, 5). The US is moving from charity rating, mainly based on efficiency, towards impact. Hence, impact researchers in the US and elsewhere – such as Social Impact Analysts Association UK and the Australasian Evaluation Society, and Giving Evidence UK – are growing.[8]

The sample of 200 charity annual reports drawn for this book suggests that while a number of large charities could meet the requirements of the ACNC return, indeed, calculate and publish various financial efficiency ratios, most failed to provide all of the information required. In terms of impact measures, Australia has not reached a level of sophistication comparable to that of the US performance evaluations.

DonorInform Limited would, in time, seek to be a repository of evaluations relevant to each sector of the charity market.

Questions to guide prospective donors

The US charity rater, *Charity Navigator*, recommends seven questions donors that should ask of prospective charities.

- What is the charity's commitment to reporting results?
- How does the charity demonstrate the demand for its services?
- Does the charity report its activities (what it does)?

8 Social Impact Analysts Association UK, http://www.siaassociation.org, Australasian Evaluation Society Inc, http://www.aes.asn.au, Giving evidence http://giving-evidence.com/about/ accessed 13 February 2014.

- Does the charity report its immediate results?
- Does the charity report its outcomes (medium- and longer-term results)?
- What is the quality of evidence for reported results?
- Does the charity adjust and improve in light of its results?[9]

GiveWell US has adopted a method that relies on less detailed analysis. The approach they apply to international aid charities is to:

- Understand the cause by reading the literature and talking to experts
- Identify charities that could *potentially* receive a top rating
- Formulate measures to prioritise some of the promising charities
- Categorise charities as 'promising' or 'not promising'
- Investigate the most promising ones in more depth
- Identify top contenders, investigate, and visit programs in the field.[10]

Charity Navigator suggests a more open set of tests that a donor may apply to charity performance than does *GiveWell.* Both, however, are working to include and encourage charities into reporting. Those that fail to report well do not receive fewer stars or a lower ranking per se. They are instead excluded from further consideration and are not recommended. Having encouraged reporting it moves the charity donor along the path to greater knowledge about charity performance. These

9 Charity Navigator, 'How To Investigate A Charity's Results', http://www.charitynavigator.org/ accessed 4 July 2013. There are attempts by the Centre for Social Impacts at the University NSW and partners to establish a Social Impact Measurement Network Australia.

10 GiveWell USA, http://www.givewell.org/international/process accessed 5 July 2013. Another method is used by New Philanthropy Capital http://www.philanthropycapital.org/ accessed 13 February 2014.

are very valuable processes and would be encouraged by DonorInform Limited in Australia.

Figure 7.2: The donor decision path

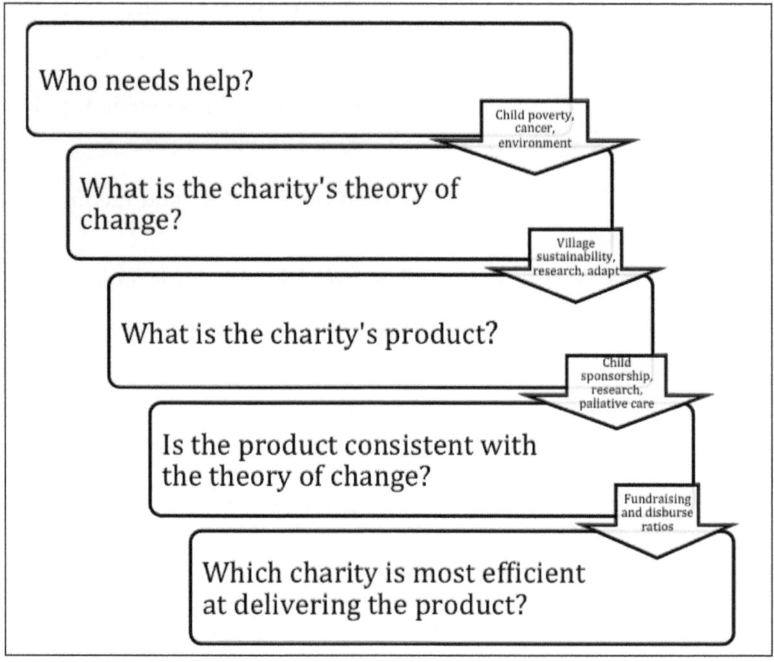

Source: author.

DonorInform Limited cannot do the work of government in defining charity. It cannot create financial ratios where no national standard is widely accepted. Neither can it hope to undertake costly evaluations. Nevertheless, DonorInform Limited can list on its site charities that have DGR status and are therefore most likely to attract the attention of donors. It can list on its website those charities that report to an agreed minimum standard. For example, the charity should have a website and an annual report containing an audit, published and available in electronic form. It must disclose any government income from all sources, including the amount.

These are simple and inexpensive measures for the charities who wish to be listed on the DonorInform Limited website. In time, and with philanthropic support, DonorInform Limited can perform more sophisticated tasks such as comparative financial performance and impact evaluation. Above all, DonorInform Limited can guide donors in their selection of a charity that suits their values and prompt them to inquire further of charity performance, as illustrated in figure 7.2.

Conclusion

Charities have worked long and hard to sell their version of need and to fashion their solutions to need. Donors have little knowledge of these matters, although they have their own perceptions of need and their own values as to who or what they consider most deserving. Donor capital flows to charities and somehow the outcome satisfies both donor and charity and their clients. That is the market at work. Information, however, is not in balance. The donor has little to work on, in lieu of which they are forced to trust the charity.

There is a great deal of impure altruism in the charity business. On the donor side there is some self-regard and some agenda chasing. On the charity side there is agenda pushing and organisation enhancement. No set of rules could hope to create a clean market of pure motives and perfect outcomes. The one thing that may help is to lower the cost to the donor of finding out what happens to their money.

Apart from fundraising and registration legislation, governments have tended to leave the charity sector to its own devices. The intention of the Abbott Government to abolish the ACNC is testament to the truth that many charities do not want any interference in their activities, despite their considerable reliance on government money. In the short term, taxpayers have to accept the decisions that governments make, but donors need not delay organising their own means of evening up the information playing field.

An Australian organisation and website, DonorInform Limited, that aims to inform donors and to assist them to decide where to invest in charity would be a valuable assist to those who rely on charities. Many people asking many questions throughout the vast array of charitable causes is a market-based way to better charity.

Appendix 1

Charity sample

Drawing a sample of Australian charities is difficult because the number and type of charities and their various forms of registration and taxation benefit is bewildering, and there is no single publicly available list.

The Australian Charities and Not-for-profits Commission has begun the task of gathering and publishing annual information returns from all charities, but a list is not available. The researcher has to know the name of the charity to enquire.

The Australian Taxation Office, which was responsible for administering charity eligibility prior to the establishment of the ACNC, does not have a readily publicly available list of charities although its statistical series, TAXSTATS (ATO, 2012), is derived from all tax eligible charities. It does, however, publish a list of those charities endorsed for donor income taxation deductions.

A guide to the types of charities and their number is in table 2.4 (page 47). A range of organisations is eligible to receive deductible gifts. All DGRs have to be endorsed by the ATO or ACNC, unless they are listed by name in the income tax law. There are 29,046 DGR organisations and these cover PBIs, HPCs, CIs and funds, overseas aid funds, registered cultural and environmental organisations and sundry others such as school building funds, libraries and research institutions.

There are also two classes of charity registration not specifically managed by the ATO; those specifically mentioned in the Tax Act (177 under 15 different headings), and those managed by an Australian Government department (seven registers covering almost 2,000 organisations). The ACNC has taken over responsibility for their registration, although the lists are no longer available from that source.

Drawing a sample of charities from this mélange was difficult. The most readily accessible organisations were charities that have DGR status, or are named in the Act, or are on departmental registers. Further, of the charities on those lists, larger charities were chosen as these were most likely to publish an annual report and host a website where there would be sufficient information to report various characteristics relevant to the study. The sample frame draws from available lists, in the proportions as shown in table A1.1. The list of charities follows immediately after.

The key issues for which evidence was sought from the annual, financial and other reports for each charity were as follows:

- Donations and grants clearly distinguished and acknowledged
- Whether activity belies purpose – advocacy versus delivery
- Any political activities or to change the law
- How and whether the charity reports impact
- What is the charity product – interpretation of purpose
- Signs of sensitivity to 'crowding out'
- Any 'indirect' activity in PBIs.

Table A1.1: Sample frame for large charities

Charity group	**Number**
Endorsed DGR entities from the ATO	108
Register of *Environmental Organisations* 583, in addition Environment groups named in the Act – WWF and ACF	27
Register of approved *Overseas Aid Funds* 219, in addition *International Affairs* groups named in the Act - *The Foundation for Development Cooperation Ltd* and *Lowy Institute for International Policy*	22
Organisations entered on the Register of *Cultural Organisations* 960	10
Register of *Harm Prevention Charitable Institutions* - Deductible Gift Register 69	5
Health Promotion Charities 1,058, but no list (use ANPHA Health Promotion Websites Database 366)	10
Education named in the Act - *Australian Human Rights Education Fund, The Constitution Education Fund*	2
Industry named in the Act - *Australian Business Week Limited, WorldSkills Australia*	2
Research named in the Act – *Centre for Independent Studies, The Menzies Research Centre Public Fund, The Sir Earle Page Memorial Trust, The Chifley Research Centre Limited, Grattan Institute, The Green Institute Limited, Institute of Public Affairs*	7
Welfare named in the Act - *Amnesty International Australia, Reconciliation Australia Limited, International Social Service (Australian Branch)*	3
The Family named in the Act - *Playgroup Australia Limited*	1
Health named in the Act – *Cancer Australia*	1
Other named in the Act - *Social Ventures Australia Limited*	1
Community Legal Centres	1
Total	**200**

Charity sample

Endorsed DGRs Charity type	
PBI	Aboriginal Legal Service
PBI	Achieve Australia
PBI	ACT for kids
PBI	Allanah & Madeline Foundation
PBI	Alzheimer's Australia
PBI	Anglicare Victoria
PBI	Annecto
CI	(ANZ) Breast Cancer Institute of Australia
PBI	Arthritis Foundation of Australia
CI	Australian Breastfeeding Association
PBI	Australian Relief and Mercy Services
PBI	Australian Volunteers International
PBI	Baptist Care
PBI	Benetas
HPC	Black Dog Institute
PBI	Boystown
PBI	Camp Quality
PBI	Carers Australia
CF	Centenary Institute
PBI	Cerebral Palsy League of Queensland

CI	Collingwood Foundation Trustee
PBI	Concern Australia
PBI	Down Syndrome Association NSW
PBI	Dress for Success
HPC	Dragons Abreast Australia
HPC	Ear Science Institute Australia
CI	Edmund Rice Foundation
PBI	Endeavour Foundation
CI	Engineers without borders Australia Ltd
HPC	Family Planning NSW
PBI	First Voice Australia
PBI	Foodbank Victoria
PBI	Foundation Housing
HPC	Gateway Community Health
PBI	Grow
PBI	Guide Dogs NSW/ACT
PBI	Guide Dogs Victoria
PBI	Habitat for Humanity
PBI	Harrison Community Services
PBI	Hear and Say
HPC	Heart Kids Australia Inc
PBI	Human Rights Law Centre
CI	Ian Thorpe's Foundation
HPC	Indigenous Allied Health Australia
PBI	Indigenous Community Volunteers
CI	Institute for Breathing and Sleep
PBI	Jewish Aid Australia
PBI	Jobs Australia Foundation
PBI	Juvenile Diabetes Research
HPC	Kids Cancer (Oncology Child)

PBI	Kids Under Cover
PBI	L'Arche Australia
HPC	Leap Frog Ability
PBI	Life Education Australia
PBI	Madec Australia
PBI	Mallee Accommodation & Support
PBI	Marist Youth Care
HPC	Mental Health Council of Australia
PBI	Menzies Caring for Kids
CI	National Trust
PBI	Neurological Council of WA
PBI	Odyssey House McGrath Foundation
PBI	One Health Organisation
PBI	Outcare
PBI	Oz Harvest
C&PAF	Peter Mac Foundation
PBI	Police Citizens Youth Clubs NSW
PBI	Quantum Support Services
CI	Queen Victoria Women's Centre
HPC	Queensland Aboriginal and Islander Health Council
PBI	Queensland Advocacy Inc.
PBI	Reconnexion
CI	Relationships Australia
CI	Relationships Australia NSW
CI	Results International
PBI	Royal Flying Doctor Service
CI	RSL National
CI	RSPCA Qld
PBI	Sacred Heart Mission St Kilda Inc.
PBI	St Vincent de Paul Society, Canberra

PBI	Second Bite
PBI	Sexual Assault Support Services
CI	Silver Chain Foundation
PBI	Springvale Community Aid
PBI	Steps Group Australia
PBI	Surf Lifesaving NSW
PBI	The Australian Kidney Foundation
PBI	The Australian Lung Foundation
PBI	The Benevolent Society
PBI	The First Step Program
PBI	The Lowitja Institute
CI	The Royal Institution of Australia
PBI	Transplant Australia
CI	United States Study Centre, University of Sydney
PBI	Uniting Communities
PBI	Variety Queensland Inc.
PBI	Villa Maria Society
PBI	Volunteering Australia
PBI	Water Aid Australia
PBI	Wesley Mission
PBI	Windana Drug and Alcohol Recovery
CI	Women's Children's Hospital Foundation
PBI	Workways Australia
CI	YMCA Community Housing
PBI	Youth and Family Services (Logan)
PBI	Youth Focus
PBI	YWCA Australia
PBI	Working it out

Register of Environmental Organisations	
CI	Australian Conservation Foundation
Other IC	Aid Watch
CI	Australian Wildlife Conservancy
CI	Birdlife Australia Ltd
CI	Carbon Neutral Ltd
CI	Conservation Council of South Australia
CI	Earthwatch Institute
CI	Foundation for National Parks & Wildlife
CI	Gondwana Link
CI	Greenpeace
CI	Keep Australia Beautiful (NSW)
CI	Mallee Sustainable Farming
Not specified	Nature Conservation Council of NSW
CI	NQ Dry Tropics
CI	Planet Ark Environmental Foundation
CI	Port Phillip EcoCentre Inc.
CI	Responsible Forest Management Ltd
CI	Save Foundation Australia
Not a charity	SEQ Catchments
CI	South West Goulburn Landcare
CI	Tasmanian Land Conservancy
CI	The Climate Institute
CI	The Keep Australia Beautiful Council
CI	The Orangutan Project
CI	Trees for Life Inc.
CI	Whale and Dolphin Conservation Society
CI	World Wide Fund for Nature Australia

Register of Approved Overseas Aid Funds	
CI	The Foundation for Development Cooperation
CI	Lowy Institute for International Policy
PBI	Adventist Development and Relief Agency
CI	African Enterprise Limited
Not a charity	ASHM International Aid
CI	Asian Aid Organisation
CI	Lasallian Foundation
PBI	Care Australia
CI	Disaster Aid Australia
PBI	ActionAid
CI	International Children's Care
CI	Mahbobas Promise
CI	Mercy Ships
PBI	Opportunity International
PBI	Oxfam Australia
PBI	RedR Australia
Charity	SIMaid Trust
CI	Anglican Overseas Aid
PBI	The Fred Hollows Foundation
CI	World Youth International
PBI	World Education Australia
PBI	World Vision Australia

Register of Cultural Organisations	
CI	National Gallery of Australia
CI	Museums Australia
Charity	Art Gallery NSW
PBI	Australian Children's Music Foundation
CI	Australian Youth Orchestra
CI	National Institute of Dramatic Art
CI	Opera Australia
CI	Sydney Dance Company
CI	Sydney Opera House Trust
CI	Queensland Ballet
Register of Harm Prevention Charitable Institutions	
CI	All Together Now
PBI	Project Respect
CI	Dunn & Lewis Youth Development
CI	White Ribbon Foundation Australia
CI	Beacon Foundation
Health Promotion Charities	
HPC	Action on Smoking and Health Australia
PBI	Asthma Foundation Victoria
HPC	Heart Foundation
PBI	Diabetes Australia
HPC	Life Education Australia
HPC	Walter+Eliza Hall Institute Medical
HPC	Foundation for Alcohol Research
HPC	Murdoch Children's Research Institute
HPC	Think Pink
HPC	Beyondblue

Education named in the Act	
Not listed	Australian Human Rights Education Fund
CI	The Constitution Education Fund
Industry named in the Act	
CI	Australian Business Week Limited
CI	WorldSkills Australia
Research named in the Act	
CI	Centre for Independent Studies
CI	The Grattan Institute
Charity	The Menzies Research Centre
Charity	The Sir Earle Page Memorial Trust
Charity	The Chifley Research Centre Ltd
CI	The Green Institute Limited
CI	The Trustee for Institute of Public Affairs Research Trust
Welfare named in the Act	
PBI	Amnesty International Australia
CI	Reconciliation Australia Limited
PBI	International Social Service
Family named in the Act	
Charity	Playgroup Australia Limited

Health named in the Act	
Not a charity	Cancer Australia
Other named in the Act	
CI	Social Ventures Australia Limited
Community Legal Centres	
PBI	Caxton Street Legal Centre

Appendix 2

Awareness calendar

February 2013

1-7 February	World Interfaith Harmony Week
1-28 February	Febfast
	International CHD Awareness Month
	Ovarian Cancer Awareness Month
	Heart Research Australia
2 February	World Wetlands Day
4 February	World Cancer Day
5 February	Safer Internet Day
6 February	International Zero Tolerance to Female Genital Mutilation
9-24 February	The Sustainable Living Festival
10-16 February	Duchenne Awareness Week
13 February	World Radio Day
14 February	International CHD Awareness Day
	National Condom Day
	Heart Research Day
	V-DAY
	1 Billion Rising
14-21 February	Sexual Health Awareness Week
20 February	World Harmony Day
	World Day of Social Justice
21 February	International Mother Language Day

22 February	Boardies Day World Thinking Day
24 Feb- 3 March	Donate Life Week
25 February	International Corporate Philanthropy Day
27 February	Teal Ribbon Day

March 2013

1 March	Schools Clean Up Day
3 March	Clean Up Australia Day
4-11 March	Hello Parks Week
8 March	International Women's Day
9 March	World Naked Bike Ride
10-16 March	World Glaucoma Week
10-17 March	Multiple Birth Awareness Week
11-17 March	Salt Awareness Week
14 March	World Kidney Day
14-17 March	World's Greatest Shave
15 March	National Day of Action against Bullying and Violence
17-24 March	National Playgroup Week
18-22 March	National Wound Awareness Week
18-24 March	Cultural Diversity Week
20 March	International Day of Happiness
21 March	World Poetry Day World Down Syndrome Day Harmony Day Intenational Day Elimination of Racial Discrimination

	World Forestry Day
	Close The Gap Day
21-27 March	Week of Solidarity with the Peoples Struggling against Racism and Racial Discrimination
22 March	Ride2School Day
	World Water Day
23 March	World Meteorological Day
	Earth Hour
24 March	International Day for the Right to the Truth concerning Gross Human Rights Violations and for the Dignity of Victims
	World Tuberculosis Day
	Run for the Kids
25 March	International Day of Remembrance of the Victims of Slavery and the Transatlantic Slave Trade
	International Day of Solidarity with Detained and Missing Staff
26 March	Purple Day (Epilepsy)
31 March	Neighbour Day

April 2013

1-30 April	Drawtism (Autism) 2013
2 April	World Autism Awareness Day
4 April	International Day for Mine Awareness and Assistance in Mine Action
	World Stray Animals Day
5-14 April	National Youth Week

7 April	Be alarmed! Change your smoke alarm battery!!
	Day of Remembrance Victims of the Rwanda Genocide
	World Health Day
10 April	Youth Homelessness Matters Day
11 April	World Parkinson's Day
17 April	World Haemophilia Day
17-23 April	International Creativity & Innovation Week
18 April	World Heritage Day
	Drawtism For Laughs (Autism)
22 April	Earth Day
	International Mother Earth Day
23 April	World Book and Copyright Day
24 April	World YWCA Day
	International Guide Dog Day
25 April	Pay it Forward Day (Random Acts of Kindness)
	Anzac Day
	World Malaria Day
26 April	World Intellectual Property Day
28 April	World Day for Safety and Health at Work
29 April	Day of Remembrance for all Victims of Chemical Warfare

May 2013

1 May	Kiss Goodbye to MS
1-7 May	Tourette Syndrome Awareness Week
1-31 May	Crohns & Colitis Awareness Month
	NF Awareness Month (Neurofibromatosis)

	Mindful in May (Charity Water)
	Miracle (Babies) Month of May
3 May	World Press Freedom Day
5 May	International Midwives Day
5-11 May	State Education Week
	Heart Week
6 May	International No Diet Day
6-11 May	International Composting Awareness Week
6-12 May	UN Global Road Safety Week
	National Family Day Care Week
7 May	World Asthma Day
8 May	World Red Cross Day
10 May	World Lupus Day
10-12 May	Disconnect to Reconnect
11-12 May	World Migratory Bird Day
12 May	International Nurses Day
	International Fibromyalgia Awareness Day
	Mother's Day Classic (Breast Cancer Research)
	International ME/CFS Awareness Day
	Mother's Day
12-18 May	Schizophrenia Awareness Week
13-19 May	National Volunteer Week
15 May	International Day of Families
17 May	World Hypertension Day
	International Day Against Homophobia
19 May	RSPCA Million Paws Walk
19-25 May	National Palliative Care Week

21 May	World Day for Cultural Diversity for Dialogue and Development
21-26 May	Thyroid Awareness Week
21-27 May	Spinal Health Week
22 May	International Day for Biological Diversity
23 May	Australia's Biggest Morning Tea (Cancer Council)
	World Turtle Day
24 May	Wear a Bear Day (Princess Margaret Hospital Foundation)
	National Walk Safely To School Day
25 May	World Thyroid Day
	International Missing Children's Day
25-31 May	Week of Solidarity with the Peoples of Non-Self-Governing Territories
26 May	World Autoimmune Arthritis Day
	National Sorry Day
26 May-1 June	Kidney Health Awareness Week
	Macular Degeneration Awareness Week
27 May-2 June	Making Music Being Well Week
29 May	White Wreath Day (Suicide Victims)
	World MS Day
31 May	65 Roses Day
	World No-Tobacco Day

June 2013

1 June	National Whale Day
1-8 June	Medical Research Week
1-30 June	Bowel Cancer Awareness Month
1-30 June	CMV Awareness Month
2 June	International Gratitude Day (Chronic illness)
3-4 June	Mabo Day
4 June	International Day of Innocent Children Victims of Aggression
5 June	World Environment Day
	Red Aussie Apple Day (Bowel Cancer)
7 June	CafeSmart (Homeless)
8 June	World Oceans Day
10-16 June	International Men's Health Week
12 June	World Day Against Child Labour
14 June	World Blood Donor Day
15 June	World Elder Abuse Awareness Day
16-22 June	Drug Action Week
	Refugee Week
17 June	World Day to Combat Desertification and Drought
17-21 June	Philanthropy Week
20 June	World Refugee Day
21 June	MND Global Day (Motor Neurone Disease)
23 June	MS Brissie to the Bay Bike Ride (Multiple Sclerosis)
	World Elder Abuse Awareness Day
	United Nations Public Service Day
	International Widow's Day

24-30 June	World Continence Week
25 June	Day of the Seafarer
26 June	International Day against Drug Abuse and Illicit Trafficking
	International Day in Support of Victims of Torture
28 June	Red Nose Day (SIDS)
29 June	World Scleroderma Day
30 June	Social Media Day

July 2013

1-31 July	JulEYE
6 July	International Day of Cooperatives
7-14 July	NAIDOC Week
11 July	World Population Day
14-20 July	National Diabetes Week
15-20 July	National Farm Safety Week
18 July	Nelson Mandela International Day
22-28 July	National Pain Week 2013
26 July	Stress Down Day
	Schools Tree Day
28 July	National Tree Day
	World Hepatitis Day
28 July-3 Aug	National Missing Persons Week
30 July	International Day of Friendship
31 July	National Stepfamily Awareness Day

August 2013

1-7 August	World Breastfeeding Week
1-31 August	Honey Money Days (End Bear Bile Farming)
	Tradies National Health Month
2 August	Jeans for Genes Day
3-10 August	OCD and Anxiety Disorders Week
4-10 August	National Healthy Bones Week
5-11 August	Homeless Persons Week
9 August	International Day of the World's Indigenous People
10-18 August	National Science Week
11-17 August	National EOS Awareness Week (Eosinophilic Gastrointestinal)
12 August	Cupcake Day (RSCPA)
	International Youth Day
12-18 August	Haemochromatosis Awareness Week
17-23 August	Children's Book Week
19 August	World Humanitarian Day
19-25 August	Keep Australia Beautiful Week
23 August	Daffodil Day (Cancer)
	International Day for the Remembrance of the Slave Trade and Its Abolition
25 August	Walk in the Park (Parkinson's)
25-31 August	Hearing Awareness Week
28 August	National Meals on Wheels Day
29 August	International Day Against Nuclear Tests
30 August	International Day of the Victims of Enforced Disappearances
31 August	International Overdose Awareness Day

September 2013

1 September	Wattle Day
	Gold Bow Day (Thyroid)
	Father's Day
	Big Red Kidney Walk
1-7 September	Legacy Week
	Spina Bifida Awareness Week
1-8 September	Adult Learners' Week
1-30 September	Biodiversity Month
	Prostate Cancer Awareness Month
	Save the Koala Month
	Heart Foundation Doorknock Appeal
	Foster Care Month
1 September-16 October	Tiwest Night Stalk (Native and Feral Animals)
3 September	National Flag Day
4 September	National Health and PE Day
5 September	Cancer Council Walk To Work Day
6 September	Footy Colours Day (Cancer)
7 September	White Balloon Day (Child Sexual Assault)
8 September	Sustainable House Day
	International Literacy Day
9 September	International Fetal Alcohol Spectrum Disorder Awareness Day
9-15 September	National Stroke Week
10 September	World Suicide Prevention Day
12 September	R U OK? Day (Suicide Prevention)

13 September	The 13th "Don't Be One Of The Unlucky Ones" (Fire Prevention)
15 September	International Day of Democracy
16 September	International Day for the Preservation of the Ozone Layer
16-22 September	Herbal Medicine Week
17 September	Australian Citizenship Day
	World Parks Day
20-21 September	Clean up the World Weekend
21 September	World Alzheimer's Day
	International Day of Peace
22 September	World Carfree Day
	International Rhino Day
23-28 September	Dementia Awareness Week
26 September	World Maritime Day
27 September	World Tourism Day
28 September	World Rabies Day
	World Heart Day
29 September	National Police Remembrance Day
	World Rivers Day

October 2013

1 October	International Day of Older Persons
1-31 October	Ocsober (Drug Misuse)
	Pink Ribbon Breakfast Campaign (Breast Cancer)
2 October	International Day of Non-Violence
4 October	World Smile Day

	Happy Tails Day (RSPCA)
	World Animal Day
4-10 October	World Space Week
4-13 October	National Organic Week
5 October	World Teachers' Day
6-12 October	Mental Health Week
	Fire Prevention Week
7 October	World Habitat Day
9 October	World Post Day
10 October	World Mental Health Day
	World Sight Day
11 October	International Day of the Girl Child
11-19 October	Anti Poverty Week
12 October	International Arthritis Day
13 October	International Day for Natural Disaster Reduction
13-19 October	Carers Week
14-20 October	National Nutrition Week
15 October	Global Handwashing Day
	International Day of Rural Women
16 October	World Food Day
	Ride2Work Day
17 October	International Day for the Eradication of Poverty
18 October	World Vasectomy Day
20 October	World Osteoporosis Day
20-26 October	National Water Week
20-28 October	Children's Week
23 October	Big Breakfast (Thyroid)

24 October	United Nations Day
	World Development Information Day
24-30 October	Disarmament Week
26 October	Garage Sale Trail
27 October	World Day for Audiovisual Heritage
28 October	Pink Ribbon Day (Cancer)

November 2013

1 November	World Vegan Day
1-30 November	Movember (Prostate Cancer and Depression)
	Lung Health Awareness Month
3-9 November	National Others Week
6 November	International Day for Preventing the Exploitation of the Environment in War and Armed Conflict
8 November	National Sunnies Day (Eye Health)
10 November	World Science Day for Peace and Development
10-16 November	International Week of Science and Peace
11 November	Remembrance Day
11-17 November	National Recycling Week
12 November	Thank U NICU Day (Neonatal Intensive Care)
	World Pneumonia Day
14 November	World Diabetes Day
16 November	International Day for Tolerance
17 November	World Day of Remembrance for Road Traffic Victims
20 November	Universal Children's Day
	World Chronic Obstructive Pulmonary Disease Day
	Africa Industrialization Day

21 November	World Philosophy Day
	World Television Day
25 November	International Day for the Elimination of Violence against Women
	White Ribbon Day (Violence Prevention)
29 November	International Day of Solidarity with the Palestinian People

December 2013

1 December	World AIDS Day
2 December	International Day for the Abolition of Slavery
3 December	International Day of Persons with Disabilities
5 December	International Volunteer Day for Economic and Social Development
7 December	International Civil Aviation Day
9 December	International Anti-Corruption Day
10 December	Human Rights Day
11 December	International Mountain Day
18 December	International Migrants Day
19 December	United Nations Day for South-South Cooperation
20 December	International Human Solidarity Day

Source: ourcommunitycalendar.com.au and various other calendars.

Appendix 3

UN years and decades

Year	
2014	International Year of Small Island Developing States
	International Year of Crystallography
	International Year of Family Farming
2013	International Year of Water Cooperation
	International Year of Quinoa
2012	International Year of Cooperatives
	International Year of Sustainable Energy for All
2011	International Year for People of African Descent
	International Year of Chemistry
	International Year of Forests
2010	International Year of Youth (August 2010 — August 2011)
	International Year for the Rapprochement of Cultures
	International Year of Biodiversity
	International Year of the Seafarer
2009	International Year of Reconciliation
	International Year of Natural Fibres
	International Year of Human Rights Learning
	International Year of Astronomy
	Year of the Gorilla (UNEP and UNESCO)
2008	International Year of Planet Earth
	International Year of Languages
	International Year of Sanitation
	International Year of the Potato
2007–08	International Polar Year (WMO)
2006	International Year of Deserts and Desertification

2005	International Year of Microcredit
	International Year for Sport and Physical Education
	International Year of Physics
2004	International Year to Commemorate the Struggle against Slavery and its Abolition
	International Year of Rice
2003	Year of Kyrgyz Statehood
	International Year of Freshwater
2002	United Nations Year for Cultural Heritage
	International Year of Mountains
	International Year of Ecotourism
2001	United Nations Year of Dialogue among Civilizations
	International Year of Volunteers
	International Year of Mobilization against Racism, Racial Discrimination, Xenophobia and Related Intolerance
2000	International Year of Thanksgiving
	International Year for the Culture of Peace
1999	International Year of Older Persons
1998	International Year of the Ocean
1996	International Year for the Eradication of Poverty
1995	United Nations Year for Tolerance
	World Year of Peoples' Commemoration of the Victims of the Second World War
1994	International Year of the Family
	International Year of Sport and the Olympic Ideal
1993	International Year for the World's Indigenous People
1992	International Space Year
1990	International Literacy Year
1987	International Year of Shelter for The Homeless
1986	International Year of Peace

1985	Year of The United Nations
	International Youth Year: Participation, Development, Peace
1983	World Communications Year: Development of Communication Infrastructures
1982	International Year of Mobilization for Sanctions Against South Africa
1981	International Year for Disabled Persons
1979	International Year of The Child
1978–79	International Anti-Apartheid Year
1975	International Women's Year
1974	World Population Year
1971	International Year for Action to Combat Racism and Racial Prejudice
1970	International Education Year
1968	International Year for Human Rights
1967	International Tourist Year
1965	International Co-operation Year
1961	International Health and Medical Research Year
1959–60	World Refugee Year

Decade

2014–2024	United Nations Decade of Sustainable Energy for All
2011–2020	Third International Decade for the Eradication of Colonialism
	United Nations Decade on Biodiversity
	Decade of Action for Road Safety
2010–2020	United Nations Decade for Deserts and the Fight against Desertification

2008–2017	Second United Nations Decade for the Eradication of Poverty
2006–2016	Decade of Recovery and Sustainable Development of the Affected Regions (third decade after the Chernobyl disaster)
2005–2015	International Decade for Action, "Water for Life"
2005–2014	United Nations Decade of Education for Sustainable Development
	Second International Decade of the World's Indigenous People
2003–2012	United Nations Literacy Decade: Education for All
2001–2010	International Decade for a Culture of Peace and Non-violence for the Children of the World
	Decade to Roll Back Malaria in Developing Countries, Particularly in Africa
	Second International Decade for the Eradication of Colonialism
1997–2006	Decade for The Eradication for Poverty
1995–2004	Decade for Human Rights Education
1994–2004	Decade of the World's Indigenous People
1993–2003	Third Decade to Combat Racism and Racial Discrimination
1991–2000	Second Industrial Development Decade for Africa
	Second Transport and Communications Decade in Africa
	United Nations Decade Against Drug Abuse
	Fourth United Nations Development Decade
1990–2000	International Decade for the Eradification (sic) of Colonialism
1990–1999	United Nations Decade of International Law
	International Decade for Natural Disaster Reduction
1990s	Third Disarmament Decade
1988–1997	World Decade for Cultural Development

1983–1993	Second Decade to Combat Racism and Racial Discrimination
1983–1992	United Nations Decade for Disabled Persons
1981–1990	International Drinking Water Supply and Sanitation Decade
	Third United Nations Development Decade
1980–1990	Second Disarmament Decade
1980s	Industrial Development Decade for Africa
1978–1988	Transport and Communications Decade for Africa
1976–1985	United Nations Decade for Women: Equality, Development and Peace
1973–1983	Decade to Combat Racism and Racial Discrimination
1971–1980	Second United Nations Development Decade
1970s	Disarmament Decade
1960–1970	United Nations Development Decade

Sources: United Nations, http://www.un.org/en/events/observances/years.shtml and United Nations http://www.un.org/en/events/observances/decades.shtml accessed 28 July 2013.

Appendix 4

Social determinants of health lobby

Each of these made a submission to the Senate Community Affairs References Committee, Australia's domestic response to the World Health Organization's Commission on Social Determinants of Health report 'Closing the gap within a generation', March 2013.

Social Determinants of Health Alliance

Beyondblue

Gippsland Women's Health Service

Hume Whittlesea Primary Care Partnership

Women's Health Victoria

Southgate Institute, Flinders University

Victorian Healthcare Association

Centre for Health Equity Training Research and Evaluation

Victorian Dental and Oral Health Therapist Association Inc

Women's Health West

Consumers Health Forum of Australia

Public Health Information Development Unit

Public Health Association of Australia

Macarthur Future Food Forum

HealthWest Partnership

Australian College of Nursing

Catholic Health Australia

Doctors for the Environment Australia Inc.

Family Planning NSW

Tasmanian Department of Health and Human Services

Merri Community Health Services Limited

Community Indicators Victoria

Tasmanian Social Determinants of Health Advocacy Network

Australian Federation of AIDS Organisations

Australian Health Promotion Association

Australian Healthcare and Hospitals Association

Australian Health Care Reform Alliance

St Vincent's Health Australia

Australian Nursing Federation

Australian Bureau of Statistics

The Pharmacy Guild of Australia

Australian Institute of Health and Welfare

Municipal Association of Victoria

Western Region Health Centre Ltd

Health in All Policies Collaboration

Gay and Lesbian Rights Lobby

Australian Women's Health Network

National LGBTI Health Alliance

Councils of Social Service

The Royal Australasian College of Physicians

Cancer Council Australia and the National Heart Foundation of Australia

Centre for Women's Health, Gender and Society

The Australian Psychological Society Limited

Victorian Gay and Lesbian Rights Lobby Policy Working Group

Australian Association of Social Workers

Appendix 5

Characteristics of charity members

Prepared by Lauren Vogel

The results outlined in this report address four independent variables relating to membership of charitable organisations taken from the 2007 and 2005 Australian Survey of Social Attitudes.

The first independent variable is from the 2007 survey and will be referred to as 'charity membership 2007' (ref: N1, Are you an active member of any of the following organisations, an inactive member or not a member? where 'charitable organisation' was one option). This independent variable of 'charity membership 2007' has three levels: 'active member'; 'inactive member'; and 'don't belong'. See table 1 for descriptives.

Table 1. Sample according to 'charity membership 2007'

	Charity membership status	Frequency	Per cent	Valid Per cent	Cumulative Per cent
Valid	Active member	384	4.7	16.8	16.8
	Inactive member	281	3.5	12.3	29.1
	Don't belong	1624	20.0	70.9	100.0
	Total	2289	28.1	100.0	
Missing	Not asked	5550	68.2		
	Missing	294	3.6		
	Total	5844	71.9		
Total		8133	100.0		

The remaining three independent variables are taken from the 2005 survey (ref: B5, We would like to ask if you are a member of any of the groups and organisations listed below. If you are a member, please try to tell us whether you are an officeholder, an active member or just a member). There were three organisations that may be considered as broadly charitable: a group that promotes rights (referred to as 'rights group 2005'); an environmental group (referred to as 'environmental group 2005'); and an aid organisation (referred to as 'aid organisation 2005'). There were very few people who indicated that they were officeholders in each of these three organisations; thus 'officeholder' and 'active member' were combined to form the variable 'active member'. As a result, each of these three independent variables ('rights group 2005', 'environmental group 2005', and 'aid organisation 2005') has three levels: 'active member'; 'member'; and 'don't belong'. See tables 2-4 for descriptives.

Table 2. Sample according to 'rights group 2005'

	Rights group membership status	**Frequency**	**Per cent**	**Valid Per cent**	**Cumulative Per cent**
Valid	Don't belong	1830	46.9	95.3	95.3
	Member	65	1.7	3.4	98.7
	Active Member	25	.6	1.3	100.0
	Total	1920	49.2	100.0	
Missing	Not asked	1914	49.1		
	Missing	68	1.7		
	Total	1982	50.8		
Total		3902	100.0		

Table 3. Sample according to 'environmental group 2005'

	Environmental group membership status	Frequency	Per cent	Valid Per cent	Cumulative Per cent
Valid	Don't belong	1769	45.3	92.0	92.0
	Member	134	3.4	7.0	99.0
	Active Member	19	.5	1.0	100.0
	Total	1922	49.3	100.0	
Missing	Not asked	1914	49.1		
	Missing	66	1.7		
	Total	1980	50.7		
Total		3902	100.0		

Table 4. Sample according to 'aid organisation 2005'

	Aid organisation membership status	Frequency	Per cent	Valid Per cent	Cumulative Per cent
Valid	Don't belong	1694	43.4	88.4	88.4
	Member	190	4.9	9.9	98.3
	Active Member	32	.8	1.7	100.0
	Total	1916	49.1	100.0	
Missing	Not asked	1914	49.1		
	Missing	72	1.8		
	Total	1986	50.9		
Total		3902	100.0		

The sample size for 'active member' was still relatively small in each of three types of groups, despite combining the two categories of most active memberships. Many of the analyses have different methods for dealing with unequal *n*; the most conservative option was used in each case, as is recommended by several researchers.

Lastly, preliminary analyses were conducted in order to check that the data met assumptions of normality, homogeneity, and covariance. In most cases the data met the required assumptions, or otherwise were within the bounds as specified by Tabachnick and Fidell.[1] In some cases, where non-normality was present, a nonparametric alternative was performed. In all cases the findings were identical and so the parametric test is reported.

Demographics according to charity membership

Social group perception – 2007

A between subjects analysis of covariance (ANCOVA) was conducted on social group perception (ref: O2 – In our society there are groups which tend to be towards the top and groups which tend to be towards the bottom. Where would you place yourself on this scale?). On this social group scale the bottom was 1 and the top was 10. The independent variable was 'charity membership 2007' and the covariate was age (year born).

Results of the ANCOVA indicated that age was not a significant covariate, where $F(1, 2023) = .13$, $p = .724$. However, self-placement on this social group scale varied significantly with charity membership, with $F(2, 2023) = 8.02$, $p < .001$, partial $\eta^2 = .008$.[2] Follow-up pairwise comparisons with a Bonferroni correction for multiple comparisons[3]

---

1 Tabachnick. B., & Linda Fidell. L. (2007). *Using Multivariate Statistics* (5th ed). Boston, MA: Pearson Education.

2 Partial η^2 is a measure of effect size or the proportion of variance explained in the dependent variables by the independent variable. In this instance, .008 of variance in the scores on the social group scale was explained by charity membership (after the variance explained by age was controlled). Eight per cent of the variance in the social group scale was explained by charity membership.

3 Conducting multiple pairwise comparisons leads to an inflated Type I error rate (incorrect rejection of a true null hypothesis). A Bonferroni correction is a conservative method of counteracting this effect. It divides the α value for significance (typically .05) by the number of pairwise comparisons. In order for a mean difference to be a significant difference, it must meet a stricter criterion (e.g. the significant α value is set at .008 instead of the standard .05).

revealed that people who were members of a charity ('active member' and 'inactive member') placed themselves significantly higher on this social group scale than those people who were not members of a charity ('don't belong'), although the mean difference was quite small. See table 5 for means, standard deviations and sample size.

Table 5. Social group self-placement descriptive statistics according to charity membership

Charity membership status	Mean	Std. Deviation	N
Active member	6.21	1.448	345
Inactive member	6.23	1.528	260
Don't belong	5.91	1.591	1460
Total	6.00	1.571	2065

Personal income – 2007

A between subjects analysis of covariance (ANCOVA) was subsequently performed on gross personal income (ref: P31 – what is your gross personal income, before tax or other deductions, from all sources?). On this scale 1 was nil income and 14 was $2,000 or more earned per week. The independent variable was 'charity membership 2007' and the covariate was age (year born).

The covariate, age, was significantly associated with gross personal income, where $F(1, 2044) = 32.10$, $p < .001$, $\eta^2 = .015$. Results indicated that, after adjustment for age, gross personal income varied significantly by charity membership, with $F(2, 2044) = 6.00$, $p < .01$, partial $\eta 2 = .006$. Follow up pairwise comparisons with a Bonferroni correction for multiple comparisons revealed that inactive members of charities earned significantly more than both active charity members and people who did not belong to a charity (see table 6 for descriptives). In these descriptive statistics, a score of 9 on the income scale equated to $600-699 per week whilst a score of 8 equated to $500-599 per week.

Table 6. Gross annual income descriptive statistics according to charity membership

Charity membership status	Adjusted Mean	Std. Error	Mean	Std. Deviation	N
Active member	8.456a	.196	8.37	3.633	346
Inactive member	9.328a	.226	9.38	3.558	259
Don't belong	8.501a	.096	8.51	3.680	1443
Total			8.60	3.667	2048

a. Covariates appearing in the model are evaluated at the following values: v559 R: year born = 1957.61.

Educational attainment – 2007

A chi-square analysis was conducted on charity membership and highest level of high school education achieved (ref: P4). The options 'did not go to school' and 'still at high school' were excluded from the analysis due to low cell counts (including them would make the results of the chi-square unreliable).

The results indicated that there was a significant association between charity membership and high school, χ^2 (4, N = 2192) = 22.36, $p < .001$, although Cramer's *V* indicated that the strength of the association was weak (*V* = .071). Examination of the adjusted standardised residuals[4] revealed that people who did not belong to a charity were more likely to not have completed high school or to have only completed high school up to year 10. They were also less likely to have completed high school up to year 12. In contrast, inactive members of a charity were more likely to have completed year 12 and less likely to not have completed high school. Active members of a charity had expected counts across the dependent variable. See table 7 for descriptives.

4 The residual is the difference between the expected count and actual count in each cell of the chi square analysis.

Table 7. Chi-square results – high school educational attainment by charity membership status

Charity membership status		Highest level of high school education completed: Did NOT complete High School to Year 10	Completed High School to Year 10	Completed High School to Year 12	Total
Active member	Count	41	110	217	368
	Expected Count	47.5	117.5	203.0	368.0
	% within Charity membership status	11.1%	29.9%	59.0%	100.0%
	Adjusted Residual	-1.1	-.9	1.6	
Inactive member	Count	19	74	178	271
	Expected Count	35.0	86.5	149.5	271.0
	% within Charity membership status	7.0%	27.3%	65.7%	100.0%
	Adjusted Residual	-3.1	-1.7	3.7	
Don't belong	Count	223	516	814	1553
	Expected Count	200.5	495.9	856.6	1553.0
	% within Charity membership status	14.4%	33.2%	52.4%	100.0%
	Adjusted Residual	3.2	2.0	-4.0	
Total	Count	283	700	1209	2192
	Expected Count	283.0	700.0	1209.0	2192.0
	% within Charity membership status	12.9%	31.9%	55.2%	100.0%

A chi-square analysis was also conducted on charity membership and highest level of education achieved since leaving high school (ref: P5). The results indicated that there was a significant association between charity membership and high school, χ^2 (8, N = 2167) = 41.35, $p < .001$, although Cramer's V indicated that the strength of the association was weak (V = .098). Examination of the adjusted standardised residuals revealed that people who did not belong to a charity were more likely to have no post-high school qualifications. If they did go on to education after high school it was more likely to be a trade qualification or apprenticeship and less likely to be a university degree (bachelor or postgraduate). In contrast, both active and inactive members of a charity were less likely to have a trade qualification or apprenticeship. In addition, inactive members were more likely to have a university degree (bachelor and postgraduate) and were less likely to have no post-high school qualification. See table 8 for descriptives.

A between subjects ANCOVA was conducted for each independent variable ('rights groups 2005', environmental group 2005' and 'aid organisation 2005') on gross personal income (ref: I33, what is your gross personal income, before tax or other deductions, from all sources?). On this scale 1 was nil income and 14 was $2,000 or more earned per week. Age was the covariate in each analysis.

Table 8. Chi-square results – post-high school educational attainment by charity membership status

Charity membership status		Highest level of education completed since leaving school					Total
		None	**Trade qualification or apprenticeship**	**Certificate or Diploma (TAFE or business college)**	**Bachelor Degree (including Honours)**	**Postgraduate Degree or Postgraduate Diploma**	
Active member	Count	102	41	106	67	48	364
	Expected Count	115.9	53.6	100.3	55.3	39.0	364.0
	% within Charity membership status	28.0%	11.3%	29.1%	18.4%	13.2%	100.0%
	Adjusted Residual	-1.7	-2.0	.7	1.9	1.7	
Inactive member	Count	65	28	72	60	38	263
	Expected Count	83.7	38.7	72.5	39.9	28.2	263.0
	% within Charity membership status	24.7%	10.6%	27.4%	22.8%	14.4%	100.0%
	Adjusted Residual	-2.6	-2.0	-.1	3.7	2.1	
Don't belong	Count	523	250	419	202	146	1540
	Expected Count	490.4	226.7	424.3	233.8	164.9	1540.0
	% within Charity membership status	34.0%	16.2%	27.2%	13.1%	9.5%	100.0%
	Adjusted Residual	3.3	3.1	-.6	-4.2	-2.9	
Total	Count	690	319	597	329	232	2167
	Expected Count	690.0	319.0	597.0	329.0	232.0	2167.0
	% within Charity membership status	31.8%	14.7%	27.5%	15.2%	10.7%	100.0%

Personal income – 2005

'Rights group 2005': Results indicated that age was a significant covariate, with $F(1, 1759) = 43.66$, $p < .001$, partial $\eta^2 = .024$. After adjustment for age, gross personal income did not vary significantly according to membership status of a rights group, with $F(2, 1759) = 1.16$, $p = .315$. See table 9 for descriptives.

Table 9. Gross annual income descriptive statistics according to membership of a rights group

Rights group membership status	Adjusted Mean	Std. Error	Mean	Std. Deviation	N
Don't belong	8.013a	.088	8.01	3.671	1679
Member	8.571a	.464	8.62	3.800	61
Active Member Total	8.760a	.756	8.74	3.137	23
Total			8.04	3.670	1763

a. Covariates appearing in the model are evaluated at the following values: v381 R: year of birth = 55.74.

'Environmental group 2005': Results indicated that age was a significant covariate, with $F(2, 1759) = 2.57$, $p = .077$. After adjustment for age, gross personal income did not vary significantly according to membership status of an environmental group, where $F(2, 1759) = 2.57$, $p = .077$. See table 10 for descriptives.

Table 10. Gross annual income descriptive statistics according to membership of an environmental group

Environmental group membership status	Adjusted Mean	Std. Error	Mean	Std. Deviation	N
Don't belong	7.978a	.090	7.97	3.664	1621
Member	8.689a	.323	8.76	3.785	126
Active Member	8.753a	.906	8.56	2.476	16
Total			8.04	3.668	1763

a. Covariates appearing in the model are evaluated at the following values: v381 R: Year of birth = 55.72.

'Aid organisation 2005': Results indicated that age was a significant covariate, with $F(1, 1753) = 43.82, p < .001, \eta 2 = .024$. After adjustment for age, gross personal income varied significantly according to membership status of an aid organisation, $F(1, 1753) = 5.91, p < .01$, partial $\eta 2 = .007$. Follow up pairwise comparisons with a Bonferroni correction for multiple comparisons revealed that people who did not belong to a charity earned significantly less than those people who were members of a charity. Active members did not differ significantly. See table 11 for descriptives.

Table 11. Gross annual income descriptive statistics according to membership of an aid organisation

Aid organisation membership status	Adjusted Mean	Std. Error	Mean	Std. Deviation	N
Don't belong	7.932a	.092	7.93	3.687	1546
Member	8.841a	.268	8.90	3.528	182
Active Member	8.870a	.672	8.76	3.101	29
Total			8.04	3.673	1757

a. Covariates appearing in the model are evaluated at the following values: v381 R: Year of birth = 55.77.

Perception of family income – 2005

A between subjects ANCOVA was conducted for each independent variable ('rights groups 2005', 'environmental group 2005' and 'aid organisation 2005') on family income perception (ref: H4, compared with Australian families in general, would you say your family income is below average, average or above average. This scale ranged from 'far below average' (1) to 'far above average' (5). Age was the covariate in each analysis.

'Rights group 2005': Results indicated that age was not a significant covariate, with $F(1, 1863) = 2.62, p = .106$. Further, perception of family income did not vary significantly according to membership status of a rights group, $F(2, 1863) = .23, p = .795$. See table 12 for descriptives.

Table 12. Perception of family income according to membership of a rights group

Rights group membership status	Mean	Std. Deviation	N
Don't belong	3.14	1.307	1778
Member	3.14	1.283	64
Active Member	3.32	1.547	25
Total	3.14	1.309	1867

'Environmental group 2005': Results indicated that age was not a significant covariate, with $F(1, 1865) = 3.12, p = .078$. Perception of family income did not vary significantly according to membership status of an environmental group, $F(2, 1865) = .43, p = .431$. See table 13 for descriptives.

Table 13. Perception of family income according to membership of an environmental group

Environmental group membership status	Mean	Std. Deviation	N
Don't belong	3.13	1.309	1718
Member	3.28	1.233	133
Active Member	3.28	1.809	18
Total	3.14	1.309	1869

'Aid organisation 2007': Results indicated that age was not a significant covariate, $F(1, 1860) = 3.22, p = .073$. Perception of family income varied significantly according to membership status of an aid organisation, where $F(2, 1860) = 5.55, p < .004$, partial $\eta^2 = .006$. Post-hoc tests with a Bonferroni correction for multiple comparisons indicated that those people who were members of a charity perceived themselves to be 'average'/'above average' in terms of family income whilst people who were active members of charities and those who did not belong to a charity perceived themselves to be 'below average'/'average' in terms of family income. See table 14 for descriptives.

Table 14. Perception of family income according to membership according to membership of an aid organisation

Aid organisation membership status	Mean	Std. Deviation	N
Don't belong	3.11	1.312	1645
Member	3.45	1.289	188
Active Member	3.00	1.095	31
Total	3.14	1.310	1864

Educational attainment – 2005

A chi-square analysis was conducted on each of the independent variables ('rights groups 2005', 'environmental group 2005' and 'aid organisation 2005') and high school educational attainment (ref: I4, what is the highest level of high school education you have completed?). The options 'did not go to school' and 'still at high school' were excluded from the analysis due to low cell counts (including them would make the results of the chi-square unreliable).

'Rights group 2005': The results of the chi-square analysis indicated that there was a significant association between membership status of a rights group and level of high school education completed, χ^2 (4, N = 1844) = 15.75, $p < .01$, although Cramer's V indicated that the strength of the association was weak (V = .065). Examination of the adjusted standardised residuals revealed that people who were members of a right group were more likely to have completed year 12 and less likely to have completed high school only to year 10 or to have not completed high school to year 10. In contrast, people who did not belong to a rights group were less likely to have completed high school or to have only completed high school to year 10. They were less likely to have completed year 12. Active members exhibited expected counts across all cells. See table 15 for descriptives.

Table 15. Chi-square results – membership status of a rights group by high school education

Rights group membership status		Highest level of high school education completed			Total
		Did NOT complete High School to Year 10	Completed High School to Year 10	Completed High School to Year 12	
Don't belong	Count	279	589	889	1757
	Expected Count	270.6	580.3	906.1	1757.0
	% within Rights group membership status	15.9%	33.5%	50.6%	100.0%
	Adjusted Residual	2.6	2.0	-3.8	
Member	Count	4	13	46	63
	Expected Count	9.7	20.8	32.5	63.0
	% within Rights group membership status	6.3%	20.6%	73.0%	100.0%
	Adjusted Residual	-2.0	-2.1	3.5	
Active Member	Count	1	7	16	24
	Expected Count	3.7	7.9	12.4	24.0
	% within Rights group membership status	4.2%	29.2%	66.7%	100.0%
	Adjusted Residual	-1.5	-.4	1.5	
Total	Count	284	609	951	1844
	Expected Count	284.0	609.0	951.0	1844.0
	% within Rights group membership status	15.4%	33.0%	51.6%	100.0%

'Environmental group 2005': The results of the chi-square analysis indicated that there was a significant association between membership status of a rights group and level of high school education completed, $\chi 2$ (4, N = 1847) = 39.90, $p < .001$, although Cramer's V indicated that the strength of the association was weak ($V = .104$). Examination of the adjusted standardised residuals revealed that people who were members of an environmental group were less likely to have not completed high school and to have completed year 10. They were more likely to have completed high school to year 12. People who did not belong to an environmental group were more likely to have not completed high school or to have completed year 10. They were less likely to have completed

Table 16. Chi-square results – membership of an environmental group by high school education

Environmental group membership status		Highest level of high school education completed			Total
		Did NOT complete High School to Year 10	Completed High School to Year 10	Completed High School to Year 12	
Don't belong	Count	277	581	840	1698
	Expected Count	261.1	561.7	875.2	1698.0
	% within Environmental group membership status	16.3%	34.2%	49.5%	100.0%
	Adjusted Residual	3.8	3.5	-6.0	
Member	Count	5	25	102	132
	Expected Count	20.3	43.7	68.0	132.0
	% within Environmental group membership status	3.8%	18.9%	77.3%	100.0%
	Adjusted Residual	-3.8	-3.6	6.1	
Active Member	Count	2	5	10	17
	Expected Count	2.6	5.6	8.8	17.0
	% within Environmental group membership status	11.8%	29.4%	58.8%	100.0%
	Adjusted Residual	-.4	-.3	.6	
Total	Count	284	611	952	1847
	Expected Count	284.0	611.0	952.0	1847.0
	% within Environmental group membership status	15.4%	33.1%	51.5%	100.0%

year 12. Active members of a rights group had expected counts across all cells. See table 16 for descriptives.

'Aid organisation 2005': The results of the chi-square analysis indicated that there was a significant association between membership status of a rights group and level of high school education completed, χ^2 (4, N = 1841) = 31.56, $p < .001$, although Cramer's V indicated that the strength of the association was weak (V = .093). Examination of the adjusted standardised residuals revealed that people who were members of an aid organisation were less likely to have not completed high school or to have completed year 10. They were more likely to have completed high school to year 12. In contrast, people who did not belong to an aid organisation were less likely to have completed 12 and more likely to have completed high school to year 10 only or to have dropped out of high school before completing year 10. Active members exhibited expected counts across all cells. See table 17 for descriptives.

A chi-square analysis was conducted on each of the independent variables ('rights groups 2005', environmental group 2005' and 'aid organisation 2005') and tertiary educational attainment (ref: I5, what is the highest level of education you have completed since leaving high school?).

'Rights group 2005': The results of the chi-square analysis indicated that there was a significant association between membership status of a rights group and level of tertiary education completed, $\chi2$ (8, N = 1799) = 47.16, $p < .001$, although Cramer's V indicated that the strength of the association was weak (V = .114). Examination of the adjusted standardised residuals revealed that people who were members of a rights group were less likely to have a trade qualification or apprenticeship and more likely to have a postgraduate degree or diploma. Active members were less likely to have no tertiary degree and more likely to have a bachelor degree. People who were not members of any rights group were more likely to have no post high school qualification or a trade

Table 17. Chi-square results – membership status of an aid organisation by high school education

Aid organisation membership status		Highest level of high school education completed			Total
		Did NOT complete High School to Year 10	Completed High School to Year 10	Completed High School to Year 12	
Don't belong	Count	266	556	802	1624
	Expected Count	248.8	537.2	838.0	1624.0
	% within Aid organisation membership status	16.4%	34.2%	49.4%	100.0%
	Adjusted Residual	3.5	2.9	-5.2	
Member	Count	13	42	131	186
	Expected Count	28.5	61.5	96.0	186.0
	% within Aid organisation membership status	7.0%	22.6%	70.4%	100.0%
	Adjusted Residual	-3.3	-3.2	5.4	
Active Member	Count	3	11	17	31
	Expected Count	4.7	10.3	16.0	31.0
	% within Aid organisation membership status	9.7%	35.5%	54.8%	100.0%
	Adjusted Residual	-.9	.3	.4	
Total	Count	282	609	950	1841
	Expected Count	282.0	609.0	950.0	1841.0
	% within Aid organisation membership status	15.3%	33.1%	51.6%	100.0%

Table 18. Chi-square results – tertiary education by membership status of rights group

Rights group membership status		Highest level of education completed since leaving school					Total
		None	Trade qualification or apprenticeship	Certificate or Diploma (TAFE or business college)	Bachelor Degree (including Honours)	Postgraduate Degree or Postgraduate Diploma	
Don't belong	Count	631	236	428	268	147	1710
	Expected Count	620.7	226.2	434.4	270.9	157.8	1710.0
	% within Rights group membership status rights	36.9%	13.8%	25.0%	15.7%	8.6%	100.0%
	Adjusted Residual	2.3	3.1	-1.6	-.9	-4.1	
Member	Count	20	1	22	6	15	64
	Expected Count	23.2	8.5	16.3	10.1	5.9	64.0
	% within Rights group membership status rights	31.3%	1.6%	34.4%	9.4%	23.4%	100.0%
	Adjusted Residual	-.9	-2.8	1.7	-1.4	4.0	
Active Member	Count	2	1	7	11	4	25
	Expected Count	9.1	3.3	6.4	4.0	2.3	25.0
	% within Rights group membership status rights	8.0%	4.0%	28.0%	44.0%	16.0%	100.0%
	Adjusted Residual	-3.0	-1.4	.3	3.9	1.2	
Total	Count	653	238	457	285	166	1799
	Expected Count	653.0	238.0	457.0	285.0	166.0	1799.0
	% within Rights group membership status rights	36.3%	13.2%	25.4%	15.8%	9.2%	100.0%

qualification or apprenticeship and less likely to have a postgraduate qualification. See table 18 for descriptives.

'Environmental group 2005': The results of the chi-square analysis indicated that there was a significant association between membership status of an environmental group and level of tertiary education completed, χ^2 (8, N = 1802) = 64.10, $p < .001$, although Cramer's V indicated that the strength of the association was fairly weak ($V = .133$). Examination of the adjusted standardised residuals revealed that people who were members of an environmental group were less likely to have no post-high school qualification and also less likely for this qualification to be in a trade or as an apprentice. Members were more likely to have either a bachelor degree or a postgraduate degree. People who did not belong to a charity were more likely to have no post high school qualification or to have a trade or apprenticeship. They were less likely to have a bachelor or postgraduate degree. Active members were less likely to have no post high school qualification. The small cell counts for both members and active members means that these trends should be taken with some caution. See table 19 for descriptives.

'Aid organisation 2005': The results of the chi-square analysis indicated that there was a significant association between membership status of an aid organisation and level of tertiary education completed, $\chi 2$ (8, N = 1796) = 73.48, $p < .001$, although Cramer's V indicated that the strength of the association was fairly weak (V = .143). Examination of the adjusted standardised residuals revealed that people who were members of an aid organisation were less likely to have no post-high school qualification and also less likely for this qualification to be in a trade or as an apprentice. Members were more likely to have either a bachelor degree or a postgraduate degree. Active members of an environmental group were less likely to have no tertiary qualification and were more likely to have a certificate or diploma. People who did not belong to an aid organisation were more likely to have no post high school qualification or a trade or apprenticeship. They were less likely to have a bachelor or

Table 19. Chi-square results – tertiary qualification by membership status of an environmental group

Environmental group membership status		Highest level of education completed since leaving school					Total
		None	Trade qualification or apprenticeship	Certificate or Diploma (TAFE or business college)	Bachelor Degree (including Honours)	Postgraduate Degree or Postgraduate Diploma	
Don't belong	Count	627	232	413	246	136	1654
	Expected Count	599.4	220.3	421.3	260.7	152.4	1654.0
	% within Environmental group membership status	37.9%	14.0%	25.0%	14.9%	8.2%	100.0%
	Adjusted Residual	4.9	3.0	-1.6	-3.5	-4.9	
Member	Count	24	5	39	33	29	130
	Expected Count	47.1	17.3	33.1	20.5	12.0	130.0
	% within Environmental group membership status	18.5%	3.8%	30.0%	25.4%	22.3%	100.0%
	Adjusted Residual	-4.4	-3.3	1.2	3.1	5.4	
Active Member	Count	2	3	7	5	1	18
	Expected Count	6.5	2.4	4.6	2.8	1.7	18.0
	% within Environmental group membership status	11.1%	16.7%	38.9%	27.8%	5.6%	100.0%
	Adjusted Residual	-2.2	.4	1.3	1.4	-.5	
Total	Count	653	240	459	284	166	1802
	Expected Count	653.0	240.0	459.0	284.0	166.0	1802.0
	% within Environmental group membership status	36.2%	13.3%	25.5%	15.8%	9.2%	100.0%

Table 20. Chi-square results – tertiary education by membership of an aid organisation

Aid organisation membership status		Highest level of education completed since leaving school					Total
		None	Trade qualification or apprenticeship	Certificate or Diploma (TAFE or business college)	Bachelor Degree (including Honours)	Postgraduate Degree or Postgraduate Diploma	
Don't belong	Count	609	222	394	228	125	1578
	Expected Count	572.0	210.0	400.7	249.5	145.9	1578.0
	% within Aid organisation membership status	38.6%	14.1%	25.0%	14.4%	7.9%	100.0%
	Adjusted Residual	5.6	2.6	-1.1	-4.3	-5.2	
Member	Count	38	13	48	50	37	186
	Expected Count	67.4	24.8	47.2	29.4	17.2	186.0
	% within Aid organisation membership status	20.4%	7.0%	25.8%	26.9%	19.9%	100.0%
	Adjusted Residual	-4.7	-2.7	.1	4.4	5.3	
Active Member	Count	4	4	14	6	4	32
	Expected Count	11.6	4.3	8.1	5.1	3.0	32.0
	% within Aid organisation membership status	12.5%	12.5%	43.8%	18.8%	12.5%	100.0%
	Adjusted Residual	-2.8	-.1	2.4	.5	.6	
Total	Count	651	239	456	284	166	1796
	Expected Count	651.0	239.0	456.0	284.0	166.0	1796.0
	% within Aid organisation membership status	36.2%	13.3%	25.4%	15.8%	9.2%	100.0%

postgraduate degree. However, again, note that the small cell counts for both members and active members means that these trends should be taken with some caution. See table 20 for descriptives.

Summary: Demographic characteristics of charity members

With regards socioeconomic data from the 2007 survey, both active and inactive members of a charity organisation perceived themselves as being significantly higher on the social group scale compared to people who did not belong to a charity. However, only those people who were inactive members actually earned more than people who did not belong to a charity.

With regards socioeconomic data from the 2005 survey, membership of an aid organisation was the only independent variable that explained significant variance in actual personal income and perceived family income. In this case, members of an aid organisation accurately perceived their income to be higher in comparison to people who did not belong to a charity. Although the personal income of active charity members did not differ significantly from either members or non-members, they perceived their family income to be less than members and on par with non-members.

With regards to educational achievement data from the 2007 survey, inactive members of a charity were more educated than people who did not belong to a charity. Inactive charity members were more likely to have completed year 12 and to have either a bachelor degree or postgraduate degree. In contrast, non-members were more likely to finish high school before year 10 or only complete up to year 10. They were less likely to have post-high school qualification; where they did, this qualification was more likely to be a trade or apprenticeship. Active members of a charity exhibited fewer deviations from the expected distributions, although they were less likely to have a trade qualification or apprenticeship.

With regards education achievement data from the 2005 survey, similar trends in explained variance were exhibited across the three independent variables of 'rights group', 'environmental group' and 'aid organisation'. Members of these groups were more likely to have completed year 12, and were less likely to have finished high school prior to year 10 or at year 10. In contrast, people who did not belong to a charity exhibited the opposite trend; they were more likely to have finished high school prior to year 10 or only to have completed year 10, and they were less likely to have completed year 12. Active members of these three types of organisations exhibited no significant deviations from expected distributions.

Although the trends in post-high school qualifications were not identical for all the three independent variables, there were some similarities. Generally, members were more highly educated whilst non-members were less educated. Members were more likely to hold bachelor or postgraduate degrees whilst non-members were unlikely to have a post-high school qualification or a trade or apprenticeship. Active members were more likely to have a post-high school qualification.

Attitudes towards government provision, taxes and services

Attitude towards paying taxes to protect the environment - 2007

Analysis

A multivariate analysis of covariance (MANCOVA) was performed on the responses to three questions about willingness to pay taxes to protect the environment. Ref: A7, How willing would you be to pay higher taxes in order to protect the quality of the:

- Local environment (i.e. your neighbourhood)
- National environment (i.e. countrywide)
- Global environment (i.e. worldwide)

The response scale ranged from 1 (very willing) to 5 (very unwilling).

In this analysis, the three dependent variables listed above were combined to form a composite dependent variable, hypothesised to be indicative of an overall attitude towards paying taxes to protect the environment in general. A MANCOVA was deemed necessary as the independent variable was likely to explain overlapping variance in each of the three separate dependent variables. A MANCOVA takes account of this overlap by analysing the effect of the independent variables on the composite dependent variable as well as on each dependent variable separately. The results of a correlational analysis (see table 21) revealed that the dependent variables of 'local environment', 'national environment' and 'global environment' were indeed significantly associated. In this MANCOVA, then, the composite dependent variable was made up of 'local environment', 'national environment' and 'global environment', the independent variable was charity membership and the covariate was age.

Table 21. Results of correlational analysis between the dependent variables

Dependent variable		Local environment	National environment	Global environment
Local environment	Pearson Correlation	1	.829**	.678**
	Sig. (2-tailed)		.000	.000
	N	--	2367	2357
National environment	Pearson Correlation	--	1	.789**
	Sig. (2-tailed)	--	--	.000
	N	--	--	2364
Global environment	Pearson Correlation	--	--	1
	Sig. (2-tailed)	--	--	--
	N	--	--	--

** Correlation is significant at the 0.01 level (2-tailed)

Results

With use of Wilks' criterion,[5] the combined dependent variables were significantly related to the covariate of age, $F(3, 2085) = 9.34$, $p < .001$, partial $\eta^2 = .013$. After adjustment for age, the composite dependent variable was significantly associated with charity membership, $F(6, 4172) = 13.59$, $p < .001$, partial $\eta 2 = .019$.

Whilst the MANCOVA indicated that the composite dependent variable was significantly associated with charity membership, it does not indicate if charity membership explains unique variance in each of the three separate dependent variables or if overlapping variance is explained that is shared between the three dependent variables. Therefore, the effect of charity membership on the three separate dependent variables, after adjustment for covariates, was investigated by way of three univariate *F* tests (ANCOVAs) and a Roy-Bargmann stepdown analysis. Univariate *F* tests the effect of the independent variable on each of the dependent variables; however, as these dependent variables are correlated, any significant amount of explained variance could potentially be shared variance.

Additionally, conducting several ANCOVAS leads to an inflation of Type I error rate (i.e. incorrect rejection of a true null hypothesis). In contrast, Roy-Bargmann analysis, which requires that each dependent variable is entered into the model sequentially, controls the explained variance of the covariate and the higher-order dependent variables (essentially the dependent variables are sequentially entered as covariates in the model). Depending on the situation, either approach (Univariate *F* or the Roy-Bargmann stepdown analysis), or both approaches in combination, is recommended. In this instance, as there was no theoretical or practical indication regarding the importance of one

5 Wilks' criterion is the standard for statistical inference given that the assumptions of the MANCOVA are met. In general, the assumptions were met in this instance, with a few minor violations of homogeneity of variance. In actual fact, the test statistic was significant for both age and charity membership regardless of which criterion was used.

dependent variable over another, both analyses are conducted in order to aid interpretation.

As there was no theoretical basis for the order in which the dependent variables were entered into the Roy-Bargmann stepdown analysis, they were entered in the order they appeared on the survey. Hence, 'local environment' was entered first, 'national environment' entered second (so that adjustment was made for 'local environment' as well as the covariate of age), and 'global environment' was entered third (so that adjustment was made for 'local environment' and 'national environment' as well as the covariate of age). Results of this analysis can be found in table 22.

Table 22. Tests of the effect of charity membership on each of the dependent variables

Dependent variable	Univariate *F*	df1	α2	Stepdown *F*	df	α	Partial η2
Local environment	29.30	2/2087	.000	29.30	2/2087	.000	.027
National environment	39.99	2/2087	.000	10.90	2/2086	.000	.037
Global environment	29.85	2/2087	.000	1.01	2/2085	.364	.028

As can be seen in this table, the results of the univariate ANCOVAs indicated that charity membership explained a significant amount of variance in all three dependent variables. The Roy-Bargmann stepdown analysis revealed, however, that charity membership explained a significant amount of variance in local and national environment only; the variance explained in global environment by charity membership was shared variance with the two previous dependent variables (local and national environment).

As the independent variable of charity membership had three levels, post hoc comparisons, with a Bonferroni adjustment for multiple comparisons, were made between each of the membership types ('active', 'inactive member', 'don't belong') for each of the dependent variables after adjustment for age. Descriptives can be found in table 23.

Table 23. Descriptives for each dependent variable according to charity membership status

Dependent variable	Charity membership status	Adjusted Mean	Std. Error	Mean	Std. Deviation	N
Local environment	Active member	2.319a	066	2.32	1.176	345
	Inactive member	2.202a	.075	2.20	1.140	266
	Don't belong	2.712a	.032	2.71	1.243	1480
	Total			2.58	1.236	2091
National environment	Active member	2.250a	.065	2.26	1.148	345
	Inactive member	2.057a	.074	2.05	1.106	266
	Don't belong	2.673a	.031	2.67	1.241	1480
	Total			2.52	1.232	2091
Global environment	Active member	2.623a	.068	2.64	1.236	345
	Inactive member	2.512a	.077	2.50	1.214	266
	Don't belong	3.036a	.033	3.03	1.274	1480
	Total			2.90	1.277	2091

a. Covariates appearing in the model are evaluated at the following values: v559 R: Year born = 1957.89.

'Local environment': Pairwise comparisons indicated that people who did not belong to a charity differed significantly from both active and inactive members of a charity. People who did not belong to a charity tended to be 'unsure' about whether they were willing to pay tax to protect the local environment whilst active and inactive members of a charity tended to be 'fairly willing' to do so.

'National environment': Pairwise comparisons indicated that people who did not belong to a charity differed significantly from both active and inactive members of a charity. People who did not belong to a charity tended to be 'unsure' about whether they were willing to pay tax to protect the local environment whilst active and inactive members of a charity tended to be 'fairly willing' to do so.

'Global environment': Although the Roy-Bargmann stepdown analysis indicated that there was no remaining variance that was explained by charity membership in willingness to pay taxes to protect the global environment, pairwise comparisons were still conducted as the order in which the dependent variables were entered into the model was completely arbitrary. The same trend occurred in the dependent variable, whereby pairwise comparisons indicated that people who did not belong to a charity differed significantly from both active and inactive members of a charity. People who did not belong to a charity tended to be 'unsure' about whether they were willing to pay tax to protect the local environment whilst active and inactive members of a charity tended to be 'fairly willing' to do so.

Attitude towards personal tax and social spending – 2005

A between-subjects ANCOVA was conducted for each independent variable ('rights groups 2005', 'environmental group 2005' and 'aid organisation 2005') on preference towards the reduction of personal income tax or increased social spending (ref: F1, if the government had a choice between reducing personal income taxes or increasing social spending on services like health and education which do you think it should do?). This scale ranged from 'strongly favour reducing taxes' (1) to 'strongly favour increasing social spending' (5). Age was the covariate in each analysis.

'Rights group 2005': Results indicated that age was not a significant covariate in this model, $F(1, 1778) = .26, p = .610$. Opinions regarding reduction in personal income tax versus increased social spending varied significantly according to membership of a rights group, where *F*(2,

1778) = 4.83, p <.01, partial η^2 = .005. Follow up pairwise comparisons with a Bonferroni adjustment for multiple comparisons revealed that those people who were members of a rights group tended to 'mildly favour increasing social spending' whilst those people who did not belong to a rights group at all tended to indicate that their preference 'depends'. Those people who were active members of a rights group did not differ from either of the other two membership types. See table 24 for descriptives.

Table 24. Reduction in personal tax vs. increased social spending descriptives according to membership of a rights group

Rights group membership status	Mean	Std. Deviation	N
Don't belong	3.22	1.511	1696
Member	3.77	1.541	62
Active Member	3.63	1.555	24
Total	3.24	1.516	1782

'Environmental group 2005': Results indicated that age was not a significant covariate, $F(1, 1779) = .38$, $p = .540$. However, opinions regarding reduction in personal income tax versus increased social spending varied significantly according to membership of an environmental group, where $F(2, 1779) = 9.22$, $p < .001$, partial η^2 = .010. Pairwise comparisons with a Bonferroni adjustment for multiple comparisons revealed that those people who were members of an environmental group tended to 'mildly favour increasing social spending' whilst those people who did not belong to an environmental group tended to indicate that their preference 'depends'. Those people who were active members of a rights group did not differ from either of the other two groups. See table 25 for descriptives.

Table 25. Reduction in personal tax vs. increased social spending descriptives according to membership of an environmental group

Environmental group membership status	Mean	Std. Deviation	N
Don't belong	3.20	1.507	1634
Member	3.79	1.499	131
Active Member	3.22	1.665	18
Total	3.24	1.515	1783

'Aid organisation 2005': Results indicated that age was not a significant covariate, $F(1, 1774) = .59$, $p = .444$. Opinions regarding reduction in personal income tax versus increased social spending varied significantly according to membership of an aid organisation, $F(2, 1774) = 16.24$, $p < .001$, $\eta^2 = .018$. Pairwise comparisons with a Bonferroni adjustment for multiple comparisons revealed that those people who were members of an aid organisation tended to 'mildly favour increasing social spending' whilst those people who did not belong to an aid organisation tended to indicate that their preference 'depends'. Those people who were active members of a rights group did not differ from either of the other two groups. See table 26 for descriptives.

Table 26. Reduction in personal tax vs. increased social spending descriptives according to membership of an aid organisation

Aid organisation membership status	Mean	Std. Deviation	N
Don't belong	3.17	1.523	1568
Member	3.81	1.313	181
Active Member	3.76	1.527	29
Total	3.25	1.515	1778

Attitude towards privatisation of government services – 2005

A between-subjects ANCOVA was conducted for each independent variable ('rights groups 2005', environmental group 2005' and 'aid organisation 2005') on attitude towards the privatisation of government services (ref: F6b, privatisation of government services has more benefits than costs, where 1 was 'strongly agree' and 5 was 'strongly disagree). Age was the covariate in each analysis.

'Rights group 2005': Results revealed that age was not a significant covariate in this model, with $F(1, 1713) = .63, p = .427$. However, attitude towards the privatisation of government services did vary significantly according to membership status of a rights group, $F(2, 1713) = 6.83$, $p < .01$, partial $\eta^2 = .008$. Follow up post hoc tests with a Bonferroni correction for multiple comparisons indicated that those people who were active members of a rights group tended to 'disagree'/'strongly disagree' with the statement, 'privatisation of government services has more benefits than costs', in comparison to those people who did not belong to a rights group. Those people who were members of a rights group did not differ significantly in comparison to the two other membership types. See table 27 for descriptives.

Table 27. Opinion regarding privatisation of government services according membership of a rights group

Rights group membership status	Mean	Std. Deviation	N
Don't belong	3.51	1.022	1634
Member	3.79	.985	61
Active Member	4.18	.733	22
Total	3.53	1.021	1717

'Environmental group 2005': Results revealed that age was not a significant covariate, with $F(1, 1716) = .77, p = .380$. Attitude towards the privatisation of government services did vary significantly according to membership status of an environmental group, $F(2, 1716) = 7.69$, $p < .001$, partial $\eta^2 = .009$. Follow up post hoc tests with a Bonferroni correction for multiple comparisons indicated that those people who were members of an environmental group tended to 'disagree' with the statement, 'privatisation of government services has more benefits than costs', in comparison to those people who did not belong to a rights group. Those people who were active members of a rights group did not differ significantly in comparison to the two other membership types. See table 28 for descriptives.

Table 28. Opinion regarding privatisation of government services according membership of an environmental group

Environmental group membership status	Mean	Std. Deviation	N
Don't belong	3.50	1.023	1579
Member	3.86	.966	124
Active Member	3.41	1.228	17
Total	3.52	1.025	1720

'Aid organisation 2005': Results revealed that age was not a significant covariate, with $F(1, 1711) = .62$ $p = .430$. Attitude towards the privatisation of government services did vary significantly according to membership status of an environmental group, $F(2, 1711) = 4.55$, $p < .05$, partial $\eta^2 = .005$. Follow up post hoc tests with a Bonferroni correction for multiple comparisons indicated that those people who were active members of an environmental group, on average, disagreed with the statement 'privatisation of government services has more benefits than costs' in comparison to those people who did not belong to a rights group. Those people who were just members of a rights group did not differ significantly in comparison to the two other membership types. See table 29 for descriptives.

Table 29. Opinion regarding privatisation of government services according membership of an aid organisation

Aid organisation membership status	Mean	Std. Deviation	N
Don't belong	3.50	1.019	1512
Member	3.64	1.084	173
Active Member	4.00	.788	30
Total	3.53	1.024	1715

Attitude towards government distribution of income – 2005

A between-subjects ANCOVA was conducted for each independent variable ('rights groups 2005', 'environmental group 2005' and 'aid organisation 2005') on attitude towards government distribution of income (ref: F6c, government should redistribute income from the better-off to those who are less well-off, where 1 was 'strongly agree' and 5 was 'strongly disagree). Age was the covariate in each analysis.

'Rights group 2005': Results indicated that age was not a significant covariate, with $F(1, 1786) = .03$, $p = .875$. Opinion regarding the redistribution of income varied significantly according to membership of a rights group, where $F(2, 1786) = 4.67$, $p < .01$, partial $\eta^2 = .005$. Post hoc tests with a Bonferroni correction for multiple comparisons indicated that those people who were active members of a rights group tended to 'agree'/'neither agree nor disagree' with the statement, 'government should redistribute income from the better-off to those who are less well-off', in comparison to people who did not belong to a rights group. People who were just members of a rights group did not differ significantly in comparison to the other two membership types. See table 30 for descriptives.

Table 30. Opinion regarding government distribution of income according to membership of a rights group

Rights group membership status	Mean	Std. Deviation	N
Don't belong	2.98	1.113	1702
Member	2.73	1.221	63
Active Member	2.40	1.041	25
Total	2.96	1.118	1790

'Environmental group 2005': Results indicated that age was not a significant covariate, with $F(1, 1787) = .004, p = .951$. Opinion regarding the redistribution of income varied significantly according to membership of a rights group, where $F(2, 1787) = 7.79, p <.001$, partial $\eta^2 = .008$. Post hoc tests with a Bonferroni correction for multiple comparisons indicated that those people who were members of an environmental group were significantly different to those who did not belong to an environmental group; however, the mean difference was not substantial enough to be meaningful. People who were just members of a rights group did not differ significantly to the other two membership types. See table 31 for descriptives.

Table 31. Opinion regarding government distribution of income according to membership of an environmental group

Environmental group membership status	Mean	Std. Deviation	N
Don't belong	2.99	1.123	1642
Member	2.65	.984	131
Active Member	2.56	1.149	18
Total	2.96	1.117	1791

'Aid organisation 2005': Results revealed that age was not a significant covariate, with $F(1, 1781) = .001$ $p = .974$. Opinion regarding the redistribution of income also did not vary significantly according to membership of an aid organisation, where $F(2, 1781) = .38, p = .681$. Descriptives can be found in table 32.

Table 32. Opinion regarding government distribution of income according to membership of an aid organisation

Aid organisation membership status	Mean	Std. Deviation	N
Don't belong	2.97	1.130	1574
Member	2.90	.998	180
Active Member	2.87	1.284	31
Total	2.96	1.120	1785

Summary: Attitudes towards government provision, taxes, and services

With regards the 2007 data, people who did not belong to a charity were less certain about paying taxes to protect the environment (local, national and global environment) whilst members and active members of a charity tended to be more in favour.

With regards the 2005 data, members of all three types of groups (rights, environmental and aid) were more in favour of increasing social spending over reducing personal income taxes in comparison to people who did not belong to any of these groups. Interestingly, active members of the three groups did not differ significantly to either members or people who did not belong.

Members of an environmental group or aid organisation, in contrast to people who did not belong to these two groups, tended to disagree with the statement that privatisation of government services has more benefits than costs. Active members of these two groups (environmental and aid) did not differ significantly from members or people who did not belong. In contrast, active members of a rights group (in comparison to people who did not belong) tended to disagree with government privatisation. Members of a rights group, in this case, did not differ significantly from active members or people who did not belong.

Finally, active members of a rights group tended to agree with government redistribution of income from the better-off to those who are less well-off. The other two groups (environmental and aid) did not exhibit meaningful differences between different types of membership.

Although the specific trends are not clear-cut across all survey questions regarding government provision, taxes and services, there was a general trend whereby members[6] and active members of the four groups (charities, rights groups, environmental groups and aid organisations) tended to have stronger opinions regarding these issues in comparison to people who did not belong.

Political attitudes and behaviours

Political ideology – 2007

A between-subjects ANCOVA was performed on political ideology (ref: O3, in politics people sometimes refer to being on the left or on the right. Where would you place yourself on a scale from 0 to 10 where 0 means left and 10 means right?). The independent variable was 'charity membership 2007' and the covariate was age (year born).

Results of the ANCOVA indicated that age was a significant covariate, where $F(1, 1565) = 93.85, p <.001, \eta^2 = .057$. After adjustment for age, political self-placement varied significantly according to charity membership, with $F(2, 1565) = 6.37, p <.01$, partial $\eta 2 = .008$. Follow-up pairwise comparisons with a Bonferroni correction for multiple comparisons revealed that people who were inactive members of a charity perceived themselves to be significantly more left-wing compared to people who were active members of a charity and to those people who did not belong to a charity. See table 33 for descriptives.

6 'Members' in this instance is intended to encompass 'inactive members' of charities (2007 survey) and 'members' of rights, environmental and aid groups (2005 survey).

Table 33. Political ideology according to charity membership.

Charity membership status	Adjusted Mean	Std. Error	Mean	Std. Deviation	N
Active member	5.178a	.125	5.27	2.354	294
Inactive member	4.712a	.142	4.63	2.318	229
Don't belong	5.270a	.066	5.26	2.131	1046
Total			5.17	2.212	1569

a. Covariates appearing in the model are evaluated at the following values: v559 R: Year born = 1955.82.

Political party identification and support – 2007

A chi-square analysis was conducted on charity membership and chosen political party (ref: O4, Generally speaking, do you usually think of yourself as Labor, Liberal, National or what?). Due to small cell counts, only the major political parties were included in the analysis. These were Liberal, Labor, National, and the Greens. An option for 'no party' was also included in the analysis.

The results of the chi-square indicated that there was a significant association between charity membership and identification with a particular political party, χ^2 (8, N = 2145) = 37.75, $p < .001$, although Cramer's V indicated that the strength of the association was weak (V = .094). Examination of the adjusted standardised residuals revealed that active members of charities were more likely to support the Liberal or National parties and less likely to support the Labor Party. In contrast, inactive members of a charity were more likely to support the Greens. People who did not belong to a charity were less likely to support any party and were less likely to support the Greens. See table 34. for descriptives.

Table 34. Chi-square results – political party preference by charity membership status

Charity membership Status		Preferred political party				
		Liberal	Labor (ALP)	National	Green	No Party
Active member	Count	136	107	24	25	59
	Expected Count	119.9	125.5	15.1	20.1	70.4
	% within Charity membership status	38.7%	30.5%	6.8%	7.1%	16.8%
	Adjusted Residual	2.0	-2.3	2.6	1.2	-1.7
Inactive member	Count	84	97	8	30	44
	Expected Count	89.9	94.0	11.3	15.1	52.7
	% within Charity membership status	31.9%	36.9%	3.0%	11.4%	16.7%
	Adjusted Residual	-.8	.4	-1.1	4.2	-1.4
Don't belong	Count	513	563	60	68	327
	Expected Count	523.2	547.4	65.7	87.8	306.9
	% within Charity membership status	33.5%	36.8%	3.9%	4.4%	21.4%
	Adjusted Residual	-1.0	1.5	-1.3	-4.1	2.4
Total	Count	733	767	92	123	430
	Expected Count	733.0	767.0	92.0	123.0	430.0
	% within Charity membership status	34.2%	35.8%	4.3%	5.7%	20.0%

A between-subjects ANCOVA was conducted on level of support for chosen political party (ref: O5, would you call yourself a very strong, fairly strong or not very strong supporter of that party?). On this scale, 1 was equivalent to 'very strong supporter' and 3 was equivalent to 'not very strong supporter'. The independent variable was 'charity membership 2007' and the covariate was age (year born).

Results of the ANCOVA indicated that age was a significant covariate, with $F(1, 1784) = 5.51, p < .05$, *partial* $\eta^2 = .003$. After adjustment for age, support for preferred political party varied significantly according to charity membership, with $F(2, 1784) = 9.78$, $p < .001$, partial $\eta 2 = .011$. Follow-up pairwise comparisons with a Bonferroni correction for multiple comparisons revealed that both active and inactive members of charities supported their preferred political party more than those people who were not members of charities. See table 35 for descriptives.

Table 35. Support for preferred political party according to charity membership

Charity membership status	Adjusted Mean	Std. Error	Mean	Std. Deviation	N
Active member	2.156a	.039	2.15	.714	315
Inactive member	2.116a	.046	2.12	.658	229
Don't belong	2.294a	.020	2.30	.692	1244
Total			2.25	695	1788

a. Covariates appearing in the model are evaluated at the following values: v559 R: Year born = 1955.96.

Political ideology – 2005

A between-subjects ANCOVA was performed for each of the independent variables ('rights groups 2005', 'environmental group 2005' and 'aid organisation 2005') on political ideology (ref: F13, in politics people sometimes refer to being on the left or on the right. Where would you place yourself on a scale from 0 to 10 where 0 means left and 10 means right?). The covariate was age.

'Rights group 2005': Results of the ANCOVA indicated that age was a significant covariate, $F(1, 1335) = 117.33$, $p < .001$, partial $\eta^2 = .081$. After adjustment for age, political self-placement varied significantly according to charity membership, with $F(2, 1335) = 17.21$, $p < .001$, partial $\eta 2 = .025$. Follow-up pairwise comparisons with a Bonferroni correction for multiple comparisons revealed that all membership types were significantly different, where those who were active members of a rights group placed themselves towards the left end of the scale, members tended towards the middle of the scale (but still on the left) and those who did not belong placed themselves towards the right end. See table 36 for descriptives.

Table 36. Political ideology according to membership of a rights group

v45 Member of: A group that promotes rights	Adjusted Mean	Std. Error	Mean	Std. Deviation	N
Don't belong	5.449a	.056	5.45	2.051	1261
Member	4.656a	.267	4.65	2.405	55
Active Member	3.291a	.413	3.22	2.044	23
Total			5.38	2.090	1339

a. Covariates appearing in the model are evaluated at the following values: v381 R: age = 54.24.

'Environmental group 2005': Results of the ANCOVA indicated that age was a significant covariate, $F(2, 1336) = 13.44$, $p < .001$, partial $\eta^2 = .020$. After adjustment for age, political self-placement varied significantly according to membership of an environmental group, with $F(2, 1336) = 13.44$, $p < .001$, partial $\eta 2 = .020$. Follow-up pairwise comparisons with a Bonferroni correction for multiple comparisons revealed that those people who were members of an environmental group placed themselves more towards the left than those who did not belong to an environmental group. Active members were not significantly different to the other two membership types. See table 37 for descriptives.

Table 37. Political ideology according to membership of an environmental group

Environmental group membership status	Adjusted Mean	Std. Error	Mean	Std. Deviation	N
Don't belong	5.478a	.057	5.48	2.059	1209
Member	4.503a	.186	4.41	2.173	114
Active Member	4.738a	.482	4.88	2.027	17
Total			5.39	2.089	1340

a. Covariates appearing in the model are evaluated at the following values: v381 R: age = 54.23.

'Aid organisation 2005': Results of the ANCOVA indicated that age was a significant covariate, $F(1, 1334) = 111.43, p <.001$, partial $\eta^2 = .077$. After adjustment for age, political self-placement varied significantly according to membership of an aid organisation, with F(2, 1334) = 4.42, p <.05, partial η2 = .007. Follow-up pairwise comparisons with a Bonferroni correction for multiple comparisons revealed that those people who were active members of an aid organisation placed themselves more towards the left than those who did not belong to an environmental group. People who were just members were not significantly different. See table 38 for descriptives.

Table 38. Political ideology according to membership of a rights group

Aid organisation membership status	Adjusted Mean	Std. Error	Mean	Std. Deviation	N
Don't belong	5.433a	.059	5.44	2.084	1162
Member	5.128a	.163	5.06	2.158	151
Active Member	4.428a	.401	4.48	1.711	25
Total			5.38	2.092	1338

a. Covariates appearing in the model are evaluated at the following values: v381 R: Year of birth = 54.28

Political party identification and support – 2005

A chi-square analysis was conducted for each of the independent variables ('rights groups 2005', 'environmental group 2005' and 'aid organisation 2005') and chosen political party (ref: F8, Generally speaking, do you usually think of yourself as Labor, Liberal, National or what?). Due to small cell counts, only the major political parties were included in the analysis. These were Liberal, Labor, National, and the Greens. An option for 'no party' was also included in the analysis. Note that some cells still have lower than expected counts (except for the analysis involving aid organisation) which means that the results should be taken with some caution.

'Rights group 2005': The results of the chi-square indicated that there was a significant association between membership of a rights group and identification with a particular political party, χ^2 (8, N = 1779) = 40.01, $p < .001$, although Cramer's V indicated that the strength of the association was weak ($V = .106$). Examination of the adjusted standardised residuals revealed that active members of a rights group were less likely to support the Liberal Party and more likely to support the Labor Party and the Greens. Members were also more likely to support the Labor Party and the Greens as well as less likely not to support any party at all. In contrast, people who did not belong to a rights group were more likely to support the Liberal Party and less likely to support both the Labor Party and the Greens. People who were not members were also more likely not to support any party at all. See table 39 for descriptives.

Table 39. Preferred political party by membership of a rights group

Rights group membership status		Preferred political party					Total
		Liberal	Labor (ALP)	National	Green	No party	
Don't belong	Count	657	550	58	95	340	1700
	Expected Count	646.9	564.8	56.4	103.2	328.7	1700.0
	% within Rights group membership status	38.6%	32.4%	3.4%	5.6%	20.0%	100.0%
	Adjusted Residual	2.4	-3.6	1.0	-4.0	3.3	
Member	Count	17	28	1	8	2	56
	Expected Count	21.3	18.6	1.9	3.4	10.8	56.0
	% within Rights group membership status	30.4%	50.0%	1.8%	14.3%	3.6%	100.0%
	Adjusted Residual	-1.2	2.7	-.7	2.6	-3.0	
Active Member	Count	3	13	0	5	2	23
	Expected Count	8.8	7.6	.8	1.4	4.4	23.0
	% within Rights group membership status	13.0%	56.5%	0.0%	21.7%	8.7%	100.0%
	Adjusted Residual	-2.5	2.4	-.9	3.2	-1.3	
Total	Count	677	591	59	108	344	1779
	Expected Count	677.0	591.0	59.0	108.0	344.0	1779.0
	% within Rights group membership status	38.1%	33.2%	3.3%	6.1%	19.3%	100.0%

'Environmental group 2005': The results of the chi-square indicated that there was a significant association between membership of an environmental group and identification with a particular political party, χ^2 (8, N = 1781) = 138.19, $p < .001$. Cramer's V indicated that the strength of the association was weak to moderate (V = .197). Examination of the adjusted standardised residuals revealed that active members of an environmental group were more to likely support the Greens. Members were less likely to support either the Liberal and National party and much more likely to support the Greens. In contrast, people who did not belong to a rights group were more likely to support the Liberal or National Party and much less likely to support the Greens. See table 40 for descriptives.

'Aid organisation 2005': The results of the chi-square indicated that there was a significant association between membership of an aid organisation and identification with a particular political party, χ^2 (8, N = 1776) = 24.06, $p < .01$. Cramer's V indicated that the strength of the association was weak (V = .082). Examination of the adjusted standardised residuals revealed that active members of an aid organisation were more likely to support the National Party. Members were more likely to support the Greens. In contrast, people who did not belong to an aid organisation were less likely to support the Greens. See table 41 for descriptives.

Table 40. Preferred political party by membership of an environmental group

Environmental group membership status		Preferred political party					Total
		Liberal	Labor (ALP)	National	Green	No party	
Don't belong	Count	648	547	59	69	319	1642
	Expected Count	626.0	544.0	54.4	99.6	318.1	1642.0
	% within Environmental group membership status	39.5%	33.3%	3.6%	4.2%	19.4%	100.0%
	Adjusted Residual	4.0	.6	2.3	-11.3	.2	
Member	Count	25	40	0	35	22	122
	Expected Count	46.5	40.4	4.0	7.4	23.6	122.0
	% within Environmental group membership status	20.5%	32.8%	0.0%	28.7%	18.0%	100.0%
	Adjusted Residual	-4.2	-.1	-2.1	10.8	-.4	
Active Member	Count	6	3	0	4	4	17
	Expected Count	6.5	5.6	.6	1.0	3.3	17.0
	% within Environmental group membership status	35.3%	17.6%	0.0%	23.5%	23.5%	100.0%
	Adjusted Residual	-.2	-1.4	-.8	3.0	.4	
Total	Count	679	590	59	108	345	1781
	Expected Count	679.0	590.0	59.0	108.0	345.0	1781.0
	% within Environmental group membership status	38.1%	33.1%	3.3%	6.1%	19.4%	100.0%

Table 41. Preferred political party by membership of an aid organisation

Aid organisation membership status		Preferred political party					Total
		Liberal	Labor (ALP)	National	Green	No party	
Don't belong	Count	609	519	53	83	306	1570
	Expected Count	596.7	521.6	52.2	95.5	304.1	1570.0
	% within Aid organisation membership status	38.8%	33.1%	3.4%	5.3%	19.5%	100.0%
	Adjusted Residual	1.9	-.4	.3	-3.9	.4	
Member	Count	55	62	3	23	33	176
	Expected Count	66.9	58.5	5.8	10.7	34.1	176.0
	% within Aid organisation membership status	31.3%	35.2%	1.7%	13.1%	18.8%	100.0%
	Adjusted Residual	-1.9	.6	-1.3	4.1	-.2	
Active Member	Count	11	9	3	2	5	30
	Expected Count	11.4	10.0	1.0	1.8	5.8	30.0
	% within Aid organisation membership status	36.7%	30.0%	10.0%	6.7%	16.7%	100.0%
	Adjusted Residual	-.2	-.4	2.1	.1	-.4	
Total	Count	675	590	59	108	344	1776
	Expected Count	675.0	590.0	59.0	108.0	344.0	1776.0
	% within Aid organisation membership status	38.0%	33.2%	3.3%	6.1%	19.4%	100.0%

Political activity – 2007

A multivariate analysis of covariance (MANCOVA) was performed on responses to a number of statements regarding political interest and activity. Ref: C1, to what extent do you agree or disagree with the following statements:

- I play an active role in one or more voluntary, local or political organisations ('active role')
- I don't like to discuss politics with other people ('discuss politics')
- I don't get involved in political protests ('political protests')
- I am generally interested in what's going on in politics ('political interest').

The scale ranged from 1 (strongly agree) to 5 (strongly disagree).

Thus, in this analysis, the four dependent variables listed above were combined to form a composite dependent variable, hypothesised to be indicative of political activism in general. A MANCOVA was deemed necessary as the independent variables were likely to explain overlapping variance in each of the four separate dependent variables. A MANCOVA takes account of this overlap by analysing the effect of the independent variables on the composite dependent variable as well as on each dependent variable separately. The results of a correlational analysis (see table 42) revealed that the dependent variables were significantly associated, except for 'I don't like to discuss politics with other people' and 'I play an active role in one or more voluntary local or political organisations'. In the MANCOVA the composite dependent variable was made up of 'active role', 'discuss politics', 'political protests', 'political interest' and 'political interest'. The independent variable was charity membership and the covariate was age.

Table 42. Results of correlational analysis between proposed dependent variables

Dependent variable		I play an active role in one or more voluntary, local or political organisations	I don't like to discuss politics with other people	I don't get involved in political protests	I am generally interested in what's going on in politics
I play an active role in one or more voluntary, local or political organisations	Pearson Correlation	1	.003	-.077**	.157**
	Sig. (2-tailed)	--	.882	.000	.000
	N	--	2435	2426	2429
I don't like to discuss politics with other people	Pearson Correlation	--	1	.241**	-.271**
	Sig. (2-tailed)	--	--	.000	.000
	N	--	--	2466	2469
I don't get involved in political protests	Pearson Correlation	--	--	1	-.077**
	Sig. (2-tailed)	--	--	--	.000
	N	--	--	--	2467
I am generally interested in what's going on in politics	Pearson Correlation	--	--	--	1
	Sig. (2-tailed)	--	--	--	--
	N	--	--	--	--

**. Correlation is significant at the 0.01 level (2-tailed).

Results: MANCOVA on combined dependent variables

With use of Pillai's criterion,[7] the combined dependent variables were significantly related to the covariate age, $F(4, 2130) = 41.68$, $p < .001$, partial $\eta^2 = .073$. After adjustment for age, the composite dependent variable was significantly associated with charity membership, $F(8,4262) = 33.80$, $p < .001$, partial $\eta2 = .060$.

As in the previous MANCOVA, effects of charity membership on the dependent variables after adjustment for covariates were investigated by way of univariate *F* and a Roy-Bargmann stepdown analysis. As there was no theoretical basis for the order in which the dependent variables were entered into the analysis, they were entered in the order they appeared on the survey. Hence, 'active role' was entered first, 'discuss politics' entered second (so that adjustment was made for 'active role' as well as the covariate of age), 'political protest' entered third (so that adjustment was made for 'active role' and ' 'discuss politics' as well as the covariate of age), and 'political interest' entered last (so that adjustment was made for 'active role', 'discuss politics' and 'political protest' as well as the covariate of age). Results of this analysis can be found in table 43. As can be seen, regardless of whether univariate or stepdown *F* is used, the independent variable of charity membership explained significant variance in all of the dependent variables.

---

7 Pillai's criterion was used in this instance as the sample sizes were unequal and there was some minor violation of the assumption of variance-covariance matrices. Pillai's criterion pools the statistics from each dimension in order to test the effect and is a more robust test when the research design is less than ideal. In this analysis, age (the covariate) and charity membership (the independent variable) had a significant effect on the composite dependent variables regardless of which criterion was employed.

Table 43. Tests of the effect of charity membership on each of the dependent variables

Dependent variable	Univariate *F*	df	α	Stepdown *F*	df	α	Partial η2
Active role	115.63	2/2133	.000	115.63	2/2133	.000	.098
Discuss politics	11.45	2/2133	.000	11.07	2/2132	.000	.011
Political protest	13.36	2/2133	.000	5.89	2/2131	.003	.012
Political interest	19.23	2/2133	.000	7.24	21/30	.001	.018

As the independent variable of charity membership had three levels, post hoc comparisons, with a Bonferroni adjustment for multiple comparisons, were made between each of the membership types ('active', 'inactive member', 'don't belong') for each of the dependent variables after adjustment for age. Descriptives can be found in table 44.

'Active role': Pairwise comparisons indicated that all membership types were significantly different to each other, such that active members were more likely to 'agree'/'neither agree nor disagree', inactive members tended towards 'neither agree nor disagree' and people who did not belong to a charity tended towards 'disagree'.

'Discuss politics': Pairwise comparisons revealed that people who did not belong to a charity tended to 'neither agree nor disagree' with this statement in comparison to inactive members who tended towards 'disagree' – although the difference was marginal in real terms. Active members of a charity were not significantly different.

'Political protests': Pairwise comparisons indicated that people who did not belong to a charity were significantly different both to active and inactive members of charities. People who did not belong to charities tended to 'agree' with this statement whilst active and inactive members tended to 'neither agree nor disagree'.

Table 44. Descriptives for each dependent variable according to charity membership status

Dependent variables	Charity membership status	Adjusted Mean	Std. Error	Mean	Std. Deviation	N
I play an active role in one or more voluntary, local or political organisations	Active member	2.601a	.064	2.57	1.409	354
	Inactive member	3.292a	.074	3.31	1.196	266
	Don't belong	3.671a	.031	3.68	1.168	1517
	Total			3.45	1.281	2137
I don't like to discuss politics with other people	Active member	3.139a	.058	3.13	1.121	354
	Inactive member	3.286a	.066	3.29	1.084	266
	Don't belong	2.971a	.028	2.97	1.075	1517
	Total			3.04	1.089	2137
I don't get involved in political protests	Active member	2.417a	.065	2.43	1.251	354
	Inactive member	2.582a	.075	2.58	1.245	266
	Don't belong	2.202a	.031	2.20	1.219	1517
	Total			2.28	1.235	2137
I am generally interested in what's going on in politics	Active member	2.050a	.049	2.01	.902	354
	Inactive member	1.978a	.056	2.00	.842	266
	Don't belong	2.288a	.024	2.29	.963	1517
	Total			2.21	.947	2137

a. Covariates appearing in the model are evaluated at the following values: v559 R: Year born = 1957.58.

'Political interest': Pairwise comparisons revealed that people who did not belong to a charity were significantly different to both active and inactive members of charities. People who did not belong to charities appeared to be significantly less interested in politics; however, all three membership types tended towards the 'agree' point on the scale.

Political activity – 2005

A chi-square analysis was conducted on each of the independent variables ('rights groups 2005', 'environmental group 2005' and 'aid organisation 2005') and participation in three different types of political activity/ activism (ref: B3, over the past two years or so, have you done any of the following things to express your views or represent your interests?

- Contact a politician or government official either in person, or in writing, or some other way ('contact politician')
- Taken part in a protests, march or demonstration ('protest march')
- Worked together with people who shared the same concern ('same concern').

'Rights group 2005': The results of the chi-square analysis indicated that there was a significant association between membership status of a rights group and participation in political activism: 'contact politician', χ^2 (2, N = 1896) = 63.26, $p < .001$, V = .183; 'protest march', $\chi 2$ (2, N = 1881) = 143.76, $p < .001$, V = .276, and; 'same concern', $\chi 2$ (2, N = 1881) =49.21, $p < .001$, V = .162. The Cramer's V values indicate weak to moderate associations. Examination of the standardised residuals revealed identical trends across these three types of political activism; both active and members and ordinary members were far more likely to contact politicians, participate in protest marches and work with people who shared the same concern. People who did not belong to a rights group were far less likely to participate in any of these activities. See table 45 to table 47 for descriptives.

Table 45. Chi-square results – membership status of rights group by contact politician

Rights group membership status		Past 2 yrs have you: Contacted a politician/official		Total
		Yes	No	
Don't belong	Count	495	1312	1807
	Expected Count	528.0	1279.0	1807.0
	% within Rights group membership status	27.4%	72.6%	100.0%
	Adjusted Residual	-7.9	7.9	
Member	Count	41	24	65
	Expected Count	19.0	46.0	65.0
	% within Rights group membership status	63.1%	36.9%	100.0%
	Adjusted Residual	6.1	-6.1	
Active Member	Count	18	6	24
	Expected Count	7.0	17.0	24.0
	% within Rights group membership status	75.0%	25.0%	100.0%
	Adjusted Residual	5.0	-5.0	
Total	Count	554	1342	1896
	Expected Count	554.0	1342.0	1896.0
	% within Rights group membership status	29.2%	70.8%	100.0%

Table 46. Chi-square results – membership status of rights group by participation in protest, march or demonstration

Rights group membership status		Past 2 yrs have you: Protest, march or demonstration		Total
		Yes	No	
Don't belong	Count	172	1621	1793
	Expected Count	205.9	1587.1	1793.0
	% within Rights group membership status	9.6%	90.4%	100.0%
	Adjusted Residual	-11.6	11.6	
Member	Count	28	36	64
	Expected Count	7.3	56.7	64.0
	% within Rights group membership status	43.8%	56.3%	100.0%
	Adjusted Residual	8.2	-8.2	
Active Member	Count	16	8	24
	Expected Count	2.8	21.2	24.0
	% within Rights group membership status	66.7%	33.3%	100.0%
	Adjusted Residual	8.5	-8.5	
Total	Count	216	1665	1881
	Expected Count	216.0	1665.0	1881.0
	% within Rights group membership status	11.5%	88.5%	100.0%

Table 47. Chi-square results – membership status of rights group by working with people who share same concern

Rights group membership status		Past 2 yrs have you: Worked with people-same concern		Total
		Yes	No	
Don't belong	Count	750	1042	1792
	Expected Count	781.2	1010.8	1792.0
	% within Rights group membership status	41.9%	58.1%	100.0%
	Adjusted Residual	-6.8	6.8	
Member	Count	47	17	64
	Expected Count	27.9	36.1	64.0
	% within Rights group membership status	73.4%	26.6%	100.0%
	Adjusted Residual	4.9	-4.9	
Active Member	Count	23	2	25
	Expected Count	10.9	14.1	25.0
	% within Rights group membership status	92.0%	8.0%	100.0%
	Adjusted Residual	4.9	-4.9	
Total	Count	820	1061	1881
	Expected Count	820.0	1061.0	1881.0
	% within Rights group membership status	43.6%	56.4%	100.0%

Table 48. Chi-square results – membership status of environmental group by contact politician

Membership status environmental group		Past 2 yrs have you: Contacted a politician/official		Total
		Yes	No	
Don't belong	Count	475	1272	1747
	Expected Count	512.0	1235.0	1747.0
	% within Membership status environmental group	27.2%	72.8%	100.0%
	Adjusted Residual	-6.9	6.9	
Member	Count	68	64	132
	Expected Count	38.7	93.3	132.0
	% within Membership status environmental group	51.5%	48.5%	100.0%
	Adjusted Residual	5.8	-5.8	
Active Member	Count	13	5	18
	Expected Count	5.3	12.7	18.0
	% within Membership status environmental group	72.2%	27.8%	100.0%
	Adjusted Residual	4.0	-4.0	
Total	Count	556	1341	1897
	Expected Count	556.0	1341.0	1897.0
	% within Membership status environmental group	29.3%	70.7%	100.0%

Environmental group 2005': The results of the chi-square analysis indicated that there was a significant association between membership status of a rights group and participation in political activism: 'contact politician', χ^2 (2, N = 1897) = 51.20, $p < .001$, V = .164; 'protest march', χ2 (2, N = 1881) = 126.32, $p < .001$, V = .258, and; 'same concern', χ2 (2, N = 1883) =76.00, $p < .001$, V = .201. The Cramer's V values indicate weak to moderate associations. Examination of the standardised residuals revealed identical trends across these three types of political activism; both active and members and ordinary members were far more likely to contact politicians, participate in protest marches and work with people who shared the same concern. People who did not belong to an environmental group were far less likely to participate in any of these activities. See table 48 to table 50 for descriptives.

Table 49 Chi-square results – membership status of environmental group by participation in protest, march or demonstration

Environmental group membership status		Past 2 yrs have you: Protest, march or demonstration		Total
		Yes	No	
Don't belong	Count	158	1574	1732
	Expected Count	199.8	1532.2	1732.0
	% within Environmental group membership status	9.1%	90.9%	100.0%
	Adjusted Residual	-11.2	11.2	
Member	Count	51	80	131
	Expected Count	15.1	115.9	131.0
	% within Environmental group membership status	38.9%	61.1%	100.0%
	Adjusted Residual	10.2	-10.2	
Active Member	Count	8	10	18
	Expected Count	2.1	15.9	18.0
	% within Environmental group membership status	44.4%	55.6%	100.0%
	Adjusted Residual	4.4	-4.4	
Total	Count	217	1664	1881
	Expected Count	217.0	1664.0	1881.0
	% within Environmental group membership status	11.5%	88.5%	100.0%

Table 50. Chi-square results – membership status of environmental group by worked with people who share same concern

Environmental group membership status		Past 2 yrs have you: Worked with people-same concern		Total
		Yes	No	
Don't belong	Count	707	1025	1732
	Expected Count	757.0	975.0	1732.0
	% within Environmental group membership status	40.8%	59.2%	100.0%
	Adjusted Residual	-8.6	8.6	
Member	Count	98	34	132
	Expected Count	57.7	74.3	132.0
	% within Environmental group membership status	74.2%	25.8%	100.0%
	Adjusted Residual	7.3	-7.3	
Active Member	Count	18	1	19
	Expected Count	8.3	10.7	19.0
	% within Environmental group membership status	94.7%	5.3%	100.0%
	Adjusted Residual	4.5	-4.5	
Total	Count	823	1060	1883
	Expected Count	823.0	1060.0	1883.0
	% within Environmental group membership status	43.7%	56.3%	100.0%

'Aid organisation 2005': The results of the chi-square analysis indicated that there was a significant association between membership status of an aid organisation and participation in political activism: 'contact politician', χ^2 (2, N = 1891) = 34.94, $p < .001$, $V = .136$; 'protest march', χ2 (2, N = 1876) = 43.15, $p < .001$, $V = .152$, and; 'same concern', χ2 (2, N = 1877) =44.57, $p < .001$, $V = .154$. The Cramer's V values indicate weak to moderate associations. Examination of the standardised residuals revealed identical trends across these three types of political activism; both active and members and ordinary members were far more likely to contact politicians, participate in protest marches and work with people who shared the same concern. People who did not belong to an aid organisation were far less likely to participate in any of these activities. See table 51 to table 53 for descriptives.

Table 51. Chi-square results – membership status of an aid organisation by contact politician

Aid organisation membership status		Past 2 yrs have you: Contacted a politician/official		Total
		Yes	No	
Don't belong	Count	457	1217	1674
	Expected Count	490.4	1183.6	1674.0
	% within Aid organisation membership status	27.3%	72.7%	100.0%
	Adjusted Residual	-5.3	5.3	
Member	Count	77	109	186
	Expected Count	54.5	131.5	186.0
	% within Aid organisation membership status	41.4%	58.6%	100.0%
	Adjusted Residual	3.8	-3.8	
Active Member	Count	20	11	31
	Expected Count	9.1	21.9	31.0
	% within Aid organisation membership status	64.5%	35.5%	100.0%
	Adjusted Residual	4.3	-4.3	
Total	Count	554	1337	1891
	Expected Count	554.0	1337.0	1891.0
	% within Aid organisation membership status	29.3%	70.7%	100.0%

Table 52. Chi-square results – membership status of an aid organisation by participation in protest, march or demonstration

Membership aid organisation		Past 2 yrs have you: Protest, march or demonstration		Total
		Yes	No	
Don't belong	Count	163	1496	1659
	Expected Count	191.9	1467.1	1659.0
	% within Aid organisation membership status	9.8%	90.2%	100.0%
	Adjusted Residual	-6.5	6.5	
Member	Count	45	141	186
	Expected Count	21.5	164.5	186.0
	% within Aid organisation membership status	24.2%	75.8%	100.0%
	Adjusted Residual	5.7	-5.7	
Active Member	Count	9	22	31
	Expected Count	3.6	27.4	31.0
	% within Aid organisation membership status	29.0%	71.0%	100.0%
	Adjusted Residual	3.1	-3.1	
Total	Count	217	1659	1876
	Expected Count	217.0	1659.0	1876.0
	% within Aid organisation membership status	11.6%	88.4%	100.0%

Table 53. Chi-square results – membership status of an aid organisation by worked with people who share same concern

Membership aid organisation		Past 2 yrs have you: Worked with people-same concern		Total
		Yes	No	
Don't belong	Count	683	976	1659
	Expected Count	725.6	933.4	1659.0
	% within Aid organisation membership status	41.2%	58.8%	100.0%
	Adjusted Residual	-6.2	6.2	
Member	Count	112	75	187
	Expected Count	81.8	105.2	187.0
	% within Aid organisation membership status	59.9%	40.1%	100.0%
	Adjusted Residual	4.7	-4.7	
Active Member	Count	26	5	31
	Expected Count	13.6	17.4	31.0
	% within Aid organisation membership status	83.9%	16.1%	100.0%
	Adjusted Residual	4.5	-4.5	
Total	Count	821	1056	1877
	Expected Count	821.0	1056.0	1877.0
	% within Aid organisation membership status	43.7%	56.3%	100.0%

Summary: Political attitudes and behaviours

In regards to political ideology, inactive members of a charity identified as more left-wing in comparison to active members and people who did not belong to a charity. Active members of a rights group identified as more left-wing, as did members, whilst people who did not belong identified as more right-wing. Members of an environmental organisation identified as more left-wing in comparison to people who did not belong who identified as more right wing. Finally, active members or an aid organisation identified as more left-wing than people who did not belong.

With regards the 2007 data, these respective political ideologies were reflected in the results regarding preferred political party, whereby inactive members of a charity preferred to support the Greens whilst active members were more likely to support the Liberal and National parties. In contrast, people who did not belong to a charity were less likely to support the Greens and more likely to have chosen not to support a party. Active and inactive members also demonstrated greater support for their preferred party in comparison to people who did not belong to a charity. These findings are consistent with the previous section in which, generally, active and inactive members of a charity appeared to exhibit stronger opinions regarding an issue (in this case, preferring a particular political party and degree of support for this party).

In terms of broad trends in the 2005 data, members of a rights, environmental or aid group were all more likely to support the Greens (compared to active members and people who did not belong). Active members of a rights group or an environmental group were also more likely to support the Greens. In contrast, active members of an aid organisation were more likely to support the National Party. However, these observations need to be read in the context of the small counts in each cell for active members of these three types of groups. Lastly, people who did not belong to any of the three types of groups were universally less likely to support the Greens.

Results from the 2007 survey indicated that there were only marginal differences exhibited in political interest and activity, whereby people who did not belong to a charity tended to be less interested in politics and less active in politics compared to active and inactive members of a charity. Differences in this regard, however, were fairly minimal.

Finally, members and active members of a rights group, environmental group or aid organisation universally exhibited more political activism in contrast to those people who did not belong to these organisations. During the past two years, both members and active members were more likely to have contacted a politician or government official, taken part in a march, protest or demonstration, and to have worked together with people who shared the same concern.

Appendix 6

SROI critique

Prepared by John Humphreys

The success of a business is easy to measure, for example, by annual profit, balance sheet, share price, or various other financial indicators. The same is not true for government or the non-profit sector.

The failure to measure the success (or failure) of government and the non-profit sector easily and clearly has been a concern for a long time. Attempts to create an alternative metric have been problematic; an example is Social Return on Investment (SROI).

Social Return on Investment

SROI attempts to place a dollar value on all the benefits that arise from a project, considering all the stakeholders. These benefits are compared with the costs to determine a SROI (benefit-cost) ratio.

Many of the benefits are hard to measure. For example, improving 'social capital' is notoriously difficult to calculate. Nevertheless, by not attempting to measure these benefits the result is an implicit assumption of zero benefit. The SROI approach is an admirable attempt to provide information about what impacts social ventures are having.

Unfortunately, the SROI approach is fundamentally wrong. The SROI approach is effectively the same as a benefit-cost analysis, with a greater emphasis on intangible impacts. In the SROI literature, there is a lack of awareness about how to measure benefits and costs correctly. Common errors are – costs incorrectly labeled as benefits; total and marginal impact confused; opportunity costs, and many direct costs, ignored. These mistakes mean that the conclusions are often meaningless or misleading.

Food Connect Sydney

In 2010, *Food Connect Sydney (FCS)* received $185,000 to start their social enterprise, which offers ethical fresh food options to Sydney consumers. In 2011, *Social Ventures Australia (SVA)* consulting undertook an SROI that found a benefit-cost ratio of 7.96, which they interpreted to mean that there was $7.96 in social value for every $1 invested. This conclusion is wrong. The *SVA* analysis compared the benefits for five years with the costs for only the first year. Indeed, no information was actually provided on the future costs of the project, except the comment that 'future year investments may be significantly lower if *FCS* can run a sustainable business' (SVA, 2011, 34).

In many instances, the report measured the benefits to a group of people without measuring the costs to the same people. One of the largest benefits of the report was for consumers, who were estimated to receive $567,708 in value over five years. However, the report did not factor in the higher costs of the *FCS* food. Using estimates provided by the report, the extra cost to consumers can be estimated at $1,271,687 over five years.[1] The point of this example is not that consumers received more costs than benefits (that is probably not the case) but to highlight the danger of incomplete SROI analysis.

In another example, the report includes the non-monetary benefits to volunteers, but neglects to measure the non-monetary costs of the time and effort from the same volunteers. It is almost certainly true that the volunteers received more benefits than costs, but it is important to include both sides of the equation.

Another problem is the assumption that the benefit of an event is equal to the cost of providing the event. For example, in the *FCS* analysis the 'financial proxy used to value [farm tours and city events] is the cost of running farm tours and city events' (SVA, 2011, 30). It is possible that

1 The report states that a $50 *FSC* food box cost $40.73 elsewhere, and gave details about the average *FSC* weekly spend and estimated number of customers per year.

the benefit to the people on tour could be much higher or lower than the cost. By assuming that benefits equal costs, the analysis is assuming the answer that it is supposed to be measuring.

A more important problem is the lack of consideration for the opportunity cost of the money spent. The money used for a social project would have been spent elsewhere, and, even if it were spent on a for-profit business, there would be some associated social benefits. This is perhaps the most serious problem with the SROI approach.

Another feature missing from SROI analysis (including the *FCS* report) is a consideration of the true cost of government funds. The deadweight loss of raising tax revenue means that spending $100 of government money actually costs society much more than simply the $100 that is spent.

Finally, while SROI literature highlights the importance of considering the counter-factual, it is often missing in practice. The *FCS* analysis looks at the benefit of providing new jobs to long-term unemployed people but it does not consider the possibility that they might have found another job without the project, that is, the net benefit. Since the average length of long-term unemployment in Australia is less than three years and the considered project was measured over five years, this is a strange omission.

This does not necessarily mean that *FCS* is a bad project. The information provided in the analysis is insufficient to draw any meaningful conclusion.

Other SROI examples

The problems of SROI analysis are not limited to the above example. A report on a project in Scotland (Durie, 2007) claimed a reduction in welfare as a benefit saving the UK Government $16,854 per participant. The report also notes, however, an increase in a different welfare scheme of $23,484 – but this is also counted as a benefit of the project.

Another common mistake is to include the total wages of newly employed people as a benefit from a project, as occurred in the SROI analysis of the *St Helens Partnership in the UK* (Lawlor, 2006) and many other reports. This is an example of confusing the total benefit with the marginal benefit. The benefit of working is the wage; while the cost of working is sometimes doing things that you do not want to do. The net benefit from working is the marginal value gained from the employee.

The mistakes found in SROI analysis are not occasional oversights, but represent a systemic problem in the approach to measuring benefits and costs. Until these are addressed, the SROI approach represents at best a pointless exercise and, at worst, a distortion of reality.

Appendix 7

Annual charity returns – Australia, UK and US

Table A7.1: ACNC 2014 annual information statement: attachment (iv) national standard charter of accounts

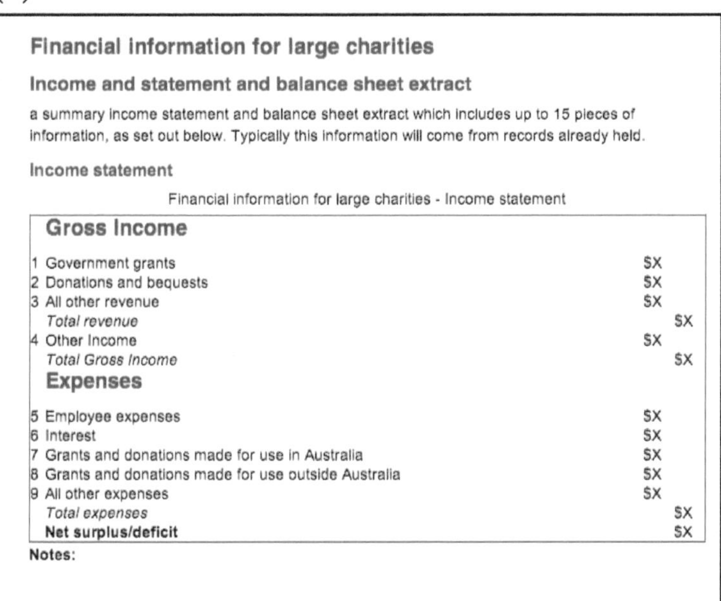

Financial information for large charities

Income and statement and balance sheet extract

a summary income statement and balance sheet extract which includes up to 15 pieces of information, as set out below. Typically this information will come from records already held.

Income statement

Financial information for large charities - Income statement

	Gross Income		
1	Government grants	$X	
2	Donations and bequests	$X	
3	All other revenue	$X	
	Total revenue		$X
4	Other Income	$X	
	Total Gross Income		$X
	Expenses		
5	Employee expenses	$X	
6	Interest	$X	
7	Grants and donations made for use in Australia	$X	
8	Grants and donations made for use outside Australia	$X	
9	All other expenses	$X	
	Total expenses		$X
	Net surplus/deficit		$X

Notes:

Source: *(Australian Charities and Not-for-profits Commission (c), 2013).*

Table A7.2: UK accounting and reporting by charities: statement of recommended practice

A	**Incoming resources**					
A1	Incoming resources from generated funds					
A1a	Voluntary income					
A1b	Activities for generating funds					
A1c	Investment income					
A2	Incoming resources from charitable activities					
A3	Other incoming resources					
	Total incoming resources					
B	**Resources expended**					
B1	Costs of generating funds					
B1a	Costs of generating voluntary income					
B1b	Fundraising trading: cost of goods sold and other costs					
B1c	Investment management costs					
B2	Charitable activities					
B3	Governance costs					
B4	Other resources expended					
	Total resources expended					
	Net incoming/outgoing resources before transfers					

Source: (Charity Commission for England and Wales, 2005).

Table A7.3: US 990 return of organization exempt from income tax

Form **990**

Department of the Treasury
Internal Revenue Service

Return of Organization Exempt From Income Tax

Under section 501(c), 527, or 4947(a)(1) of the Internal Revenue Code (except black lung benefit trust or private foundation)

▶ The organization may have to use a copy of this return to satisfy state reporting requirements.

OMB No. 1545-0047

2012

Open to Public Inspection

A For the 2012 calendar year, or tax year beginning , 2012, and ending , 20

B Check if applicable:
☐ Address change
☐ Name change
☐ Initial return
☐ Terminated
☐ Amended return
☐ Application pending

C Name of organization
Doing Business As
Number and street (or P.O. box if mail is not delivered to street address) | Room/suite
City, town or post office, state, and ZIP code

D Employer identification number

E Telephone number

G Gross receipts $

F Name and address of principal officer:

H(a) Is this a group return for affiliates? ☐ **Yes** ☐ **No**
H(b) Are all affiliates included? ☐ **Yes** ☐ **No**
If "No," attach a list. (see instructions)

I Tax-exempt status: ☐ 501(c)(3) ☐ 501(c) ( ) ◀ (insert no.) ☐ 4947(a)(1) or ☐ 527

J Website: ▶

H(c) Group exemption number ▶

K Form of organization: ☐ Corporation ☐ Trust ☐ Association ☐ Other ▶ | L Year of formation: | **M** State of legal domicile:

Part I Summary

Section	Line	Description		Prior Year	Current Year
Activities & Governance	1	Briefly describe the organization's mission or most significant activities:			
	2	Check this box ▶ ☐ if the organization discontinued its operations or disposed of more than 25% of its net assets.			
	3	Number of voting members of the governing body (Part VI, line 1a)	3		
	4	Number of independent voting members of the governing body (Part VI, line 1b)	4		
	5	Total number of individuals employed in calendar year 2012 (Part V, line 2a)	5		
	6	Total number of volunteers (estimate if necessary)	6		
	7a	Total unrelated business revenue from Part VIII, column (C), line 12	7a		
	b	Net unrelated business taxable income from Form 990-T, line 34	7b		
Revenue	8	Contributions and grants (Part VIII, line 1h)			
	9	Program service revenue (Part VIII, line 2g)			
	10	Investment income (Part VIII, column (A), lines 3, 4, and 7d)			
	11	Other revenue (Part VIII, column (A), lines 5, 6d, 8c, 9c, 10c, and 11e)			
	12	Total revenue—add lines 8 through 11 (must equal Part VIII, column (A), line 12)			
Expenses	13	Grants and similar amounts paid (Part IX, column (A), lines 1–3)			
	14	Benefits paid to or for members (Part IX, column (A), line 4)			
	15	Salaries, other compensation, employee benefits (Part IX, column (A), lines 5–10)			
	16a	Professional fundraising fees (Part IX, column (A), line 11e)			
	b	Total fundraising expenses (Part IX, column (D), line 25) ▶			
	17	Other expenses (Part IX, column (A), lines 11a–11d, 11f–24e)			
	18	Total expenses. Add lines 13–17 (must equal Part IX, column (A), line 25)			
	19	Revenue less expenses. Subtract line 18 from line 12			
				Beginning of Current Year	End of Year
Net Assets or Fund Balances	20	Total assets (Part X, line 16)			
	21	Total liabilities (Part X, line 26)			
	22	Net assets or fund balances. Subtract line 21 from line 20			

Part II Signature Block

Under penalties of perjury, I declare that I have examined this return, including accompanying schedules and statements, and to the best of my knowledge and belief, it is true, correct, and complete. Declaration of preparer (other than officer) is based on all information of which preparer has any knowledge.

Source: (Department of the Treasury Internal Revenue Service, 2012).

Bibliography

Aaberge, R., Mogstad, M., & Peragine, V. (2011). Measuring Long-term Inequality of Opportunity. *Journal of Public Economics, 95*(3-4), 193-204.

Acemoglu, D., & Robinson, J. A. (2012). *Why Nations Fail.* London: Profile Books.

ACIL Allen. (2014). *Counting the Costs of Alcohol Policy: Relevant Costs.* Sydney.

Anderson, G. (2013). *Where the Money Goes: Private Wealth for Public Good.* Sydney: Centre for Social Impact University of NSW.

Andreoni, J., & Payne, A. (2011). Is Crowding Out Due Entirely to Fundraising? *Journal of Public Economics, 95*, 334-343.

Assistant Treasurer, Australian Government. Private Ancillary Fund Guidelines (2009). Australia: Federal Register of Legislative Instruments.

Atkinson, A. B., Backus, P. G., Micklewright, J., Pharoah, C., & Schnepf, S. V. (2012). Charitable Giving for Overseas Development: UK Trends Over a Quarter Century. *Journal of the Royal Statistical Society: Series A (Statistics in Society), 175*(1), 167-190.

Auditor General. (2010). *Administration of Deductible Gift Recipients (Non-profit Sector).* Canberra.

Australian Bureau of Statistics. (2006). *Personal Safety Survey.* Canberra.

Australian Bureau of Statistics. (2008). *National Survey of Mental Health and Wellbeing: Summary of Results.* Canberra.

Australian Bureau of Statistics. (2009). *Australian National Accounts: Nonprofit Institutions Satellite Account.* Canberra.

Australian Bureau of Statistics. (2011). *Methodological Review of Counting the Homeless, 2006.* Canberra.

Australian Bureau of Statistics (a). (2012). *Census of Population and Housing: Estimating Homelessness.* Canberra.

Australian Bureau of Statistics (b). (2012). *Measures of Australia's Progress.* Canberra.

Australian Bureau of Statistics (c). (2012). *Causes of Death.* Canberra.

Australian Bureau of Statistics (a). (2013). *Counts of Australian Businesses, Including Entries and Exits.* Canberra.

Australian Bureau of Statistics (b). (2013). *Household Income and Income Distribution, Australia, 2011-12, Fact Sheet 5.* Canberra.

Australian Charities and Not-for-profits Commission (a). (2013). *Not-for-profit Reform and the Australian Government.* Melbourne.

Australian Charities and Not-for-profits Commission (b). (2013). *2014 Annual Information Statement: Public Consultation Paper.* Melbourne.

Australian Charities and Not-for-profits Commission (c). (2013). *2014 Annual Information Statement: Attachment (iv) National Standard Charter of Accounts.* Melbourne.

Australian Communities Foundation. (2012). *Taking the Plunge.* Fitzroy.

Australian Government. (2011). *National Compact: Working Together.* Canberra.

Australian Human Rights Commission. (2008). *Sexual Harassment: Serious Business.* Canberra.

Australian Institute of Grants Management. (2011). *Grantmaking Manifesto.* North Melbourne.

Australian Institute of Health and Welfare. (2012). *Australia's Health 2012.* Canberra.

Australian Taxation Office. (2007). *Taxation Statistics 2005-06: Charities and Deductible Gifts.* Canberra.

Australian Taxation Office. (2011). *Tax Basics for Non-profit Organisations.* Canberra.

Australian Taxation Office. (2012). *Taxation Statistics 2009-10: Charities and Deductible Gifts.* Canberra.

Australian Taxation Office. (2013). *Taxation Statistics 2010-11.* Canberra.

Baber, W., Daniel, P., & Roberts, A. (2002). Compensation to Managers of Charitable Organizations. *The Accounting Review*, *77*(3), 679-693.

Baber, W., Roberts, A., & Visvanathan, G. (2001). Charitable Organizations' Strategies and Program Spending Ratios. *Accounting Horizons*, *15*(4), 329-343.

Barla, P., & Pestieau, P. (2005). *The Optimal Number of Charities. Unpublished.* University of Liege.

Barman, E. (2007). With Strings Attached: Nonprofits and the Adoption of Donor Choice. *Nonprofit and Voluntary Sector Quarterly*, *37*(1), 39-56.

Barnden, D., & Sivaraman, G. (2011). Aid/Watch and the Public Benefit of

Advocacy for the Extra-territorial Relief of Poverty. *Cosmopolitan Civil Societies Journal, 3*(3), 9-19.

Begg, S., Vos, T., Barker, B., & Stevenson, C. (2003). *The Burden of Disease and Injury in Australia 2003*. Canberra: Australian Institute of Health and Welfare.

Bekkers, R., & Wiepking, P. (2010). A Literature Review of Empirical Studies of Philanthropy: Eight Mechanisms That Drive Charitable Giving. *Nonprofit and Voluntary Sector Quarterly, 40*(5), 924-973.

Benzing, C., & Andrews, T. (2004). The Effect of Tax Rates and Uncertainty on Contributory Crowding Out. *Atlantic Economic Journal, 32*(3), 200-214.

Berber, P., Brockett, P. L., Cooper, W. W., Golden, L. L., & Parker, B. R. (2011). Efficiency in Fundraising and Distributions to Cause-Related Social Profit Enterprises. *Socio-Economic Planning Sciences, 45*(1), 1-9.

Berman, G., & Davidson, S. (2003). Do Donors Care? Some Australian Evidence. *VOLUNTAS: International Journal of Voluntary and Nonprofit Organizations, 14*(4), 421-429.

Bernholz, L. (2012). *Philanthropy and the Social Economy: Blueprint 2013*. Grantcraft Stanford Center on Philanthropy and Civil Society.

Best, J. (2012). *Dammed Lies and Statistics: Untangling Numbers from the Media, Politicians, and Activists* (electronic.). Berkeley: University of California Press.

Bhattacharya, R., & Tinkelman, D. (2008). How Tough are Better Business Bureau/Wise Giving Alliance Financial Standards? *Nonprofit and Voluntary Sector Quarterly, 38*(3), 467-489.

Boscarino, J. E. (2009). Surfing for Problems: Advocacy Group Strategy in U.S. Forestry Policy. *The Policy Studies Journal, 37*(3), 415-434.

Bougheas, S., Dasgupta, I., & Morrissey, O. (2007). Tough Love or Unconditional Charity? *Oxford Economic Papers, 59*(4), 561-582.

Bowman, W. (2006). Should Donors Care About Overhead Costs? Do They Care? *Nonprofit and Voluntary Sector Quarterly, 35*(2), 288-310.

Breen, O. B. (2013). The Disclosure Panacea: A Comparative Perspective on Charity Financial Reporting. *VOLUNTAS: International Journal of Voluntary and Nonprofit Organizations, 24*(3), 852-880.

Brodie, S. (2010). The Charity Commission: Politicised and Politicising. *Economic Affairs, 3*, 9-13.

Brooks, A. C. (a). (2007). Does Giving Make Us Prosperous? *Journal of Economics and Finance*, *31*(3), 403-411.

Brooks, A. C. (b). (2007). *Who Really Cares: The Surprising Truth About Compassionate Conservatism* (Electronic.). New York: Basic Books.

Brown, C. (2012). From Ideas to Action: Insights for Community Foundations. In *Australian Community Foundation Forum*. Mackay: Philanthropy Australia.

Bruce, I., & Chew, C. (2011). Debate: The Marketization of the Voluntary Sector. *Public Money & Management*, *31*(3), 155-157.

Bryce, H. J. (2012). *Players in the Public Policy Process* (Electronic.). New York: Palgrave Macmillan.

Buteau, E., & Buchanan, P. (2011). *The State of Foundation Performance Assessment: A Survey of Foundation CEOs*. Cambridge MA: The Center for Effective Philanthropy.

Butterfly Foundation. (2012). *Paying the Price: the Economic and Social Impact of Eating Disorders in Australia*. Melbourne.

Cassells, R., McNamara, J., Gong, C., & Bicknell, S. (2011). *Unequal Opportunities: Life Chances for Children in the "Lucky Country"*. Sydney: The Smith Family.

Centre for Social Impact. (2012). An Australian Snapshot: Social Impact Bonds. In *Perspectives from the Social Finance Forum 2012*. The Centre for Social Impact.

Chamberlain, C., & MacKenzie, D. (2003). *Counting the Homeless 2001*. Canberra: Australian Bureau of Statistics.

Chamberlain, C., & MacKenzie, D. (2008). *Counting the Homeless 2006*. Canberra: Australian Bureau of Statistics.

Chambers, C., & Parvin, P. (2010). Coercive Redistribution and Public Agreement: Re-evaluating the Libertarian Challenge of Charity. *Critical Review of International Social and Political Philosophy*, *13*(1), 93-114.

Charity Commission. (2008). *Speaking Out: Guidance on Campaigning and Political Activity by Charities*. London.

Charity Commission for England and Wales. (2005). *Accounting and Reporting by Charities: Statement of Recommended Practice*. London.

Chen, G. (2009). Does Meeting Standards Affect Charitable Giving? *Nonprofit Management & Leadership*, *19*(3), 349-365.

Chevalier-Watts, J. (2011). Charitable Trusts and Political Activity: Time for a Change? *Waikato Law Review*, *19*(2), 145-159.

Chew, C., & Osborne, S. P. (2007). Identifying the Factors that Influence Positioning Strategy in U.K. Charitable Organizations that Provide Public Services. *Nonprofit and Voluntary Sector Quarterly*, *38*(1), 29-50.

Chia, J., & O'Connell, A. (2010). Charitable Treatment?: A Short History of the Taxation of Charities in Australia. Melbourne: University of Melbourne.

Child, C., & Gronbjerg, K. (2007). Nonprofit Advocacy Organizations: Their Characteristics and Activities. *Social Science Quarterly*, *88*(1), 259-281.

Chung, D. (2013). *Understanding the Statistics About Male Violence Against Women.* Sydney: White Ribbon.

Cnaan, R. A., Jones, K., Dickin, A., & Salomon, M. (2011). Nonprofit Watchdogs: Do They Serve the Average Donor? *Nonprofit Management & Leadership*, *21*(4), 381-397.

Cobb-Clark, D. (2013). *The Case for Making Public Policy Evaluations Public.* Canberra: The Productivity Commission.

Collier, P. (2013). *Exodus: Immigration and Multiculturalism in the 21st Century* (Electronic.). Penguin.

Commission on Social Determinants of Health. (2008). *Closing the Gap in a Generation.* Geneva: World Health Organization.

Community Affairs References Committee, Australian Senate. (2013). *Australia's Domestic Response to the World Health Organization's Commission on Social Determinants of Health Report "Closing the Gap Within a Generation".* Canberra.

Community Council for Australia. (2012). Submission: Not-for-profit Sector Tax Concessions Working Group. Canberra.

Comptroller HR Revenue & Customs and Auditor General. (2013). *Gift Aid and Reliefs on Donations.* London: National Audit Office.

Copps, J., & Vernon, B. (2010). *The Little Blue Book.* London: New Philanthropy Capital.

Cordery, C. (2013). Regulating Small and Medium Charities: Does It Improve Transparency and Accountability? *VOLUNTAS: International Journal of Voluntary and Nonprofit Organizations*, *24*(3), 831-851.

Core, J. E., & Donaldson, T. (2010). An Economic and Ethical Approach to Charity and to Charity Endowments. *Review of Social Economy*, *68*(3), 261-284.

CPA Australia. (2013). *Charities: A Guide to Financial Reporting and Assurance Requirements.* Melbourne: CPA.

Crampton, E., Burgess, M., & Taylor, B. (2011). *The Cost of Cost Studies*. Christchurch: University of Canterbury.

Craven, R., Dillon, A., & Parbury, N. (Eds.). (2013). *In Black and White: Australians All at the Crossroads*. Ballan: Connor Court.

Dalton, P., & Lyons, M. (2005). *Representing the Disadvantaged in Australian Politics: for the Democratic Audit of Australia* (No. 5). Canberra: ANU.

Dalton, R., Scarrow, S., & Cain, B. (2004). Advanced Democracies and the New Politics. *Journal of Democracy*, *15*(1), 124–138.

Dasgupta, I., & Kanbur, R. (2009). Does Philanthropy Reduce Inequality? *The Journal of Economic Inequality*, *9*(1), 1–21.

Daza, J. (2010). Economy of Non-profit Organizations Charities and Donations. *International Research Journal of Finance and Economics*, *52*, 1–13.

Deloitte Access Economics. (2011). *Dementia Across Australia: 2011-2050*. Canberra: Alzheimer's Australia.

Department of the [US] Treasury Internal Revenue Service. (2012). *Return of Organization Exempt From Income Tax*. Washington DC.

Dhanani, A. (2009). Accountability of UK Charities. *Public Money & Management*, *29*(3), 183-190.

Dhanani, A. (2012). Discharging Not-for-profit Accountability: UK Charities and Public Discourse. *Accounting, Auditing & Accountability Journal*, *25*(7), 1140-1169.

Disley, E., Rubin, J., Scraggs, E., Burrowes, N., & Culley, D. (2011). *Lessons Learned from the Planning and Early Implementation of the Social Impact Bond at HMP Peterborough*. London: Ministry of Justice.

Doyle, L., & Hill, R. (2012). *An Overview of Approaches for Philanthropic Investment in Aboriginal Women and Girls*. Sydney: AMP Foundation.

Dunn, A. (2008). Demanding Service or Servicing Demand? Charities, Regulation and the Policy Process. *The Modern Law Review*, *71*(2), 247-270.

Durie, S. (2007). *North Ayrshire Fab Pad Project Impact Arts Social Return on Investment Report*. Scotland: Forth Sector Development.

Ebrahim, A. and V. K. R. (2010). *The Limits of Nonprofit Impact: A Contingency Framework for Measuring Social Performance*. Boston: Harvard Business School.

Eckerd, A., & Moulton, S. (2011). Heterogeneous Roles and Heterogeneous Practices: Understanding the Adoption and Uses of Nonprofit Performance Evaluations. *American Journal of Evaluation*, *32*(1), 98-117.

Edna McConnell Clark Foundation. (2012). *2011 Annual Report.* New York.

Endeavour Foundation. (2011). *Advocacy Manual and Workbook.* Brisbane.

Falkiner-Rose, L. (2007). *Funding Advocacy for Social Change: Clarifying the Rules for Grantmakers.* Changemakers Australia.

Ferdinand, A., Paradies, Y., & Kelaher, M. (2013). *Mental Health Impacts of Racial Discrimination in Victorian Aboriginal Communities.* Melbourne: The Lowitja Institute.

Ferris, J. S., & West, E. G. (2003). Private Versus Public Charity: Reassessing Crowding Out From the Supply Side. *Public Choice*, *116*, 399-417.

Fiennes, C. (2012). *It Ain't What You Give: It's How you Give It: Making Charitable Donations Which Gets Results* (Electronic.). London: Giving Evidence.

Foundation for Alcohol and Research Education. (2013). *The Foundation for Alcohol Research and Education's 2013 Election Platform.* Canberra.

Fukuyama, F. (2012). *The Origins of Political Order.* London: Profile Books.

Garrett, T., & Rhine, R. (2010). Government Growth and Private Contributions to Charity. *Public Choice*, *143*(1-2), 103-120.

Givewell (Australia). (2009). *Australian Charities Financial Analysis.* Sydney: Givewell (Australia).

Goggins Gregory, A., & Howard, D. (2009). The Nonprofit Starvation Cycle. *Stanford Social Innovation Review*, 49-53.

Goldberg, S. H. (2009). *Billions of Drops in Millions of Buckets: Why Philanthropy Doesn't Advance Social Progress* (Electronic.). New Jersey: Wiley.

GPOBA. (2012). *The Global Partnership on Output-Based Aid: Annual Report 2012.* Washington DC: World Bank.

Halsbury's Laws of Australia. (2013). LexisNexis Butterworths.

Hamilton, C., & Maddison, S. (2007). *Silencing Dissent.* Sydney: Allen & Unwin.

Harding, M. (a). (2011). What is the Point of Charity Law? In *Curent Legal Issues Seminar.* Brisbane: Bar Association of Queensland.

Harding, M. (b). (2011). Finding the Limits of Aid/Watch. *Cosmopolitan Civil Societies Journal*, *3*(3), 34-45.

Harding, M., O'Connell, A., Stewart, M., & Chia, J. (2011). *Taxing Not-for-profits*. Melbourne: Melbourne Law School.

Harris, M. (2001). This Charity Business: Who Cares? *Nonprofit Management & Leadership*, *12*(1), 95-110.

Harrison, T. D., & Laincz, C. A. (2008). Entry and Exit in the Nonprofit Sector. *The B.E. Journal of Economic Analysis & Policy*, *8*(1).

Heard, G., Birrell, B., & Khoo, S. (2009). Intermarriage Between Indigenous and Non-Indigenous. *People and Place*, *17*(1), 1-14.

Heckelman, J. C., & Wilson, B. (2013). Institutions, Lobbying, and Economic Performance. *Economics & Politics*, *25*(3), 360-386.

Hind, A. (2011). Increasing Public Trust and Confidence in Charities. *Public Money & Management*, *31*(3), 201-205.

Hollway, S., Howes, S., Reid, M., Farmer, B., & Denton, J. (2011). *Independent Review of Aid Effectiveness*. Canberra: Australian Government.

Hope Consulting. (2011). *Money for Good II: Driving Dollars to the Highest Performing Nonprofits*. San Francisco.

Husock, H. A. (2007). The Politics of Philanthropy: Stockmarkets for Nonprofits. *Social Science and Modern Society*, *44*(3), 16-23.

Hyndman, N., & McMahon, D. (2011). The Hand of Government in Shaping Accounting and Reporting in the UK Charity Sector. *Public Money & Management*, *31*(3), 167-174.

Independent Commission Against Corruption. (2012). *Funding NGO Delivery of Services in NSW: A Period in Transition. Consultation Paper*. Sydney.

Iwaarden, J. Van, Wiele, T. Van Der, Williams, R., & Moxham, C. (2009). Charities: How Important is Performance to Donors? *International Journal of Quality & Reliability Management*, *26*(1), 5-22.

J B Were. (2011). *What is Impact Investment?*. Sydney.

Johns, G. (2006). Party Organisations and Resources: Membership, Funding and Staffing. In I. Marsh (Ed.), *Political Parties in Transition?*. Sydney: Federation Press.

Johns, G. (a). (2012). Paved With Good Intentions: The Road Home and the Irreducible Minimum of Homelessness in Australia. *AGENDA*, *19*(1), 41-59.

Johns, G. (b). (2012). When Too Much Social Justice Is Never Enough. In G. Johns (Ed.), *Right Social Justice: Better Ways to Help the Poor.* Ballan: Connor Court.

Jones, C. L. & Roberts, A. A. (2006). Management of Financial Information in Charitable Organizations: The Case of Joint Cost Allocations. *The Accounting Review*, *81*(1), 159-178.

Jones, E. (2013). Biodiversity Does Not Matter: Revealed Biodiversity Matters. In G. Johns (Ed.), *Really Dangerous Ideas!*. Melbourne: Connor Court.

Judd, Stephen, Robinson, Anne, Errington, F. (2012). *Driven by Purpose: Charities That Make the Difference.* Sydney: Hammond Press.

Jung, T., Kaufmann, J., & Harrow, J. (2014). When Funders Do Direct Advocacy. *Nonprofit and Voluntary Sector Quarterly*, *43*(1), 36-56.

Kahneman, D. (2012). *Thinking Fast and Thinking Slow* (Electronic.). Allen Lane.

Khanna, J., & Sandler, T. (2000). Partners in Giving: the Crowding-in Effects of UK Government Grants. *European Economic Review*, *44*, 1543-1556.

Kitching, K. (2009). Audit Value and Charitable Organizations. *Journal of Accounting and Public Policy*, *28*(6), 510-524.

Kramer, M. R. (2009). Catalytic Philanthropy. *Stanford Social Innovation Review*, (Fall), 30-35.

Kurti, P. (2013). *In the Pay of the Piper: Governments, Not-for-profits, and the Burden of Regulation.* Sydney: Centre for Independent Studies.

Laslett, A., Catalano, P., Chikritzhs, T., Dale, C., Doran, C., Ferris, J., Wilkinson, C. (2010). *The Range and Magnitude of Alcohol's Harm to Others.* Canberra: Alcohol Education and Rehabilitation Foundation.

Lawlor, E., & Nicholls, J. (2006). *Hitting the Target, Missing the Point: How Government Regeneration Targets Fail Deprived Areas.* London: New Economics Foundation.

Leggat, S. (2011). *Childhood Heart Disease in Australia: Current Practices and Future Needs.* Sydney: HeartKids Australia.

Leigh, A. (2007). Intergenerational Mobility in Australia. *The B . E . Journal of Economic Analysis & Policy*, *7*(2), 1-28.

Li, S. X., Eckel, C. C., Grossman, P. J., & Brown, T. L. (2011). Giving to Government: Voluntary Taxation in the Lab. *Journal of Public Economics*, *95*(9-10), 1190-1201.

Lohmann, R. A. (2007). Charity, Philanthropy, Public Service, or Enterprise: What Are the Big Questions of Nonprofit Management Today? *Public Administration Review*, May-June, 437-444.

Lomborg, B. (Ed.). (2013). *How To Spend $75 Billion To Make The World A Better Place* (Electronic.). Washington DC: Copenhagen Consensus Center.

Mayer, L. H. (2011). Charities and Lobbying: Institutional Rights in the Wake of Citizens United. *Election Law Journal*, *10*(4), 407-426.

McCormack, S. W. (2010). Taking the Good With the Bad: Recognizing the Negative Externalities Created by Charities and Their Implications for the Charitable Deduction. *Arizona Law Review*, *52*, 977-1026.

McGregor-Lowndes, M., & Turnour, M. (2012). Wrong Way Go Back! Rediscovering the Path for Charity Law Reform. *University of New South Wales Law Journal*, *35*(3), 810-845.

McLachlan, R., Gilfillan, G., & Gordon, J. (2013). *Deep and Persistent Disadvantage in Australia.* Canberra: Productivity Commission.

Merchant, A., Ford, J. B., & Rose, G. (2011). How Personal Nostalgia Influences Giving to Charity. *Journal of Business Research*, *64*(6), 610-616.

Mourâo, P. R. (2008). What Has the Economics of Giving Given to Economics? The Contemporary Situation. *Journal of Economic and Social Research*, *10*(1), 1-33.

Munk, N. (2013). *The Idealist: Jeffrey Sachs and the Quest to End Poverty* (Electronic.). New York: Doubleday.

National Cancer Institute. (2012). *Cancer: Changing the Conversation.* US Department of Health and Human Services.

nfpSynergy. (2013). *The Politics of Charities: What do the Public, MPs and Journalists Think of Campaigning and Political Activity by Charities?*. London.

Nicholls, J., Lawlor, E., & Neitzert, E. (2012). *A Guide to Social Return on Investment.* UK: The SROI Network.

Nicholson-Crotty, J. (2011). Does Reported Policy Activity Reduce Contributions to Nonprofit Service Providers? *Policy Studies Journal*, *39*(4), 591-607.

Not-for-profit Sector Tax Concession Working Group. (2013). *Fairer, Simpler and More Effective Tax Concessions for the Not-for-profit Sector*. Canberra: Treasury.

Null, C. (2011). Warm Glow, Information, and Inefficient Charitable Giving. *Journal of Public Economics*, *95*(5-6), 455-465.

Office of Charities. (2002). *Charitable Fundraising: Best Practice Guidleines for Charitable Organisations*. Sydney: Department of Gaming and Racing NSW.

Office of Liquor Gaming and Racing. (2010). *Charitable Fundraising General Information*. Sydney: Department of Communities NSW.

Omura, T. (2010). *Competition Between Charitable Organisation for Private Donations*. Griffith University.

Ostrander, S. A. (2007). The Growth of Donor Control: Revisiting the Social Relations of Philanthropy. *Nonprofit and Voluntary Sector Quarterly*, *36*(2), 356-372.

Pallotta, D. (2008). *Uncharitable: How Restraints on Nonprofits Undermine Their Potential* (Electronic.). Medford: Tufts University Press.

Pestieau, P., & Sato, M. (2006). Limiting the Number of Charities. *SSRN Electronic Journal*, *September*, 1-14.

Petrovits, C., Shakespeare, C., & Shih, A. (2011). The Causes and Consequences of Internal Control Problems in Nonprofit Organizations. *Accounting Review*, *86*(1), 325-357.

Philanthropy Australia. (2009). *Submission to the Productivity Commission Review into the Contribution to the Not-for-Profit Sector*. Melbourne.

Philanthropy Australia. (2011). *Strategies for Increasing High Net Worth and Ultra High Net Worth Giving*. Melbourne.

Pincus, Jonathan, J. (2013). *The Wellbeing of the Australian People: Comments on the Treasury's Framework*. University of Adelaide.

Pinker, S. (2012). *The Better Angels Of Our Nature*. London: Penguin.

Prime Minister's Community Business Partnership. (2005). *Giving Australia: Research on Philanthropy in Australia*. Canberra.

Productivity Commission. (2003). *Social Capital: Reviewing the Concept and its Policy Implications*. Canberra.

Productivity Commission. (2010). *Contribution of the Not-for-Profit Sector*. Canberra.

PWC. (2013). *Investing in Vision: Comparing the Costs and Benefits of Eliminating Avoidable Blindness and Visual Impairment*. The Fred Hollows Foundation.

Rajan, S. S., Pink, G. H., & Dow, W. H. (2008). Sociodemographic and Personality Characteristics of Canadian Donors Contributing to International Charity. *Nonprofit and Voluntary Sector Quarterly*, *38*(3), 413-440.

Reich, R. (2013). Toward a Political Theory of Philanthropy. In P. Illingworth, T. Pogge, & L. Wenar (Eds.), *Giving Well: the Ethics of Philanthropy*. Oxford: Oxford University Press.

Ryan, A. (2012). *On Politics: A History of Political Thought from Herodotus to the Present*. London: Allen Lane.

Ryan, C., & Irvine, H. (2012). Not-for-profit Ratios for Financial Resilience and Internal Accountability: A Study of Australian International Aid Organisations. *Australian Accounting Review*, *22*(2), 1-45.

Sargeant, A., Lee, S., & Jay, E. (2008). Communicating the "Realities" of Charity Costs: An Institute of Fundraising Initiative. *Nonprofit and Voluntary Sector Quarterly*, *38*(2), 333-342.

Scharf, K. (2010). *Public Funding of Charities and Competitive Charity Selection*. University of Warwick. Coventry.

Schizer, D. (2009). Subsidizing Charitable Contributions: Incentives, Information, and the Private Pursuit of Public Goals. *Tax Law Review*, *62*(2), 221-268.

Seddon, N. (2007). Who Cares?: How State Funding and Political Activism Change Charity. London: Civitas.

Showers, V. E., Showers, L. S., Beggs, J. M., & Cox, J. E. (2011). Charitable Giving Expenditures and the Faith Factor. *American Journal of Economics and Sociology*, *70*(1), 152-86.

Sloan, M. F. (2009). The Effects of Nonprofit Accountability Ratings on Donor Behavior. *Nonprofit and Voluntary Sector Quarterly*, *38*(2), 220-236.

Snowdon, C. (2012). *Sock Puppets: How the Government Lobbies Itself and Why*. London: Institute of Economic Affairs.

Social Ventures Australia. (2011). *Forecast SROI Report.* Sydney.

Standing Committee on Economics, Australian Senate. (2008). *Disclosure Regimes for Charities and Not-for-profit Organisations.* Canberra.

Steinberg, R. (1986). Should Donors Care About Fundraising? In S. Rose-Ackerman (Ed.), *The Economics of Nonprofit Institutions.* New York: Oxford University Press.

Sunstein, C. (2002). *Risk and Reason: Safety, Law, and the Environment.* Cambridge: Cambridge University Press.

Sutton, D., Baskerville, R., & Cordery, C. (2010). A Development Agenda, the Donor Dollar and Voluntary Failure. *Accounting, Business & Financial History, 20*(2), 209-229.

Szper, R., & Prakash, A. (2009). Is Sunlight the Best Disinfectant? Charity Watchdogs and the Limits of Information-Based Regulation. In *Proceedings of the Midwest Political Science Association.* Chicago: The Midwest Political Science Association.

Szper, R., & Prakash, A. (2011). Charity Watchdogs and the Limits of Information-based Regulation. *VOLUNTAS, 22*(1), 112-141.

Trussel, J. (2003). Assessing Potential Accounting Manipulation: the Financial Characteristics of Charitable Organizations with Higher than Expected Program-Spending Ratios. *Nonprofit and Voluntary Sector Quarterly, 32*(4), 616-634.

Trussel, J. M., & Parsons, L. M. (2007). Financial Reporting Factors Affecting Donations to Charitable Organizations. *Advances in Accounting, 23*, 263-285.

Trust Company (a). (2012). *Social Impact Report: Engaged Philanthropy in Practice.* Sydney.

Trust Company (b). (2012). *The Trust Company Limited Annual Review 2012.* Sydney.

Tuan, M. T. (2008). *Measuring and/or Estimating Social Value Creation: Insights Into Eight Integrated Cost Approaches.* Bill & Melinda Gates Foundation.

Turnour, M., & Turnour, E. (2012). Archimedes, Aid/Watch, Constitutional Levers and Where We Now Stand. In *Defining Taxing and Regulating Not for Profits in the 21st Century.* Melbourne: Melbourne University.

UK Government. (2013). *Responses to The Public Administration Select Committee's Third Report of 2013-14: The Role of the Charity Commission and Lord Hodgson's Statutory Review of the Charities Act 2006*. London.

Van der Heijden, H. (2013). Charities in Competition: Effects of Accounting Information on Donating Adjustments. *Behavioral Research in Accounting, 25*(1), 1-13.

Van Puyvelde, S., Caers, R., Du Bois, C., & Jegers, M. (2011). The Governance of Nonprofit Organizations: Integrating Agency Theory With Stakeholder and Stewardship Theories. *Nonprofit and Voluntary Sector Quarterly*, *41*(3), 431-451.

Van Voss, L. H., & Van Leeuwen, M. H. D. (2012). Charity in the Dutch Republic: an Introduction. *Continuity and Change*, *27*(02), 175-197.

Ward, D. (2008). *Trustee Handbook: Roles and Duties of Trustees of Charitable Trusts and Foundations in Australia.* Sydney: Philanthropy Australia.

Washington State Institute for Public Policy. (2013). *Benefit-Cost Technical Manual Methods and User Guide.* Olympia.

Waters, R. (2011). Increasing Fundraising Efficiency Through Evaluation: Applying Communication Theory to the Nonprofit. *Nonprofit and Voluntary Sector Quarterly*, *40*(3), 458-475.

Whitman, J. R. (2009). Philanthropic Foundations. *Nonprofit Management & Leadership*, *19*(3), 305–325.

Williams, G. (2011). The Australian Constitution and the Aid/Watch Case. *Cosmopolitan Civil Societies Journal*, *3*(3), 1-8.

Wixley, S., & Noble, J. (2014). Mind the Gap: What the Public Thinks About Charities. London: New Philanthropy Capital.

Yi, D. T. (2010). Determinants of Fundraising Efficiency of Nonprofit Organizations: Evidence from US Public Charitable Organizations. *Managerial and Decision Economics*, *31*(April), 465-475.

Index

- **Q**

- **R**

www.ingramcontent.com/pod-product-compliance
Ingram Content Group UK Ltd.
Pitfield, Milton Keynes, MK11 3LW, UK
UKHW042007190726
13854UKWH00005B/2197